Making Participatory Management Work

Leadership of Consultive
Decision Making
in Academic Administration

David R. Powers
Mary F. Powers

Making Participatory Management Work

MAKING PARTICIPATORY MANAGEMENT WORK
*Leadership of Consultive Decision Making
in Academic Administration*
    by David R. Powers and Mary F. Powers

Copyright © 1983 by: David R. Powers

&

Mary F. Powers

Originally published by Jossey-Bass Publishing, San Francisco,1983
Now available through Whidbey Publishing LLC, Clinton WA, 2012
www.whidbeypublishing.com

Library of Congress Cataloging in Publication Data

Powers, David R.
        Making participatory management work.

        Bibliography: p. 233
        Includes index.
        1. Universities and colleges—United States—
Administration—Decision making. I. Powers, Mary F.
II. Title.
LB2341.P64   1983   378.73   82-49282
ISBN 9780985794644

Manufactured in the United States of America

JACKET DESIGN BY WILLI BAUM

FIRST EDITION

Code 8315

We dedicate this book to our fathers

Franklin P. Ferguson
Professor Emeritus of Agricultural Journalism
The Pennsylvania State University

William H. Powers (deceased)
Former Associate Dean of the College of Science
and Professor of Chemistry
The Pennsylvania State University

With love, respect, and gratitude . . .

Preface

Since the early 1960s, much has been written about problems of university governance and failures of leadership. Presidents are rarely allowed to dominate their institutions as they once did. At many universities, decision making is decentralized on a variety of issues. Participatory governance is accepted by many administrators and faculty members as the preferred way for a university to operate. This conviction, however, is tempered by lack of certainty that participatory governance can be undertaken effectively. Opponents worry that proposed changes cannot be instituted without dangerously slowing decision making and implementation. Proponents of participatory governance also worry because changes they favor are being proposed at a time when universities are having difficulty balancing their budgets. During periods of constrained funds, the tendency is to move toward centralization of decision making and toward authoritarian governance, rather than in the other direction. Centralization is also strengthened by faculty apathy toward governance and by easy availability to high-level administrators of more accurate and revealing information from all sectors of the university. These factors are conducive to sweeping, unilateral decision making by central administrations.

Although countervailing forces against participatory decision making are strong, the trend persists. Participatory governance is becoming increasingly popular in corporations. How can participatory governance be undertaken effectively on university campuses? What factors favor such an effort and which tend to block it? This book offers some answers to these questions by describing an administrative practice that requires that the persons who will be affected by decisions or who will have to implement them play roles in making them.

In a consultive process, a leader is not simply a decision maker who gives orders to others, as he is in classic authoritarianism.* Instead, a leader orchestrates, evaluates, and coordinates implementation of decisions made in consultation with concerned individuals and permanent or *pro tem* advisory bodies, which include representatives of constituencies that have stakes in the problems at hand. Consultive processes place administrators under an obligation to try their best to comply with decisions that are referred to them for approval except when those decisions are counter to the mission or best interests of the university, when they are impossible to implement (perhaps owing to lack of funds), or when they infringe on the rights or responsibilities of other units. Consultive processes place constituents under an obligation to forward to administrators decisions of sufficient wisdom that administrators are not forced to take command of malfunctioning subunits that should be self-governing in order that the affairs of the institution may progress.

The consultive process involves a model of governance that is both conservative and innovative. It is conservative in that it maintains a hierarchal view of university organization, retains most existing governance structures, and strongly upholds

*Throughout the book, the singular masculine pronoun is used to denote an individual member of the human race. Sexism is neither implied nor intended by this usage. The term *consultive* is a legitimate short form of *consultative*.

university traditions such as collegial governance. Further, it maintains that ethics are as important to governance as they are to all other cooperative human activities. Consultation is innovative in that instead of requiring establishment of new structures to broaden participatory governance, as was the trend during the 1960s and early 1970s, it advocates development of new procedures and routines through which representatives of all constituencies of the university community can play roles in governance to maintain and improve their institution.

An underlying premise of this book is the optimistic view that, conceptually and philosophically, nothing much is wrong with the governance structures, traditions, or goals of universities. This is not to say that no problems exist, however. Changes in governance processes are needed, accompanied by necessary changes in attitudes and behavior of members of university communities, if existing structures are to operate in a manner that honors the traditions of democratic and collegial governance and provide a work climate that is both personally sustaining and conducive to productivity.

In a 1982 report the Carnegie Foundation for the Advancement of Teaching described current problems in academic governance as follows: "Traditional structures do not seem to be working very well. Faculty participation has declined, and we discovered a curious mismatch between the agenda of faculty councils and the crisis now confronted by many institutions. . . . The inadequate state of campus governance should not be attributed to faculty alone. Some administrators still appear to be too authoritarian or too bureaucratic to consult openly and honestly with colleagues. The chair of the faculty budgetary affairs committee at one major university reported a feeling of futility about the consultation process: 'Our work on program review, many of us felt, was used as a shield for unpopular administrative decision making and some of our most important suggestions were ignored' " (p. 74). In answer to this problem, the foundation recommends "no less than a rebirth of leadership in higher education" (p. 89).

This book is subtitled *Leadership of Consultive Decision Making in Academic Administration.* It attempts to give insight into principles of behavior, attitudes, and components of consultation that will help administrators initiate or improve consultive decision making at their institutions. Only experience in conducting consultive processes, however, can teach an administrator what works best at his particular institution with its unique individuals, issues, governance bodies, and traditions. The organization of the book is straightforward: The consultive process is described (Chapters One through Four); leadership of consultive processes is explored (Chapter Five); ethics of the consultive process are discussed (Chapter Six); use of consultive decision making in crises is analyzed (Chapter Seven); and potential drawbacks and benefits of consultation and ways to overcome potential drawbacks are examined (Chapter Eight). Discussions are confined to information pertinent to consultation; exhaustive descriptions are not attempted. Practicing administrators at any level, faculty members who care about their institutions, and anyone investigating participatory decision making may possibly find this book of interest. Readers are assumed to be familiar with the literature and techniques of university administration and with the structures and functions of governance mechanisms on their own campuses, since such background knowledge and skills are required to understand fully and to apply the principles of consultation, if so desired.

The authors offer special thanks to Professor Alasdair MacIntyre for allowing us to quote extensively from his remarkable book *After Virtue*. We have attempted to put his ethical theory to good use. We also thank most sincerely the people who helped prepare the manuscript, in particular Betty Jenks, who patiently dealt with revisions and typed the final draft. Aiko Miller, Nancy White, Carmel Vlha, Sandy Berdux, and Jean Kelly also gave us assistance and encouragement. Franklin P. Ferguson, professor emeritus of agricultural journalism at the Pennsylvania State University, edited the manuscript.

Charleston, West Virginia   David R. Powers
February 1983   Mary F. Powers

Contents

The Authors

David R. Powers is vice-chancellor for academic affairs of the West Virginia Board of Regents, a state system of sixteen colleges and universities. He is also adjunct professor of public administration at West Virginia University. He received his B.A. (1963), his M.A. (1965), and his Ph.D. (1971) degrees in political science from the University of Pittsburgh.

Powers's teaching and research activities have been in public administration, politicomilitary strategy, and international affairs, concentrating on China. His administrative experience includes service as assistant dean of the faculty (1968–70), assistant to the chancellor (1970–76), and vice-provost (1976–79) at the University of Pittsburgh and vice-president for academic affairs (1979–82) at George Mason University, the state university in northern Virginia. His published articles in academic administration include "Beyond the Carnegie Commission Reports" (*Educational Planning,* 1975) and "Reducing the Pain of Retrenchment" (*Educational Record,* 1982).

While at the University of Pittsburgh, Powers led consultive processes to develop long-range academic program plans, guidelines for program evaluation, a faculty appointment and appeals system, academic integrity guidelines for students and faculty, an office of research, an undergraduate honors program, and retrenchment guidelines. At George Mason University, by means of consultive processes, he developed a long-range plan for the institution, led a governance study, established several governance councils and research centers, developed policies for a research grants program and a study-leave program, and established an institute to link industry with the university. In West Virginia, he has used consultive processes to develop policies governing statewide program planning and program evaluation and to coordinate efforts fostering collaboration with industry through research and training programs.

Mary F. Powers is a free-lance writer and editor. She received her B.S. degree (1961) from the Pennsylvania State University in bacteriology and engaged in graduate study in philosophy of science and educational research at the University of Pittsburgh and in experimental psychology at George Mason University. She served as instructor in microbiology for the Pennsylvania State University from 1961 through 1968, developed a syllabus used statewide for teaching microbiology to student nurses, and was a contributor to *Reid's Microbiology* (R. L. Maginnis, Ed., 1965).

Powers has edited numerous program proposals, articles, and reports in the area of academic administration. She has also undertaken such varied projects as coordinating committee reports leading to Middle States reaccreditation, writing on affirmative action (*College Management,* 1971), submitting a report to the Ministry of Education of the People's Republic of China on teaching English, and coordinating volunteer efforts to establish campus enrichment programs, including lecture series and campus meetings on governance.

Together, the Powerses produced one of the first affirmative action programs accepted by HEW (1970), worked on major grant proposals to foundations and government agencies, and developed one of the first exchange programs by an American university with the People's Republic of China (1978), among other projects.

Making Participatory Management Work

Leadership of Consultive Decision Making in Academic Administration

1

Using Consultive Processes Successfully

A desire for participatory governance is arising not merely on university campuses, but across the United States and around the world. In a 1982 article in the *AAHE Bulletin,* Cleveland identified the phenomenon as part of a "macrotransition in American life." He also stated: "We are moving *from* doctrines of centralized power *to* notions of decentralization, devolution, separatism, and a broadened participation. . . . Power is leaking out of national governments to local communities determined to exercise more jurisdiction over their own destinies. The formulation of public policy is increasingly done by nongovernments (profit and nonprofit) which can more easily think further ahead, and experiment more flexibly, than governments can. And the yen to participate keeps spreading—through what the Communists call collective leadership and the Japanese call consensus and we call committee work—so that the key dilemma of the new era is how to get everybody in on the act and still get some action" (p. 11).

On university campuses, the trend toward participatory governance became evident during the student demonstrations of the 1960s. Before that period, governance of universities generally was conducted somewhat differently. In a classic study published in 1960, Corson identified the system of institutional decision making that he named "organizational dualism" (p. 43). For the most part, the executive/administrator is the crucial decision maker in the dual-organization model. The following characteristics are also integral:

1. Faculty and institutional management bureaucracies function as parallel, but separate and distinct hierarchies.
2. As professional experts on curricula, admissions, and other matters integral to the educational side of the duality, faculty members and academic administrators have primary responsibilities for determining operating modes, decision-making criteria, and "product quality" within their units and programs.
3. Although a management bureaucracy differs from a faculty in essence, duties, and expertise, it also operates in an essentially hierarchal style, with clearly delimited power to make decisions, aside from occasional exceptions allowed to recognize special talents.
4. Very different skills and backgrounds are expected of administrators such as the chief academic officer and the senior business officer, just as in any major corporation.
5. Administrators defer to technical and professional expertise of appropriate colleagues when problems occur that fall into special areas of understanding.
6. A board of directors or trustees of an institution has ultimate power but is concerned mainly with fiduciary responsibilities, broad mission, range of degree programs, and election of senior officers.

In *New Structures of Campus Power* (1978), John Millett claimed that "the dual-organization model of university governance failed in practice when subjected to the stress of student disorder and disruption during the 1960s" (p. 13). Millett made this claim while introducing a study of the various organs of campus governance that were adopted by colleges and universities following failure of the dual-organization model. He found that, for the most part, attempts to reform campus governance had involved efforts to centralize decision making by establishing councils or committees of representatives from various constituencies, which deliberated on issues of universitywide importance and served in an advisory capacity to their presidents. The success of these bodies had been limited. As Millett put it, "the performance of campuswide governance in general from 1966 to 1976 was somewhat checkered" (p. 221). Millett's underlying concern that stable systems of governance be developed by universities to meet the problems of the future is shared by many administrators and faculty members.

The "Statement on Government of Colleges and Universities" issued jointly in 1966 by the American Association of University Professors, the American Council on Education, and the Association of Governing Boards of Universities and Colleges has been accepted by administrators as standard guidelines for university governance. The statement endorses participation in decision making by interdependent constituents with common interests. Authority of each constituent depends on the responsibility borne by the constituent for the matter under consideration. The definitions of primary responsibility of major constituents given in a 1970 report of the American Association of University Professors also have become generally accepted. In most universities, faculties are responsible for curriculum development, authorization boards are responsible for increasing and managing the endowment, and so forth. For both the 1966 and the 1970 statements, efforts to put principles into practice have been only partly successful on many campuses.

What has been needed to enact the statements is well-established procedures that guarantee constituents effective roles in decision making and implementation. As Millett concluded, campuswide senates have not adequately filled this need. Beyond the realm of negotiating terms of employment, faculty unions too are inadequate by definition because unions operate according to adversarial principles often incompatible with those of traditional collegial governance. Any system of democratic decision making that is devised for collegiate needs cannot be so free-form as to be inefficient and, therefore, eventually self-destructive; nor can it produce only decisions that are arrived at through such murderous compromise that instead of pleasing everyone, they please no one. Furthermore, the problem that has to be addressed in such a system is of broad scope, according to Millett. He pointed out that "the problems of governance of colleges and universities need to be approached, I believe, in a larger context ... it is a context of government, not just of governance, and embraces the functions of guidance and performance as well as the structures and processes of decision making. Governance within a college or university is not enough; government is also essential" (1978, p. 12). The consultive process brings to campuses a system of government that does more than give constituencies a greater role in decision making. It preserves necessary hierarchies and provides new routes for exerting leadership in planning for the future and in implementing policies thereby responding to Millett's concern.

Failure of the dual-organization model under stress during the protest era does not imply that the model is no longer descriptive of university governance. The two hierarchies, learning and management, still exist, though not as separate and distinct entities. Formal and informal ties prevail among various units in the hierarchies, allowing consultation and shared decision making on matters of common interest. The consultive process, which will be discussed in this book, not only utilizes to excellent advantage existing ties among units but builds new ones. The result is an effective system of ensuring constituencies a greater role in decision making.

The purpose of the consultive model is to open the decision-making process without irrevocably separating from it responsibility for making sure that institutional objectives are met as a result of decisions being made. Just as consultation does not require dismantling of legitimate, effective hierarchies within the administration, it does not focus on eliminating existing governance structures of the institution or on adding new structures. Nor does it require displacement of loci of final authority; that is, administrators retain their function of approving decisions and policies. Established governance bodies may be used in different ways in the consultive process, and new memberships may be drawn into them. Those bodies may deliberate on wider varieties of questions involving subjects heretofore not considered the responsibility of certain elements of the membership, and they may make decisions that affect far broader segments of the university community. In a university, in which processes of consultation have become routine, established routes are readily available through which faculty power can be exercised and the interests of affected constituencies can be taken into account in decision making. Of course, like all structures and forms of government, no matter how well intentioned or finely designed, the success of consultation fundamentally depends on the integrity and dedication of the persons at various levels of an institution who take part.

Millett identified establishment of new campuswide decision-making organs as the most common response to deficiencies in the dual-organization model. Establishment of such decision-making organs is an example of modifying governance through change in structure. Governance may also be modified by changing process, by bringing together existing campus decision-making organs in different ways to deliberate issues of interest to many constituencies. In the systems studied by Millett, stability is defined through the unchanging continuity of particular deliberative bodies. In systems that involve process modifications, changes may occur constantly in membership, interrelationships, and focus of deliberative bodies, depending on the issues under consideration. Stability does not depend on these factors but on the endurance of the processes by which constituencies express their will and conduct their common business to produce outcomes that are generally accepted.

In a process model of governance, process is defined as the means by which inputs are converted to outputs—that is, as the mechanisms and activities through which opinions, facts, and values are brought to bear on problems and decisions are made that lead to action to overcome the problems. Being rooted in a process model of governance, consultation assumes that people operate in organized groups to make decisions that guide the course of the institution and that the relational processes by which they operate reveal more about governance

than do the formal charters or structures, the particular interpersonal or group relationships, or the kind of decision models
according to which they are operating.

As Cohen and March (1974) point out, understanding the
social system in which processes occur is crucial. Consultive processes attempt to modify the culture within a university community to establish an obligation of members of the community
to exercise the self-discipline and objectivity required to participate in consultation and an obligation of administrators to facilitate consultation and to be responsive to its outcomes. Deliberation about alternatives, implementation of outcomes, and
responsibility for success or failure of efforts are shared. Neither
constituencies nor administrators may sidestep their responsibilities or fulfill them unilaterally or independently.

In a university, as in a factory, hospital, or any other kind
of institution, consultive decision making evokes a sense of partnership, of community, of working together for the common
good. It increases freedom but requires all participants to fulfill
concomitant responsibilities so that the process can remain
healthy. It does not give power to the people, as was the cry on
university campuses in the 1960s, as little evidence exists that
faculty members want the administrative responsibilities that go
with power. It requires administrators to listen carefully and
constantly to the people and makes it easy for those concerned
with, knowledgeable about, or affected by issues to speak on
them. Cleveland (1982, p. 12) noted, "With nobody in general
charge but everybody partly in charge, more participatory decision making implies a need for much feedback information
widely available. That means more openness, less secrecy—
not as an ideological preference but as a technological imperative."

Successful practitioners of consultive decision making do
not view human nature simply as a wellspring of creativity,
energy, and potential for achievement, as is the tendency of
some advocates of organizational development. Realities of human behavior and organizational dynamics are accepted for
what they are, inherent weaknesses and problems included.
Consultation also is not based on idealized models of govern-

ance. It involves a pragmatic quest for effective governance and refining of organizational activity, to be achieved within the constraints of human nature and by virtue of its strengths. Walker (1979) observed:

> It is relatively profitless to spend time trying to get people to be "better" or trying to head off their anticipated bad behavior. An advantage of the democratic political style is that the emphasis is elsewhere. In a sense, the basic character of people is irrelevant when this style is being used. People are not presumed to be either naturally good or naturally bad. Administration is simply not approached in this way. The best administrators of my acquaintance seem to accept people as they are and to work from that point. . . .
>
> Several implications derive from this point of view. When one accepts the principle of taking people as they are, the question of "who is responsible" becomes unimportant. The relevant question when something goes wrong is . . . "How can we improve our performance and solve the problem?" When this outlook is adhered to over a period of time, a kind of nonpersonal nonblaming approach to problems develops. Members of work teams accept and recognize their limitations as well as their strengths. . . . People do not hesitate to own part of a problem if personal judgments of blame are not being used as weapons. . . .
>
> Experienced administrators . . . may object, "But people don't always do right. Sometimes a president or a dean has to step in to prevent total disaster. . . ."
>
> The more administrative intervention occurs, the more it will be required. Without shunning intervention strategies entirely, I must stress that such strategies must have a low priority on the master agenda that informs administrative efforts. If the dominant assumption being pushed and worked with is that bad people are at the heart of every problem and that they cannot be trusted, then it becomes important to prevent them from hurting themselves and others. Played out, that assumption can become the total game.

Thus, the most effective administrators I know seem to perceive institutional problems as basically suprapersonal or impersonal. People are accepted as they are [pp. 160-161].

Model of the Consultive Process

When shared decision making was less common in universities and presidents had more sweeping powers, so-called group decision making often consisted merely of endorsement and implementation by group members of decisions made unilaterally by leaders. Authoritarian administration is a rudimentary style of leadership. Because of its simplicity, it is attractive to fledgling administrators, who find, on trying it, that it inevitably can cause more problems than it resolves. Issuing orders is easy enough, but getting people to follow them is another matter on most university campuses.

When decisions result from consultive processes, more than one person is involved in defining the problem, in weighing alternative courses of action, in determining the implications of proposed solutions, and in structuring the response to be implemented. Constituencies are persuaded, not ordered, to cooperate in implementation. Successive iterations of drafts of policies eventually lead to a version that can be accepted by key parties. All existing feedback loops are called on for information and analysis, which are used to weigh alternatives and to evaluate progress in the collaborative effort as it develops. Throughout the process, only moderate attention is paid to what the highest-ranking leader prefers. He should avoid an imperial style, which can nullify many of the benefits of consultation and shared decision making.

There is no question that the goals of some autocratic leaders are altruistic and are designed to be in the best interests of their universities. Nevertheless, differences between autocratic and democratic approaches are reflected in outcomes, which are rarely identical, although they may appear to be. If representatives of the university community are involved in decisions, needs of the institution and of broader ranges of constituencies are more likely to be met by outcomes, rather than personal needs or notions of the president or of any other individual or single constituency. In addition, consultation brings broader ranges of expertise to bear on problem definition and on identification and consideration of alternative solutions. Consultation also can add to the decision-making process an error-correction factor, which occurs as various constituencies examine and weigh alternatives, cross-checking each other in the process. This factor is lacking in autocratic, unilateral decision making. In addition, decisions that result from democratic processes are more likely to be supported by constituencies they affect and by personnel responsible for their implementation. This last statement assumes that, for the most part, faculty members value traditional collegial governance, not authoritarianism, since Vroom and Mann (1960) have presented evidence that authoritarian leaders can be more effective than democratic leaders in dealing with authoritarian subordinates.

In a highly simplified form, from which successive iterations and feedback loops have been eliminated, as well as the multiple levels of review and approach that may be customary in real settings, a consultive process may be described as follows:

1. *Identification of a problem.* From the lowest-ranked member of the community to the leaders, anyone may be responsible for calling attention to a problem or need. An advantage of the consultive process is that communications networks are maintained continuously among all levels of the management and teaching hierarchies and among all constituencies so that everyone willing to speak up can be heard.

2. *Problem definition.* Consultation, carried out by telephone or by other informal procedures, such as raising the subject informally at meetings convened for other purposes, is undertaken to define the problem more clearly and to determine breadth of interest in it. At this early stage, the problem usually is not called to the attention of an appropriate governance council or advisory board, because it easily could prove to be much ado about nothing. Instead, persons are contacted who

are sure to be concerned with the problem, if it exists, and are asked to give their views of the nature of the problem and its importance.

3. *Analysis of alternatives.* Examination of alternative courses of action may be combined with the preceding step of bringing the problem into clear focus, but most often, measured and thoughtful analysis is carried out after the problem has been defined. Again, this process is carried out through extensive, informal consultation to identify many, if not all, possible alternatives and to weigh the positive and negative aspects of each.

4. *Drafting a position paper.* The position paper that must usually be drafted at this stage states the problem and identifies one or more possible policies, actions, or programs that would redress it. This paper must be composed with great care. It is a rough draft in one sense, in that it may present only in general form a position that could be proposed in the final draft of the paper. From another point of view, it cannot be considered a rough draft, because it must be composed with precision. Since its purposes are to broaden communication and the consultive base, its wording must not foreclose discussion or preempt alternative solutions. Sensitivity to the needs of various constituencies must be displayed, and an invitation to join in the process of solving the problem must be extended.

Position papers are of great importance because they serve two purposes: (1) to present a perception of the problem and one or more apparently reasonable solutions so that those consulted are given a clear idea of the exact situation they are being asked to address and (2) to solicit participation, since in most endeavors, volunteers are scarce creatures, even when the issue is self-governance.

5. *Circulating the position paper.* Circulation of a position paper is an art that requires sensitivity to the power structures of a university. It involves knowing who the effective, not the titular, representatives of key constituencies are and understanding the sequence in which various representatives should be contacted to produce an effective solution efficiently. No leader of a consultive process should ever be without a word processor or photocopier and a "draft" stamp.

Art is involved in knowing whether to send a draft statement to representatives early on, so that they will not be surprised when the problem becomes public, or to try to coopt their staffs so that they will prepare the representatives to respond sensitively when the time comes. Understanding roles played by potential supporters and how best to approach them is as important as avoiding enemies. Solutions may be rejected not because they would not be effective but because they were shown to the wrong people, in the wrong fashion, at the wrong time. The credibility of the representatives who are contacted is extremely important to the acceptance of solutions, no matter how good the solutions may be. Furthermore, status and credibility of the individual or constituency who gives voice to a problem can be more important to its resolution than its intrinsic importance. The nature of the inquiry, the position and reputation for fair action of the addressee, the signator or author of a position paper, the person circulating the draft, and the reputation of the person convening the discussions are important considerations at this stage of the process. Not only opinions of key informants but opinions of large cross-sections of constituencies having an interest in a problem may be collected. Large-scale meetings may be convened for this purpose, questionnaires may be distributed, or numerous interviews may be conducted. If questionnaires are used, the Delphi technique may be applied to build consensus, if desired. The point is to elicit reactions to the solutions suggested by a position paper from as many people as possible to gain a sense of the outcomes that are generally desired and the actions to attain them which are preferred or on which consensus can be built.

6. *Referral to governance bodies.* The consultive process becomes highly visible and formal when a draft statement is referred to appropriate deliberative bodies. A question concerning university policy may require endorsement by a faculty senate and several committees thereof, by a universitywide council, by the council of the graduate school, science faculty, or other collegial units, by the administrative council, and eventually, perhaps, by trustee and even state authorizing groups. In such cases, careful orchestration of the sequence of presentation and questions posed to each is essential. The architect of the process

must understand the consequences of subsequent or simultaneous reviews. If this step involves only a faculty senate, the university president may be charged with referring the draft statement to the group and requesting its review.

7. *Deliberation of governance bodies.* Bylaws, rules of order, and past practice regulate deliberations of governance bodies, but other influences have effect as well. When an executive committee assigns a question to a strong and competent faculty senate committee that has a sympathetic and responsible membership, many potential problems are obviated. Committee review is usually the first stage in deliberation of a governing body. Representative bodies operate most effectively if small subgroups analyze and recommend policies to the group at large. Not only is such an approach efficient in terms of hours of work required, but committee-size groups usually do a better job of analysis and revision of draft statements. Compromises with other constituencies are more easily negotiated and consensus is more easily built. Rules or organization committees have an innate capacity to kill deliberation and to ensure inaction by a deliberative body. Sensitive attentiveness to leadership of that committee is wise.

A full review process carried out by the entire membership of a faculty senate, complete with debate, amendments from the floor, and motion to approve, provides some of the more fascinating and colorful moments of the consultive process. Literate, logical, and persuasive committee reports are essential at this stage. Some senators are influenced more readily by style than by content. Evidence of trustworthy deliberation, careful research, and sensitive drafting of resolutions will convince most senators that faculty interests are being protected. Lobbying, mobilizing turnout of voting blocs, or arranging speeches by respected representatives on behalf of committee reports is necessary when approval of the reports may be essential to approval of the policy itself. Drafting an effective policy that represents the best possible compromise among competing constituents does not guarantee that the proposal will be approved. The need for extensive preparation depends on how controversial the report is and whether opponents have mobilized to challenge desired policy changes.

8. *Final approval.* Final approval of policies usually comes from an executive such as the president of the university, although some policies require governing board or state approval. An administrator is wise not to give a politicized committee a chance to forward policies to him that he knows he will have to reject outright. Reliable intelligence sources and careful orchestration throughout the consultive process, accompanied by clear articulation of the administrator's opinions, often avoid confrontation during later stages. Throughout the process, feedback from administrators should enable personnel who have been assigned to prepare drafts of proposed policies to make successive modifications so that consensus among the faculty senate and the president of the university, or the chairman of the governing board or state coordinating board, as required, eventually is achieved. Problems with implementation will also be reduced if administrative opinion has been sought at all levels throughout the deliberative process. This gives all administrators involved ample opportunity to decide whether new policies are affordable, whether new programs can be staffed, and whether leaders of new efforts can be identified. Plans for implementing new policies and gathering sufficient resources will be completed before the end of the deliberative process. In consultive as in authoritarian decision-making processes, administrators often take the lead in establishing new units and legitimizing new advisory bodies, as well as in finding resources to implement changes, but they do so by initiating cooperative efforts, not unilaterally.

9. *Evaluation.* Senate committees often request feedback evaluation or program reports on an annual basis. Progress or the lack thereof is made transparent by these reports. An executive should request periodic review and evaluation of programs if the senate does not. Sunset laws that set a date of expiration of a unit, program, or policy ensure review at regular intervals before continuation can be endorsed. When an executive is satisfied that a unit, program, or policy has matured to a point at which it would not be damaged seriously by evaluation and might benefit from it, he should encourage sunset provisions. When he fears that politicization will harm a worthy unit or an effective program, sunset provisions should not be encouraged,

and greater direct control should be sustained in his own or in another trusted office.

The steps of a consultive process are not themselves remarkable, since, like any classic problem-solving model, they involve problem identification, problem resolution, and implementation and evaluation of a selected solution. The difference in consultation lies instead in how each step is carried out. An authoritarian administrator could follow the same sequence of steps but might identify and define a problem himself, order his staff to analyze alternatives but choose a solution he himself prefers regardless of their recommendations, order his staff to compose a position paper announcing his choice, make it known to any governing bodies mandated to examine problems such as the one at hand that they are expected to approve his choice to avoid causing problems for themselves, formally approve the measure himself, and evaluate the results if and when they fail to serve his needs and interests. Unlike a consultive administrator, an authoritarian administrator does not feel obligated to ask anybody's opinion at any step in the process.

Consultive decision making draws on the most enduring and useful elements of other models. It also recognizes that for certain issues and under particular conditions a dual-organization, a collegial, and in some cases even an autocratic model of decision making may be appropriate. All models promise to become more effective, however, with the addition of extensive consultation. Although consultive leaders do not use consultive processes in making all decisions, especially on routine matters, whenever possible they are guided by principles established through consultation.

Understanding the consultive process, its mechanisms, its internal dynamics, and its consequences is necessary for proper use and application. Consultation must not be thought of as a fixed pattern of structural or functional relationships but as an ongoing process with constantly evolving participants and interconnections. In every consultive process undertaken to resolve a particular problem, the following elements integral to consultation can be observed:

- *Information exchange.* The consultive process provides opportunities to involve representatives of various constituencies with different perspectives in examining problems and in proposing and evaluating alternative solutions. Exchange of information encompasses examination of the impacts of options and communication of decisions to groups represented. Improved understanding of the needs, goals, and interests of constituencies also occurs, which is a worthwhile outcome in itself.

- *Coalition building.* Support generated by the consultive process for a policy or program change may lead to consensus on an issue. Failing that, in the course of building coalitions, associated problems are isolated and pressure is brought to bear on dissenting constituencies to cooperate in implementing solutions.

- *Task orientation.* Consultation focuses attention on outcomes, transcending problems of individual egos and territoriality.

- *Accommodation of conflicting needs.* Otherwise irreconcilable institutional or structural needs can be accommodated through consultation by making necessary changes in functions or leadership.

- *Alteration of power distribution.* Consultation fundamentally alters the distribution of power while not displacing legitimate authority. The process allows cooperation among decision makers of remote or nonparallel units. Fluidity within and permeability between divisions in an organization are improved, to the advantage of all sectors.

- *Flexibility.* A broad range of functions can be performed using the consultive process, including formulating goals, determining policies, planning, undertaking some elements of implementation and evaluation, and devising internal appellate procedures. For each function, procedures must be designed to govern consideration of topics and selection of participants.

- *Institutionalization of group processes.* Constituencies must be assured the right and the opportunity to participate in consultation. Institutionalization of group processes requires development of guidelines to govern timing of deliberations, to define acceptable procedures and behavior, and to establish legitimate channels of reporting or recommendation.

- *Orchestration and coordination of process by leaders.* Energetic leadership of the consultive process is required to avoid intolerable slowing of decision processes and to prevent duplication or contradiction among deliberative efforts. Leadership in this model must be confident, tireless, tolerant of diversity and contradiction, task-oriented, and logical.

Consultive Networks

The broad range of topics that can be addressed by consultation cuts across the structural jurisdictions of a university. To produce consistently fair settlements of problems, consultive networks must be established throughout an institution. Elements of consultive processes are easy to define when they parallel vertical interconnections of the administrative hierarchy. Examples of vertical consultation include department chairpersons conferring with the dean of their school or a director consulting with staffs of several units that report to him. Another necessary part of consultive networks is the horizontal element, which involves persons of equal status conferring on issues of common concern. When a department chair confers with the chair of another department in the same or a different school of a university on subjects such as sharing a new facility, jointly appointing a faculty member, or cooperatively preparing a grant proposal, horizontal interconnections of a consultive network are being used.

The third element of networks can be extremely diverse, since its form is not determined by organizational structure, by functional assignment, or by common interests shared by equals, as in the first two elements mentioned. The third network element cuts diagonally across jurisdictional boundaries of units to match needs of persons who are responsible for solving problems with expertise of persons of any rank who are capable of providing solutions to various elements of the problems. When a vice-president for business affairs who is responsible for efficient operation of the physical plant confers with an energy expert on the faculty, when the manager of the campus bookstore confers with librarians, or when faculty members who are computer experts advise the manager of the campus computer center, diagonal consultation is occurring. Specialists who cannot commune with ordinary people are often parodied in technological societies. Frequently the problem is not that specialists cannot make themselves understood but that adherence to traditional jurisdictional boundaries prevents development of the sophisticated communications networks necessary in putting to use the knowledge of specialists. Adding diagonal elements to consultive networks helps to resolve this problem.

Vertical organization and coordination of consultive processes are well established and well understood. Reporting lines on a classic university table of organization suggest that consultation may proceed in both directions, up and down within structures. Department chairs advise their deans, who, in turn, advise the vice-president for academic affairs, and vice versa. Sound management techniques, efficient leadership, and effective human relations practices suggest that vertical consultation is essential for efficient orchestration of task-oriented activities. Few leaders still believe that commands are effective if issued without vertical consultation within the hierarchy. Likert offered support for this point of view in a 1967 study in which he developed a scale of leadership that contrasted "participative" leadership on one end with "exploitative-authoritarian" leadership on the other. An exploitative-authoritarian leader relies on threats and punishment to command compliance with his orders. He interrupts communication and cooperation to render subordinates powerless. As a result, they become hostile to him and to the organization. Exploitative-authoritarian management is the least effective style, according to Likert (pp. 14–25).

If shown at all, horizontal elements of consultive networks are represented on tables of organization by wandering dotted lines or other obscure indicators. For example, a space planner's functions may cut across all schools and departments, without displacing the lines of authority and responsibility represented on the table. His role is to deal in a coordinated fashion with disparate goals, needs, and concerns of units that apparently are fairly independent. When new quarters are constructed for a unit and space previously occupied by that unit is freed for use by an unrelated unit, a space planner must examine the whole of space in use and available in his entire institution versus the needs of every unit to determine to whom to assign the newly available area. A space planner may have de facto power over space that transcends the de jure authority of the dean and vice-president for the particular unit occupying the space. He does not outrank these administrators but has been given an assignment that is not defined by traditional vertical lines of authority. Usually, his delegated authority encompasses a very narrow jurisdiction with fixed boundaries. He designates which space and how much of it will be assigned to a unit, but he has no voice in determining the activities that will occur therein. Carrying out his responsibilities properly, satisfying the real needs of all, while surviving the hornets' nests of anguished competition that immediately develop at many campuses the instant a bit of space is vacated, can be difficult.

In decisions on space allocation, consultation with all interested parties is necessary, regardless of traditional jurisdictions in which their units are located. The most complex and significant part of the process is discussion of all points of view on all aspects of the problem with all those who will be affected by the decision or wish to be. Frequently, persons greatly in need of additional office or laboratory space for their units will be willing to concede available space to a more needy unit if they can be assured that the other unit actually is more needy and that their request will be first to be considered next time an allocation is made. They also must be given a chance to bargain with someone in authority who is willing to take the time to hear them out. Giving all parties a chance to articulate needs or complaints is extremely important to successful resolution of problems.

Examples of diagonal networks are easily imagined. A vice-president for academic affairs who wishes to design a system for evaluation of programs should begin by assembling a panel that includes not only staff experts on evaluation but persons who understand the impact that proposed approaches will have on the faculty and on the university as a whole. Thus, representatives from the budget, planning, registrar's, and governmental relations offices of the institution may be included. Rank of administrators who are chosen to represent their offices is not an important consideration. Instead, administrators are included in consultive groups on the basis of expertise. Not only can diagonal consultation angle across all levels of administrative jurisdictions so that it involves administrators of every rank in a variety of units, it simultaneously can involve various areas and levels of faculty governance structures. For example, a consultive body concerned with design of an evaluation system may include the chairman of the faculty affairs committee of the senate, the chairman of the committee on program approval of the graduate council, and faculty members with academic credentials in evaluation or statistical analysis. These representatives can reassure the university community that the effort is being undertaken properly. Consultive bodies in general may include as members vice-presidents and deans and/or members of their staffs (of any rank), department chairmen, officers of faculty governing bodies, faculty members, and bureaucrats and technicians (also of any rank). From discussions of groups with such diverse membership, understanding emerges of the operational implications of proposed policy details and appreciation develops of the difficulties that will be encountered by other affected constituencies. Similarly, if a university president wishes to improve relations with an external constituency such as funding agencies, he is wise to consult persons internal or external to the university who are knowledgeable about the agencies, as well as persons who are knowledgeable about the research and program development potential of faculty members.

The goals of consultation, whether vertical, horizontal, or diagonal, are to define issues and needs, to solicit opinions, to draw on expertise, and to establish legitimacy through cooperative analysis of problems by all who are concerned with their solution. Horizontal and vertical consultation usually satisfy many of these goals. In diagonal consultation, interest in the problems at hand by the experts consulted is less important than the knowledge they can bring to bear on them.

Networks vary not only in direction but in duration as useful entities. Some channels endure for long periods, become formalized, and are ignored at one's peril. Routinized, much-used channels usually exist between a vice-president for academic affairs and a vice-president for financial affairs, for example. In such cases, when a matter of common concern arises, consultation is required even when the answer to be obtained can be predicted because the parties are thoroughly familiar with each other's competencies, needs, and viewpoints. To neglect to do so could be insulting or could cause irritation at being ignored when an important decision is being made. Often, maintenance of the network takes precedence over solving a particular problem.

When formal channels have been established, consultation is essential, whether a problem of broad significance must be solved or a consultive network must be maintained. In many other cases, consultation is informal and contingent on interest. Persons interested in a problem may be consulted not because they will contribute to a solution but merely out of courtesy because they have displayed concern. When networks are informal and ad hoc, much contingent consultation occurs. The bulk of this may take place as a part of a screening process that must become a way of life for everyone who plays a role in any consultive network. Preferences and dislikes, interests and prejudices, skills and the lack thereof are among the qualities that may make colleagues useful or harmful if they are included in a particular consultive network. Informal, ad hoc networks are constantly being formed and dissolved in any organization, and these can be much more productive if members are selected according to sound assessment of their abilities and if each member has some realization of the fundamental viewpoints and principles from which others in the network are arguing alternative views.

Over two decades ago, Pfiffner and Sherwood described various purposes that overlays may serve (1960, pp. 18-19): "The formal structure of an organization represents as closely as possible the deliberate intention of its framers for the processes of interaction that will take place among its members. In the typical work organization this takes the form of a definition of task specialties and their arrangement in levels of authority. . . . Coexisting with the formal structure are myriad other ways of interacting for persons in the organization. . . . The idea that these processes are overlays upon the conventional job-task pyramid does not require that the latter take a subordinate position. . . . The overlay approach aims to be realistic in recognizing that organization also consists of a wide variety of contacts that involve communication, sociometry, goal-centered functionalism, decision making, and personal power."

The overlay model developed by Pfiffner and Sherwood does not displace the job-task hierarchy of an organization. Instead, the model portrays the job-task hierarchy as being overlaid by patterns: "(a) the sociometric network, (b) the system of functional contacts, (c) the grid of decision-making centers, (d) the pattern of power, and (e) channels of communication" (p. 19). The consultive process also does not displace the job-task hierarchy, although it does redefine collocation of authority, responsibility, and resources. That is, while consultation allows more decisions to be proposed at lower levels and more policies to be developed that are acceptable to constituencies affected by them, approval of decisions and policies by high-ranking administrators remains necessary for legitimization and to allow coordination of activity across the organization. Cooperation of administrators in implementing decisions is also essential in a consultive system.

2

Attitudes and Skills
of Effective Leaders

~~~~~~

Consultive decision making is portrayed in this book as an effective alternative to authoritarianism. But why is an alternative needed? Many of the greatest leaders in higher education were authoritarian. They had visions of what they wanted their institutions to become and had their way in bringing their visions into being. Throughout much of the twentieth century, the need to develop more and better institutions of higher education was acute, and need can make it easier to believe that ends justify means. Current pressures on higher education have shifted from a need to expand to serve a growing college-age population to a need to contract as college-age population or state funding declines. Pressures on universities are more acute than ever, since contraction tends to be more painful than expansion. Aren't powerful authoritarian leaders who can make tough decisions and stand by them needed more than ever to meet the crises in enrollment and state funding that beset many institutions? Many administrators believe that when authority and responsibility are shared by groups rather than vested in group leaders, nothing gets done. That can be so, although it need not be.

Authoritarian Versus Consultative Leadership

Situations do exist in which authoritarian leadership is the most effective way to achieve desired outcomes—the classic example being a battlefield. Because certain tasks that university administrators must perform, such as balancing the budget, evaluating programs, and lobbying the legislature, can be extremely stressful, administrators may develop a sense of working on a battlefield. But very seldom do conditions occur on university campuses that are so extreme that grim directives are necessary to put them right. Authoritarianism is often manifested by coercive or confrontational acts, and a case can be made that a university campus is not an appropriate setting for aggressive behavior by any member of a university community, including arrogant administrators, faculty union organizers, or student protesters. Such behavior draws attention and resources away from the important business at hand, of transmitting and expanding knowledge.

Apparently such puritan arguments carry little weight, for authoritarianism is common. Struggles for dominance among individuals and among groups occur constantly on university campuses. Frequently, the issue at stake in such struggles is who shall be in charge, not how cooperation can be improved or problems solved most effectively. The rewards of dominance can be great. Giving orders instead of having to take them, not being required to explain or defend oneself routinely, and being subject to the whims of fewer superiors can be very pleasant. Probably, many administrators who defend their style as more effective or as necessary to bring order out of chaos actually are authoritarian because they enjoy it. Others may be authoritarian because they assume that they can be leaders if and only if they behave that way.

As Yukl (1981, p. 207) points out, the autocratic versus participation dichotomy traditionally used to classify leaders' decision-making styles does not tell the whole story about their decision-making behavior. No administrator is autocratic or participative all the time. Many make the majority of their decisions in either an autocratic or participative manner. However, the distinction remains useful because it provides a backdrop against which consultive leadership can be examined and put in perspective. Authoritarianism and consultive decision making are not polar entities. On a continuum of administrative style, consultive decision making lies midway between autocratic decision making, or strict authoritarianism on one extreme, and governance by committee, or true group decision making, on the other. Consultive decision making differs from governance by committee in two major respects. First, the decision rule that is used whenever possible in consultive processes is decision by consensus or mutual accommodation, whereas the decision rule ordinarily used by committees is majority vote. Second, groups consulted do not have final authority over decisions to be enacted or policies to be adopted, as in governance by committee. Although group decision making does occur routinely in consultive processes, administrators retain their authority to reject decisions of consultive groups. The position of consultive groups that recommend and endorse is hardly weak, however. Administrators in a consultive system who persist in ignoring the advice of consultive bodies may be committing professional suicide and/or authorizing policies that lack the popular support required to be effective.

Three factors are particularly useful in pinpointing differences in outlook between authoritarian administrators and administrators who operate through consultation. These differences in outlook are important because they are key factors in defining the kinds of processes and activities in which each type of administrator considers it legitimate to engage to influence governance proceedings. Because administrators of both types occupy the same positions, operate through the same university governance bodies, and perform the same activities, methods of analyzing administrative behavior based on structure or function can be of reduced value in distinguishing between them. A more helpful approach may be to examine differences in underlying assumptions that guide their behavior.

The most fundamental of these assumptions arises out of a need shared by all administrators, the need to retain authority. Authoritarian administrators must maintain dominance over others, since to lose that power entails loss of ability to give orders that will be obeyed. Authoritarian administrators believe that such a loss renders them impotent. Many operate fundamentally through coercion, relying on punishment, threats, or associated techniques to have their way, although their behavior may not ever be blatantly aggressive or explicit.

Duberman (1968, pp. 321-322) has made an important point that should be emphasized: "A crucial distinction must be made between authority and authoritarianism. The former represents accumulated experience, knowledge, and insight. The latter represents their counterfeits: age masquerading as maturity, information as understanding, technique as originality. Authoritarianism is forced to demand the respect that authority draws naturally to itself. The former, like all demands, is likely to meet with hostility; the latter, like all authenticity, with emulation. Our universities—schools at every level—are rife with authoritarianism, all but devoid of authority."

For many people, one of the most disturbing aspects of the student protests of the 1960s was the disregard for organizational and statutory authority that was displayed. Since then, although means of displaying such disregard have become less violent, suspicion remains common of authority that is not earned by an individual through proving his worth but is assumed merely because he has been appointed to a particular position that entails performance of particular tasks. Yet, identifying authority born of competence is no easy matter in an era of exploitative news media and advertising and of streamlined political salesmanship of candidates and issues. Under conditions in which many things cannot be counted on actually to be what they are made to appear, it becomes extremely difficult for an administrator to offer proof of competence, because evidence automatically is discounted by many as only more hyperbole. Some administrators may resort to some form of authoritarianism because they cannot figure out any other way to get anything done. Involving individuals throughout an organization in decision making is an alternative that works not only because it satisfies Americans' democratic leanings by sharing responsibility and authority but because it gives people chances to see for themselves why events are progressing as they are. Orchestrating a consultive process is a complex task that affords administrators constant opportunities to demonstrate their skills and to gain authority thereby, without having to resort to authoritarian tactics.

An authoritarian administrator may hold high office and be extremely competent, and yet for some reason—perhaps lack of confidence or a belief that bosses are supposed to behave in an authoritarian manner—he may continually feel a need to make his subordinates conscious of his power over them. If he is sufficiently competent, his behavior may be accepted as a necessary burden so that the institution can benefit from his ideas. If he is not particularly competent, his tenure in office will be marked at the least by hard feelings and discord and at the most by hatred and fear that can paralyze the operation he is supposed to make more efficient by his management. Both authoritarian administrators and administrators who operate through consultive decision making may dream of being charismatic leaders, so magnetic that they collect followers like Pied Pipers. Authoritarian administrators, however, overlook a well-established principle of human behavior—namely, that positive reinforcement generally is more effective in inducing desired responses than is punishment or threats.

An extremely authoritarian administrator may adopt a stereotypical Marine colonel approach, publicly harassing and maligning instead of complimenting effective elements of projects or behavior and offering concrete advice, in private, on how to counteract weaknesses. He may lose his temper violently or may deny promotions, raises, or tenure to faculty or staff members who disagree with him on issues. He may reduce funding or authorize closing of units whose personnel manifest independence; he may even fire a few administrators or staff to make the point clearly to all employees that pleasing him personally, not excellence of performance or dedication to the institution, is the key to success under his command. Or he may enact his rites of dominance in more subtle ways, by not bothering to read position papers or listen to complaints or analyses of problems, by constantly interrupting or correcting colleagues' state-ments, by publicly chiding overworked assistants for trivial in-fractions, or by using any of an infinite variety of other devices that are geared to impressing on subordinates how insignificant they are and how important he himself is by comparison.

Use of dominance ploys is common, and it may be that no administrator can or should be free of them. Subordinates will always interpret certain of an administrator's idiosyncrasies in such a light, in any case. Dominance ploys need not be overtly aggressive. Even details of physical appearance such as a suntan or the clothing an administrator wears can serve the purpose. The problem lies in the type and frequency of ploys that are used and the purpose to which they are directed. An extremely authoritarian administrator who does not balk at frequent use of threats and punishment to have his own way can debilitate his institution not because his policies are misguided, although they may be, but because his behavior reduces his vice-presi-dents and deans to spending major proportions of their time at-tending to his whims instead of devoting themselves to manag-ing their areas as well as they can. Such a president may impress his board of trustees favorably with his tough, no-nonsense methods and gain considerable job security. Leaders of consul-tive processes must shun many dominance ploys used regularly by authoritarian administrators. Behavior that disrupts group processes, impedes cooperation, or damages motivation is coun-terproductive in consultive decision making.

The second major difference between authoritarian ad-ministrators and leaders of consultive processes lies in the for-mer's love of the "lone-wolf" role, contrasted with the latter's reliance on following accepted processes and involving in deci-sions those who will be affected by them. The classic lone-wolf authoritarian holds himself aloof to maintain his impartiality so that he can make sound judgments about what is best for all parties, unswayed by whether the decisions he makes are praised or criticized. An authoritarian administrator can assume a moral imperative through a lone-wolf role. His aloofness can be interpreted by himself or by others as implying lack of stake in outcomes and may be used to justify his taking control of situations and deciding what should be done about them. Consultive decision making assumes that those who will be affected by decisions should share in making them and does not regard detachment as a virtue. An authoritarian administrator can take the lone-wolf approach to extremes and consider decisions in the system legitimate only if he himself made them. Decisions in consultive systems are accepted by everybody in the system as legitimate if they are made by accepted processes.

Third, authoritarian and consultive administrators differ in how they view the hierarchy of an organization. Drucker (1974) has this to say about hierarchies: "A hierarchy does not, as the critics allege, make the superior more powerful. On the contrary, the first effect of hierarchical organization is the protection of the subordinate against arbitrary authority from above. A scalar or hierarchical organization does this by defining carefully the sphere within which the subordinate has the authority, the sphere within which the superior cannot interfere. . . . The first organization structure of the modern West was laid down in the canon law of the Catholic Church eight hundred years ago. It set up a strictly scalar organization. . . . Even the Pope has to be formally invited by the individual priest before he can officiate in a priest's parish" (p. 525).

Consultive administrators must operate in accordance with the distribution-of-power function that Drucker claims is intrinsic to hierarchies, because filtering up of decisions from below, as opposed to imposition from above, is intrinsic to consultation. Some authoritarian administrators also operate according to Drucker's concept of hierarchy. They are satisfied making broad decisions, such as allocation of funds to units, and leaving internal decisions, such as disbursement of the allocations to areas within the units, to unit-level administrators. Other authoritarian administrators do whatever they want to do at any level in the portions of the hierarchy that are under their control. They may not be satisfied with modifying policy to meet a newly emerging type of problem, for example, but may insist on dictating proper application of the outmoded policy on a case-by-case basis. Extremely authoritarian administrators fail their institutions not only by causing all the problems associated with meddling but by not protecting their units from meddling by their superiors. Such an administrator often takes it as a fact of life that he will be treated as callously by his superiors as he treats his subordinates. For this reason, two-faced behavior is not uncommon in the type—a harsh manner for subordinates and an ingratiating manner for superiors.

Corson (1960, p. 15) and Millett (1962, p. 27) observed that viewing the organization of universities as strictly hierarchal is a mistake. They were correct, in a sense, in noting that no universitywide hierarchy exists, because in the learning structure of a university, in which collegial governance prevails, instructors do not report to full professors, who do not report to deans. A well defined subhierarchy with clear differentiation in roles does exist in the administrative structure of a university, however, and in fact describing universitywide organization as hierarchal is not inaccurate. In the process of explaining this statement, another difference in attitude toward hierarchies between authoritarian and consultive administrators can be discussed.

A hierarchy is commonly depicted, especially by authoritarian administrators, as pyramid-shaped, with a leader positioned at the top of the pyramid, practicing what Walker calls "administration from the top down" (1979, p. 103). He and many constituencies find this style of administration unsatisfactory. When a hierarchy is examined in detail, it turns out to be a complex, three-dimensional network with multiple horizontal, vertical, and diagonal interconnections and many foci of control. Information and decisions may pass up, down, horizontally, and diagonally through networks. Many subnetworks may permeate a network, within discrete sections or throughout the whole. The span of control of many foci is limited to a single person's activities, while other foci may coordinate activities of entire subunits. Interconnections among foci of control are multiple and complex. Hierarchies are necessary because assignment of responsibility and authority is essential for group activity to progress efficiently and for contractual purposes. In a network view of a hierarchy, responsibility and authority can be seen as distributed throughout an organization, yet definitely and clearly assigned. Ironically, an administrator who is assured of legal, constitutional, structural, or cultural authority finds that being gentle and persuasive is a relatively easy task, compared with an administrator who must function without clear-cut authority in an institution that claims to have done away with hierarchal organization.

The problem with using the concept of a hierarchy as a pyramid of networks to describe university organization is not that it necessarily misrepresents interrelationships of subunits. Administrators, faculty members, and staff personnel do fill positions in intertwined but distinct subnetworks that permeate the organization, each subnetwork having its own peculiar ways of conducting its affairs. Consultive administrators believe, however, that the hierarchy pyramid should not be diagrammed with the chief of all administrators of the university—the president—at the peak, as commonly depicted. Instead, the pyramid should be diagrammed with the university *in toto* at the peak because it embodies every subnetwork of all the systems depicted by the pyramid. An obvious analogue is the human body, which, like a university, may be viewed as being constituted of a hierarchy of systems and subsystems. The peak of a pyramid diagram depicting an organismic hierarchy is the entire body (Koestler, 1978, pp. 28-29), not the brain, even though the brain is the control center of the nervous system, which coordinates the activities of various other systems and subsystems.

Consultive administrators find an organismic concept of a hierarchy more useful because it emphasizes that the welfare of the total entity is of prime importance, not any individual part of it. Moreover, such a view of hierarchies is compatible with the ideas basic to consultive processes that power centers should be spread throughout an organization, not concentrated at a so-called top, and that a primary duty of a consultive administrator is to help to maintain power centers in balance with one another. Consultive processes make a university hierarchy more effective by making it more responsive to the needs of its constituencies. Although consultation provides guidance to the hierarchy, it is not intended to replace it or hobble it. Unbridled authoritarianism is seldom permitted by the dynamics of consultation, but exertion of influence does occur in proportion to the standing of each member of a consultive group.

Maintaining balance of authority is of particular importance because pressures on administrators of modern universities can be of the sort that breeds bullies. Clamoring for scarce resources by constituents who may overlook the welfare of the institution in their drive to get as much as they can for themselves sets the stage for presidents who would be kings to rule by authority, not reason. Even presidents who do not want to be kings may be forced to become authoritarian because faculty members refuse to fulfill their responsibilities in governing the university or fail to carry out their governance responsibilities in a civilized fashion.

Etzioni contrasted professional authority with administrative authority: "The ultimate justification for a professional act is that it is, to the best of the professional's knowledge, that right act. . . . The ultimate justification of an administrative act, however, is that it is in line with the organization's rules and regulations, and that it has been approved—directly or by implication—by a superior rank" (1964, p. 77).

Mortimer and McConnell use Etzioni's distinction between authority of knowledge and authority of invested power to develop a parallel distinction between professional and administrative authority (1978, pp. 19-20). They claim (pp. 23-24) that conflict between professional and administrative authority is currently a central problem of university management: "The basic problem of academic authority relations is this fundamental conflict between those who value formal authority and those who legitimize compliance on functional grounds. It is not possible to operate a complex organization without a substantial degree of formal authority. Yet, it would destroy the intellectual vitality of an educational organization to smother the functional authority of those who perform its most valued functions—teaching, research, and service. How, then, can a balance be achieved that will provide sufficient administrative authority to operate the institution effectively without destroying that degree of functional authority necessary for a dynamic academic environment? In more conventional terms, how can decision making be shared among inescapably interdependent parties to the academic enterprise?"

Consultation utilizes the services of an institution's best-established governance structures and most-respected individuals in providing an answer to this question. Energy need not be diverted to succoring newly formed structures but may be focused immediately on actual problem solving. Administrators or other persons do not need to wait years until they have acquired seniority in structures or in their units to add the status to their opinions that is needed to allow them to become leaders. Instead, whenever their particular expertise is needed, they temporarily enter into deliberations of established bodies that have the resources or influence needed to resolve current problems. Influence exerted by particular bodies depends on their standing in the university community and their stake in the outcomes. Their decisions may carry formal or functional authority, depending on their memberships' charters. When their charters do not grant them formal authority, their decisions are referred to appropriate administrators for evaluation. The 1966 joint statement of the AAUP, ACE, and AGB (Section V) affirmed that in matters that are the primary responsibility of the faculty "the power of review or final decision lodged in the governing board or delegated by it to the president should be exercised adversely only in exceptional circumstances." Administrators who ignore the advice of authorized advisory bodies of any type quickly lose support, trust, respect, and cooperation.

Consultation relies heavily on principles of human behavior, but it does not involve an exclusively people-oriented approach to administration. If the consultive process is to be effective, all participants must assume a task-oriented stance. Emphasis must be placed on solving problems of common interest, not primarily on serving needs of participants—although participants must be reinforced to the extent necessary to keep them functional. Emphasis must also be placed on serving the institution as a whole, in consonance with its goals and traditions. Selfish goals of individuals or units take precedence only when meeting them is necessary to meet a more general need. Assuming a task-oriented stance bypasses innumerable problems of conflict of interest that can bring any system of governance to a standstill. Drucker (1974) points out that the battle that has been waged in organizational theory between task focus and person focus is "pure sham" and should be forgotten. Drucker states, "Work . . . is objective and impersonal; the job itself is done by a person" (pp. 524-525).

Consultation requires all constituents to adhere to other basic operating principles. Faculty members and other constituents must be willing to contribute their knowledge through consultive processes to solve problems to the benefit of the university community. However, they must not assume authority on subjects beyond their disciplines or units. Faculty members can be prone to the error of assuming that scholarly expertise in their disciplines somehow makes them experts on matters beyond their departments. Even as a tenured full professor, survival as a faculty member requires a strong ego. Concentrated study can produce sensations of intellectual certainty, whether or not truth of some sort can be demonstrated as the result of one's labors. Some professors become sure not only of their expertise in their specialties but of everything. Administrators should expect this while remaining aware that quite often faculty members are indeed correct in their assessments of problems and potential solutions.

In return for devoting their knowledge and skills through consultation to institutional problem solving, faculty members must be assured that their functions of teaching and research, as the primary missions of the university, will always be given appropriate priority by the administrative hierarchy. They must also be given assurance that administrators value their advice and that taking part in university governance through consultation is not a waste of time. Other constituents likewise must be assured of the importance of their functions and of their roles in the consultive process. Consultation cannot be a *pro forma* process. If advice offered by constituencies is requested by administrators but too often ignored once obtained, the process will fail. Administrators who rely on consultation must believe firmly in democracy, in spite of its deficiencies.

In sum, the traditional conflict between the need of ad-

ministrators to control institutional systems and the need of
faculty members for academic control can be resolved by building and maintaining consultive networks throughout an institution. The networks operate best by focusing always on tasks, by
respecting bureaucrats in their role of performing vital supportive
functions, and by developing in faculty and other constituents a
heightened sense of responsibility for governance. The consultive process was developed in the value-laden environment of
the last two decades, but it is a reasonably bias-free model of
organizational decision making. It is the core of a stable form of
governance that protects collegiality while allowing each constituency an appropriate role in institutional decision making.
Energetic university presidents and other administrators who
are committed to democratic governance can use the consultive
process to provide institutional leadership of a quality that for
years has been in short supply on many campuses.

Basic Skills Required for Consultive Leadership

An authoritarian system provides few checks and balances to control incompetent or unprincipled leaders. Leaders
can withhold from subordinates critical information, resources,
and power to act or to plan for the future. Certain checks and
balances are intrinsic to consultive decision making as a function of a consultive system's characteristic filtering up of decisions from below, as opposed to imposition from above. But
individuals in a consultive system must take part in governance
processes regularly and demand of their leaders what is needed
to make sound judgments, or such checks and balances will fail.
The fact is that even when checks and balances are built into
university governance systems, they are no substitute for competence of key personnel. No other single factor is as important in preserving an organization and maximizing its productivity as the presence of excellent people in key posts.

Leadership of consultive processes does not reside in a
single visionary administrator; it places a responsibility on all
administrators to involve constituencies in helping to plan the
future and make it come into being. Consensus in these activi-

ties is sought when possible. Whereas authoritarianism casts senior administrators as dictators, consultive leadership casts leaders of consultive processes in a multifaceted role of initiator/facilitator/judge/implementer. Consultive leadership requires that a set of attitudes suggested by democratic ideals become commonplace—in particular, that all members of university communities work together to manage, direct, and improve their systems. Consultation has long been used by competent administrators as an effective tool in problem solving. But consultation is more than a tool. It is more, even, than an administrative style. It is a philosophy of administration that is best suited to idealistic pragmatists, optimistic enough to keep hoping for the best but practical enough to realize that nurturing the conditions required to allow effective and enduring systems to materialize is more important and more difficult than dreaming of particular outcomes.

Administrators who wish to exercise leadership in collegiate governance through leadership of consultive processes must be able to articulate goals and objectives. This initial step may be one of the most crucial in any consultive process, since the question that is asked always sets limits on the answers that will be supplied. Problems in early stages tend to be amorphous, difficult to describe in terms of both cause and effect. Different constituencies may perceive different aspects of a common problem, depending on how it initially affects them. As a problem comes into sufficient focus to be addressed meaningfully, a leader must identify constituencies who should, by virtue of a stake in the outcome and/or their expertise, take part in the process of deciding what to do about the problem, and, if necessary, the leader must persuade them to do so. The leader then orchestrates the process by providing necessary background information, by designing and controlling agendas, and by perceiving unspoken individual needs and constituent goals, which must be brought to the fore if they are integral to solving the problem or settled as separate issues if they are unrelated sources of distraction. A leader may be required to synthesize group recommendations that accurately portray the decisions of the group regarding the problem at hand. He then takes charge of presenting these recommendations to appropriate legitimizing councils or individuals. When a recommendation has been approved, a leader's job still is not done. He must understand how to implement the recommendation and how to obtain the resources and cooperation that are needed to do so.

Leaders of consultive processes must possess, in addition to the aforementioned skills related directly to the process itself, background knowledge in four major areas. Knowledge in these areas is not required only of leaders but is valuable to some degree to everyone who wishes to play a productive role in consultation. The areas are characteristics of groups, communication, dynamics of group decision making, and university constituencies.

Characteristics of Groups. Innumerable characteristics of groups must be considered when undertaking consultive processes. Some of the most important are size of the group, characteristics of its members, group cohesiveness, and group operating principles. In a large group, communication problems occur. Not all members can express opinions or are willing to speak up. Meetings are longer and coalitions often form, which can produce disruption. A broader range of analytic perspectives is brought to bear on problems, however, and a greater variety of worthwhile solutions may be suggested. Member characteristics are very important to group functioning. Expertise of members, status, personality traits such as aggressiveness, and personal goals that members wish to achieve through group membership (which may or may not correspond to group goals) all affect interactions.

Cohesive groups are easier to manage in the sense that their members try not to disagree strenuously. In fact, as Janis (1972) has pointed out, a phenomenon called "groupthink" can develop in highly cohesive groups. Members of groups in such a state bolster each other's views uncritically, often resulting in decisions that are unrealistic and have negative consequences. In consultive processes, the needs and interests of the constituencies that group members represent are an added factor. Operating principles that a group obeys may be informal and merely a matter of habit but may be as rigid as any codified set of procedures. Groups that believe in majority rule may interpret a call for consensus as a call for majority rule, rather than near unanimity. Groups that are accustomed to careful deliberation of issues are unlikely to rubber-stamp orders of an authoritarian president who believes in only *pro forma* consultation. Good or bad habits, once instilled, may be difficult to change. Anyone interested in conducting consultive processes effectively must become an attentive student of group dynamics. Hare's (1976) review of research on groups provides a detailed survey of studies done in the field.

Communication. Communication links, networks, and procedures are vital to the success of participative governance and group decision making and implementation. In an excellent review of the literature on communication, Porter and Roberts (1976) point out that since McGregor, Argyris, and Likert popularized a human relations approach to the study of organizations, the study of communications no longer focuses on formal systems but now focuses on interpersonal behavior within organizations (pp. 1556-1557). They also note that research in communication systems has ranged over structure of systems, modes of information processing, organization of institutions, and communication between and within subunits.

Although communication networks may not be highly visible, they lubricate decision-making processes by keeping involved individuals, governance structures, and administrative groups informed throughout the system. Conversations in faculty clubs among leaders, unscheduled debates in department meetings, phone calls between administrators and faculty members, negotiations by researchers with directors of laboratory facilities, and even news stories, memoranda, and announcements regarding drafts of policy statements all are events in the communication networks that pervade a university. Portions of communication networks may coincide with an institution's consultive networks. This complex web may be confusing to a constitutional lawyer and may complicate the sociograms of decision making, but it enables an assistant professor to bring problems to a vice-president, a director of a service unit to talk to a department chairman, and other individuals and groups to make important contacts outside normal reporting lines. Communication networks are particularly important in a university because acquiescence to policies and programs by numerous semiautonomous professors is vital to the success of the enterprise.

Decision Making. Decision-making processes include examination of objectives and of costs and risks of alternatives. They involve evaluating all available evidence and developing contingency plans to fall back on should consequences of a decision prove unsatisfactory. Simplified models of decision making merely hint at the continued analysis that may go on during a decision-making process. Feedback loops may be traversed repeatedly; evidence may be gathered, added to, examined, and reexamined; a decision is made, reexamined, made again, modified, and checked again. Much pondering, construction of straw men, analysis and reanalysis of cost/benefit implications, wondering how persons affected by the decision will react to it, and worrying about how one's personal image will be affected if positive or if negative consequences result tend to be part of a decision process if one is determined to look at a problem from all sides.

In a 1976 article on decision making, MacCrimmon and Taylor summarized the thrusts of the extensive research in this area by compiling a list of more than seventy strategies that decision makers can use in dealing with situations that involve uncertainty, complexity, and conflict. They point out (p. 1399) that the strategy that is required to reach a solution is determined by the decision problem, the decision environment, and the current state of the decision maker. Attributes of decision makers that have been studied include perceptual ability, information capacity, risk-taking propensity, aspiration level, and influence of these four attributes on mode of decision making. Modes of decision making include (1) *maximizing,* which involves surveying all alternatives and choosing the one that most nearly meets the ideal; (2) *satisficing,* which has a lower information-processing requirement than maximizing because it involves choosing a feasible aspiration level, searching for alternatives until one that meets that aspiration is identified, and then terminating the search; and (3) *incrementalizing,* which involves taking small steps, or increments, toward a desired goal, which is chosen by considering only a few alternatives familiar to the decision maker that can be generated by local search.

Group decision-making processes are infinitely more complicated than individual processes because more than one person is involved and because a variety of group attributes and dynamics must be added to the equation. Perhaps in some groups every person makes up his mind to some degree independently of other members. In extreme cases, members may enter a group with such strong opinions on the subject to be discussed that, for them, decisions on the matter are predetermined. Or a group may serve, for some independent souls, as just another source of information about definition of the problem and alternative solutions. Such persons may listen and decide for themselves. In such cases, a decision rule adopted by the group allows it to agree on a common opinion. A majority rule is adopted or a rule of consensus that requires everyone either to endorse the group decision or at least not to harbor serious objections to it.

At the other end of the spectrum are groups in which no one has strong opinions on the subject at hand, perhaps because members know little about it, are not interested in it, do not care about the outcome, or never before had cause to think about the matter. It may be possible that in some such groups, because the members have open minds and are detached, group discussions may mold the opinions of each member so that each reaches a common decision for the same reasons and by the same processes utilized by fellow group members. In such cases, overt or covert agreement may occur at the beginning of the process to use a satisficing mode or perhaps to rely on incremental "muddling through" because the problem at hand is so complex and contains so many ambiguous elements.

Most groups probably contain elements of both the extremes just described. Conceivably, some group members may be making up their own minds, influenced by group processes, but carrying on parallel decision procedures of their own, while others in the group are entering into common decision procedures that are being developed. Comprehensive models of group decision making, which would begin to make intelligible some of the multitude of factors that influence group decision making, have not come into common use. Even in rudimentary forms, such models would be of help to leaders of democratic and consultive processes in understanding group decision processes as they occur.

Leaders who understand the common modes and models of decision making are able to take specific action to facilitate decision processes. Another reason that knowledge of decision-making procedures is important to leaders of consultive processes has been pointed out by Yukl (1981, p. 220): "Hardly any correlational or experimental studies have examined the effect of the pattern of decision procedures used in relation to the different kinds of decisions a leader must make. Some decisions are best made in an autocratic manner, some are best made by consultation, some are best made jointly, and some are best delegated to individual subordinates. . . . Most prior research on participation simply doesn't answer the most relevant question about it, namely, 'When is each decision procedure appropriate?' "

Yukl cites Vroom and Yetton's (1973) normative model of leadership as an answer to his question. The model includes five decision methods that a leader can follow to make decisions. The methods involve subordinates in the decision process in varying ways and to varying degrees. Vroom and Yetton define these procedures as follows (p. 13):

AI.   You solve the problem or make the decision yourself, using information available to you at the time.

AII. You obtain the necessary information from your subordinates and then decide the solution to the problem yourself. You may or may not tell your subordinates what the problem is in getting the information from them. The role played by subordinates in making the decision is clearly one of providing the necessary information to you, rather than generating or evaluating alternative solutions.

CI.   You share the problem with the relevant subordinates individually, getting their ideas and suggestions without bringing them together as a group. Then *you* make the decision, which may or may not reflect your subordinates' influence.

CII. You share the problem with your subordinates as a group, obtaining their collective ideas and suggestions. Then you make the decision, which may or may not reflect your subordinates' influence.

GII. You share the problem with your subordinates as a group. Together you generate and evaluate alternatives and attempt to reach agreement (consensus) on a solution. Your role is much like that of chairman. You do not try to influence the group to adopt "your" solution, and you are willing to accept and implement any solution that has the support of the entire group.

Vroom and Yetton offer some rules to help leaders determine which of these procedures should be avoided under certain conditions as too risky and some decision flow charts to help them apply the rules. The model illustrates two decision mechanisms (CI, CII) that a leader can rely on in orchestrating a consultive process. AI and AII depict authoritarian modes of decision making, while GII depicts true group decision making. For GII to be effective, group members must be skilled in group decision making, responsible, capable, and committed to solving the problem at hand rather than satisfying selfish motives.

University Constituencies. Understanding constituencies is integral to understanding how the consultive process operates. By understanding constituencies, administrators can learn to identify circumstances in which conferring with them is essential. Such contacts allow problems to become apparent and to be defined. Through further consultation, problems may even be resolved. An administrator who understands constituencies understands that even though the legitimate needs and interests of various groups may appear wholly inconsistent, accommodation by most parties need not be impossible to achieve.

Each constituency of a university community has its own special interests, attitudes, authority and power, and even blind spots. Every problem, even every instance of a recurring problem, requires that a different set of constituencies be consulted to resolve it. Concerns of constituencies change, as do loci of responsibility for resolution of particular issues. In such a state of fluidity, the only generalization that can be made is that parties traditionally responsible for outcomes of the kind of issue that is in question are always consulted. Selection of additional parties to consultation depends on the particular interest groups or individuals who currently are finding it rewarding to play active roles in deciding university policies.

Internal constituencies of a university include faculty, students, administrators, bureaucratic staff, trustees, and minorities and special-interest groups. External constituencies include the federal and state government, the local community, the courts, institutional benefactors, prospective employers, alumni, and accrediting associations. Basic needs and interests of constituencies tend to remain fairly stable over time, although they may change in emphasis depending on the problem at hand. In meeting new problems, experienced administrators can predict with fair accuracy how proposed solutions will strike various constituencies affected and thus will be able to suggest modifications that will make measures more acceptable to all before firm commitments regarding the issue have been made.

Theories, Observations, and Commentaries on Participatory Management

Theory Z. In 1981 a book by Ouchi about participatory management in the business world became a best-seller. His Theory Z, an extension of McGregor's Theory Y (p. 58), is based on a form of management that has been extremely successful in Japan in boosting productivity. According to Ouchi, Japanese management techniques cannot be transplanted in their entirety to business firms in the United States, because the two cultures differ too much. Theory Z is an effort both to modify Japanese management techniques to fit the American culture and to point out changes in assumptions about management that can be made within the American business community that would subtly change the culture of the workplace and make it possible for Japanese management techniques to succeed. Many of Ouchi's comments describing Theory Z illuminate consultive processes in general, in any organization, including universities as well as business firms:

> In Type Z organizations ... the decision-making process is typically a consensual, participative one. Social scientists have described this process as a democratic (as opposed to autocratic or apathetic) process in which many people are drawn into the shaping of important decisions.... In Type Z companies, the decision making may be collective, but the ultimate responsibility for decision still resides in one individual.... Each person will come from the meeting with the responsibility for some individual targets set collectively by the group. The consensual process, as defined by ... Schein (1969) ..., is one in which members of the group may be asked to accept responsibility for a decision [that] they do not prefer but that the group, in an open and complete discussion, has settled upon. This combination of collective decision making with individual responsibility demands an atmosphere of trust. Only under a strong assumption that all hold basically compatible goals and that no one is engaged in self-serving behavior will individuals accept personal responsibility for a group decision and make enthusiastic attempts to get this job done....
>
> The wholistic orientation of Type Z companies ... inevitably maintains a strong egalitarian atmosphere.... An organization that maintains a wholistic orientation and forces employees at all levels to deal with one another as complete human beings creates a condition in which depersonalization is impossible, autocracy is unlikely, and open communication, trust, and commitment are common.... The natural force of organizational hierarchy promotes a segmented relationship and a hierarchical attitude. A wholistic relationship provides a counterbalance that encourages a more egalitarian attitude.
>
> Egalitarianism is a central feature of Type Z

organizations. Egalitarianism implies that each person can apply discretion and can work autonomously without close supervision, because [he is] to be trusted. Again, trust underscores the belief that goals correspond, that neither person is out to harm the other. This feature, perhaps more than any other, accounts for the high levels of commitments, of loyalty, and of productivity in Japanese firms and in Type Z organizations. . . .

Type Z organizations, unlike utopian communities, do employ hierarchical modes of control, and thus do not rely entirely upon goal congruence among employees for order. Nevertheless, they do rely extensively upon symbolic means to promote an attitude of egalitarianism and mutual trust, and they do so in part by encouraging a wholistic relation between employees. Self-direction replaces hierarchical direction to a great extent, which enhances commitment, loyalty, and motivation.

Argyris challenged managers to integrate individuals into organizations, not to create alienating, hostile, and impersonally bureaucratic places of work. In a real sense, the Type Z organization comes close to realizing that ideal. It is a consent culture, a community of equals who cooperate with one another to reach common goals. Rather than relying exclusively upon hierarchy and monitoring to direct behavior, it relies also upon commitment and trust [pp. 66-70].

Nichols (1982) argues that colleges and universities should "set the example in participatory management" and "develop an educational equivalent of the quality circle" (p. 72). A quality circle consists of Japanese workers who meet regularly to determine how products or production methods can be improved. Nichols lists a number of difficulties that must be overcome if universities are to develop places where quality circles can flourish: (1) current lack of participatory management in higher education, (2) lack of participatory leadership models, (3) general inexperience in group decision making based on consensus rather than voting, (4) confusion over who is responsible for quality control in academe, and (5) the problem of defining what "product" consists of in higher education. Nichols's second point, about the lack of participatory leadership models, is relevant to the present discussion. He states:

> Academe seems either to suffer from very indecisive leaders or, like the business world, to employ chief executives who see themselves as "Lone Ranger" bosses who are paid to make the tough, quick decisions. These rapid-fire commanders tend not to last very long. Their hasty, uninformed decisions often backfire, and they may spend months mending shattered morale and back-pedaling in a fashion that eventually destroys their dynamic image. Nevertheless, the Lone Ranger is probably our dominant leadership model.
>
> In the ideal Theory Z organization, decision-making processes are purposely slow. The participatory manager tolerates disciplined and purposeful disorder that is anything but chaotic. It is aimed at gathering facts, seeking opinions, discovering relationships, and building a consensus that gives the decision, once made, a real chance for successful implementation. That kind of leadership is not weak or confused. It sets clear goals. It reaches for quality. It provides clearly articulated purposes around which people can organize their work. It is patient enough to wait until a good decision can be made, yet strong enough to insist on reaching it [p. 75].

Some Research Findings on Consultive Leadership. Leaders play initiating and coordinating roles that are crucial to flexible processes such as consultation. Together with the preceding overview of some of the major premises of consultation, the following brief overview of certain highlights of the literature on leadership has been included to help place the consultive process in theoretical context.

Lewin and Lippitt (1938) performed the first study that distinguished between autocratic and democratic leadership. Since then, the dichotomy has persisted in the literature, although names and concepts used to describe both sides have varied markedly from time to time. Bales and Strodtbeck (1951) distinguished between task-oriented and people-oriented leadership, for example. In leadership studies conducted at Ohio State University by Halpin and Winer (1952), factor analysis revealed that two factors ("initiating structure" and "consideration") accounted for over 80 percent of the variance in leadership style. Fiedler (1964) carried on the tradition of assuming a dichotomy of leadership styles in his studies involving Least Preferred Coworker scores, calling the two types of leadership task-oriented and relationship-oriented. Vroom and Yetton (1973) also worked within the dichotomy, although their approach was very different in that they assumed the most basic function of a leader is to make decisions. In general, in the literature, task orientation, initiating structure, or other such concepts are presumed to be essential elements of an authoritarian style of leadership, while people orientation or considerations related directly to meeting workers' needs and only indirectly to task accomplishment are presumed to be essential elements of a democratic style.

McGregor (1960), in his Theory Y view of human beings, described members of organizations as possessing wide ranges of resources, which included not merely job skills but creativity, self-direction, and responsibility. McGregor stated, "Acceptance of Theory Y does not imply abdication or 'soft' management or 'permissiveness' . . . such notions stem from the acceptance of authority as the *single* means of managerial control and from attempts to minimize its negative consequences. Theory Y assumes that people will exercise self-direction and self-control in the achievement of organizational objectives *to the degree that they are committed to those objectives.* If that commitment is small, only a slight degree of self-direction and self-control will be likely, and a substantial amount of external influence will be necessary. If it is large, many conventional external controls will be relatively superfluous and to some extent self-defeating. Managerial policies and practices materially affect this degree of commitment" (1969, p. 201).

McGregor's work was influential in the early stage of an antibureaucratic, human relations trend in management studies and theories that explored means of developing workers' potential to the fullest through management techniques. Ouchi (1981,

p. 69) pointed out that McGregor's work drew heavily on the work of a former student, Chris Argyris. Argyris (1964, 1971) and Argyris and Schön (1974) advocated a people-oriented style, which they presented as a learning model to be used to improve leadership skills. They named the dichotomy Model I versus Model II, or "theory-in-use" versus "theory espoused." They described and compared the two models in terms of governing variables, action strategies, consequences for the behavioral world, consequences for learning, and effectiveness (1974, pp. 68-69, 87). They argued that Model II behavior is more effective and can be learned and that professional education should be redesigned accordingly.

Some studies of participative leadership were extremely people-oriented, while others straddled the dichotomy, being task-oriented as well. Likert (1961, 1967) contrasted a participatory leadership style with the authoritarian style, which he divided into three substyles (exploitative, benevolent, and consultive), thus creating a four-value scale of good to bad leadership. He considered participative management effective in all kinds of organizations, for all kinds of tasks. Likert argued against the view that managers should move toward a participative style only after a high level of productivity is achieved (1967, p. 11). He believed that an interest-in-people approach is not a luxury but a necessity.

Bennis (1969) took a people-oriented stance as an advocate of organizational development, an approach in which the role of the administrator is seen as changing the organization to allow members to achieve their full potential. Bennis identified one characteristic of organizational development as "an *educational strategy* adopted to bring about a *planned organizational change*" (p. 10). He said, "The only viable way to change organizations is to change their 'culture,' that is, to change the systems within which people work and live" (p. v). He advocated accomplishing this by an individual approach in which people in a workshop setting or other small learning group are stimulated to change their behavior, which initiates changes in their attitudes, which, in turn, changes the "culture" of their organizations as more individuals undergo metamorphosis. Initiating consultive processes also requires change in the culture, but a formal "educational strategy" has not been attempted. Instead, consultation, like innumerable subjects, can be taught effectively in an organizational setting by example—by doing it, pointing out positive results, and helping others to imitate the process.

Stogdill (1974) has been critical of a purely participative approach to management. He stated, "Results . . . do not confirm any simplistic or polarized theory of leader behavior and group response. The results suggest, rather, the operation of interaction effects. A pattern of behavior effective in one situation is not necessarily effective in other situations. In view of the complexity of leader behavior and the variety of situations in which it functions, a conditional and multivariate hypothesis seems more reasonable than a simplistic, bipolar view of the leader-follower relationship" (p. 407).

Cohen and March (1974) advocated a leadership strategy that does not straddle the authoritarian/participative dichotomy so much as transcend it. Their model, which has been adapted to higher education administration by Baldridge and others (1978), focused less on normative aspects of administration—that is, on what constitutes a "good" manager. Instead, they described what a manager must do to stay in power, so that whatever managerial skills he may possess will have a chance to have an impact. Baldridge and his associates described the leader (in their "political model" of governance) as "a mediator, a negotiator, a person who jockeys between power blocs trying to establish viable courses of action for the institution" (p. 45). Walker (1979) also adopted a political model that is basically similar to Cohen and March's approach. He described the differences thusly: "For example, Cohen and March stress the underuse of the 'competitive market, anarchy, independent judiciary, and plebiscitary autocracy models of governance in the universities.' I include at least a portion of these models in the democratic political concept offered here. . . . I propose that the political perspective has not been sufficiently explored as the basis on which we can make sound predictions concerning university behavior and . . . as the basis on which administrators can construct an effective style" (p. 11).

Blake and Mouton's managerial grid (1964) treats task orientation and people orientation, or "concern for people," as orthogonal dimensions of leadership style. Both their managerial grid and their adaptation of it to academic administration (Blake, Mouton, and Williams, 1981) straddle the task/people orientation dichotomy and are learning models to improve managerial skills. While the consultive process has quite a bit in common with Blake and Mouton's grid, it probably resembles most closely the approach of Mortimer and McConnell (1978). They also emphasize process as the most promising route to improving governance. They state that "the sharing of formal authority, the scope and form of internal participation in governance, and the vertical distribution of authority should be characterized by full and open consultation with an emphasis on joint endeavor. Consultation and joint effort should be built on a high degree of trust. Trust can be encouraged by an emphasis on process" (p. 275).

Although Mortimer and McConnell do not explore the practice of consultation in depth, they emphasize that "ensuring adequate consultation has six elements: consultation should occur early in the decision-making process; procedures for consultation should be uniform and fair to all parties; there must be adequate time to formulate a response to the request for consultation; information relevant to the decision should be freely available; advice rendered must be adequately considered and feedback given; and the decision, when made, should be communicated to the consulting group" (p. 275). In the next chapter, some further considerations will be mentioned that are important in conducting consultive processes through various kinds of campus governance bodies.

3

Working with University Governance Bodies

The basic and most commonly used form of consultation consists simply of two or more persons talking together. Exchanges may be formally structured, planned, and conducted through written documents or unstructured, serendipitous, and conducted orally. The most common purposes of individual consultation are to elicit ideas or reactions on issues from others and to solicit support for one's own ideas. Such consultation may preclude, be preparatory to, or be simultaneous with consultation in a formal setting. Even when formal structures for consultation exist that have been legitimized by use over time, individuals must continually consult informally to settle matters of common concern.

Individual consultation is greatly affected by the personal characteristics of the parties involved. Congeniality, mutual respect and trust, familiarity with each other's agendas and principles, and knowledge of the subject under consideration color outcomes and determine effectiveness of consultation. A respected administrator can strongly influence the leaders of a faculty senate. A respected faculty leader can sway an administrative council. Although neither party may have final authority over an issue, either can initiate further consultation through formal structures or preclude the need for such consultation by resolving the issue informally. Legitimacy of individual consultation depends on a variety of elements. Ranks and expertise of officials and primacy and jurisdiction of the constituencies they represent are critical. Centrality of an issue to the interests or charges of officials and constitutional groups is crucial to the binding quality of the results agreed on. Place and setting also have definite effects on legitimacy of consultation. For example, a conversation in a hallway may not carry the influence of an exchange in a prearranged meeting in a boardroom.

If the objective of a concerned party is to halt change in a policy or program, informal consultation may resolve the issue. But informal consultation may not be adequate to initiate change in policy, since change of any significance usually requires formal endorsement by a consultive body. Similarly, if misinformation rather than conflicting interests creates a need for consultation, informal processes may resolve the issue. But when constituency needs and positions are at stake, although informal process can reveal the real issues and perhaps facilitate compromise, formal consultation through appropriate structures most likely will be required for resolution.

Charters or bylaws of structures separate many issues that can be settled only through formal consultation from issues that can be settled by informal means. A dean is usually prohibited from changing curricula without approval of appropriate faculty committees. A president may be required to consult the faculty senate before amending the tenure code or to seek the approval of the board of trustees or state administration in order to modify building programs. An administrator should be familiar with all charters and mandates of all governance structures on his campus and should develop a fine sense of each structure's relative legitimacy and influence. Details of charters may differ significantly from one institution to another. Charters of many faculty senates, for example, claim extremely broad jurisdiction over all topics important to the academic community and over all matters affecting the welfare of faculty members; other charters define jurisdictional boundaries in less sweeping terms. Authority of faculty senates can be as inclusive or as exclusive as faculties wish to make it or as past practices dictate. As a result, substantial differences exist among institutions in how extensively and on what issues faculty senates consult or are consulted.

Although a faculty senate has overall jurisdiction on most issues that affect the academic area, it should not substitute its judgment for that of curriculum committees, admissions committees, or appeals committees of colleges and schools. Similarly, collegial faculty assemblies should not frequently or casually intervene in departmental committee processes, even when empowered to do so by their charters. Senates and assemblies should behave as the broad governance structures that they are and not attempt to operate programs or manage projects.

Executive functions may be performed by committees especially constituted for that purpose—for example, a computer policy committee. Such committees may include as members persons who are involved in various governance structures to ensure that jurisdictional networks are not violated, that communications networks function efficiently, and that executive implementation of policies is congruent with the intentions of the governance structures that drafted the policies. Some executive committees that are not charged with policy making do so nonetheless by establishing practice. A research council may establish priorities for seed grants, which may seem to be an innocuous and entirely legitimate move but which may have considerable effect on shaping the mission of the institution. The research council also may determine who is awarded seed grants —which is an executive function. Subsequently, it may review performance of the researchers, an activity that overlaps the authority of other units or groups. Working in a network that includes many groups with complex structure and function is neither impossible nor undesirable. Improvement in outcomes can make worthwhile the additional time that must be spent in coordinating such groups' activities.

Evolving Behavior of Deliberative Bodies

As charters of deliberative bodies are modified by amendments to bylaws, legislation, regulation, or interpretation through common practice, the bodies change accordingly. Deliberative bodies also evolve through stages of maturation and cycles of re-vitalization, even if their charters are not modified. A delibera-tive body may be established initially in response to a perceived need or an issue requiring immediate action. In its initial phase, the body is enamored of its power, convinced of its relevance, and confident of its wisdom. It spends its first months seeking a clearer definition of its purpose. It asks, "Why are we here?" It also spends a good deal of time defining formal and informal rules according to which it will conduct its business.

Soon after, like all adolescents, it may begin to test appro-priate authority figures by overstepping bounds and carefully observing their reactions to its misbehavior. It wants to know whether its efforts are appreciated and respected and whether its recommendations will be taken seriously and funded. The adolescent deliberative body vacillates among states of confu-sion, frustration, euphoria, and self-aggrandizement.

As a group matures, members jockey for position of lead-ership or influence. The group gradually organizes a base of common knowledge of facts and issues and develops, through much interaction, a style of working together as a committee. It builds a sense of mutual trust and confidence by exchanging perceptions of values, purposes, and experiences and by testing individual members' reactions to problems brought before it. Unless a group is an ad hoc committee or task force, these stages appear to be necessary to its development, but their dura-tion can be shortened if committee members bring a sense of urgency to their task, convene frequently, or have worked to-gether before.

The mature deliberative body has accepted its charter, understands its responsibilities, is convinced of its legitimacy, knows that its recommendations will be taken seriously, and understands its limitations and its boundaries of authority. Through experience, its members have become comfortable with one another. Periodic turnover, if spread over time to en-sure continuity, usually is not disruptive. New members are ex-pected to exercise self-restraint until they master the game. Meeting times, agenda format, and rules of order have become routinized and are no longer the objects of serious discussion.

On occasion, when a mature deliberative body attempts

to reach beyond its jurisdiction or substitute its judgment for that of another legitimate group, reminding it of its proper sphere of influence is necessary. An attentive administrator who, in the earlier, more insecure stages of a group, may have been regarded as threatening or interfering may be regarded in the mature stage of a deliberative body as cooperative and facilitative. The consultive process is most successful when mature consultive bodies are involved. They provide a medium in which constituencies can work well together toward common goals in an open, mutually supportive fashion and can resolve conflicts without permanent damage to relationships.

A deliberative body in the gerontological stage demonstrates very different behavior. A primary determinant of behavior at this stage is whether its mandate, or purpose for being, remains important. If events or policies have passed it by, and the issues it addressed are no longer central to the mission of the university, a deliberative body may slide into a stage of dormancy. Its chairman or leader convenes meetings infrequently and does not prepare significant agendas. Its members lose interest in committee business, and their deliberations become desultory. Natural leaders or key figures decline to serve as officers or stop attending meetings. As outcomes become less significant, recommendations are not acted on promptly by the administration.

Can a body in such a state be rejuvenated? One growth potion is to give it a new mandate, such as a broader charter to deal with more central or more controversial issues. Another stimulative is to appoint a proactive, or at least energetic, chairman who can revitalize the agenda, stimulate attendance, and make sure recommendations are implemented. A third salutary action is to alter the membership of the group, if its charter so allows, to foster intelligent and informed dialogue on appropriate issues by people who are opinion leaders in the university community.

Rejuvenating a council past its time may not be wise. There can be merit in change for change's sake. For example, creation of a new council that takes over the functions of several others can eliminate dormant structures while revitalizing the consultive process. The relative wisdom of changing committee names must be weighed against drawbacks. Certain constituencies may want the presence and name of a particular committee preserved. They may argue for retaining the name while making fundamental alterations in the committee's charter, functions, and membership, so that it is new in all but name. In such cases, wisdom may not dictate a new name for the group and a new charter. Usually, however, an appearance of substantive change helps to stimulate the body to reenter an adolescent phase and begin a new life cycle.

Types of Deliberative Bodies

Six types of deliberative bodies play major roles in university governance: task forces and ad hoc committees, policy councils, advisory boards, executive management committees, governing boards, and coordinating councils. Understanding the functions of each major type of deliberative body is essential to understanding how to conduct consultive processes.

Task Forces and Ad Hoc Committees. Task forces and ad hoc committees have relatively short life spans. They are created in response to particular needs, and once the needs have been met, the bodies are dissolved. Such groups are given specific, narrowly defined charges. Particular issues are addressed that may range from defining problems to agreeing on or cooperatively implementing solutions. Because their life spans are limited by the charges they are given, and because their assigned tasks are well defined, task forces and ad hoc committees may pass through their adolescent stages quite quickly.

Of all structures serving the consultive process, none is more subject to the vagaries of human behavior, the dynamics of personalities, and the impact of individual leadership than an ad hoc group. Whereas policy councils and boards tend to have formal charters and bylaws or rules of order, ad hoc groups have few constraints imposed by appointing authorities and usually are free to determine their own means of achieving their assigned goals. Therefore, style and personality of chairmen and members are central to the deliberative processes of these groups and to the quality and nature of their recommendations. The fact that wise appointees are more likely to make wise decisions is another reason that composition of a task force or ad hoc committee is the most important single determinant of its effectiveness. If members are well informed and experienced, they can be expected to perform adequately even if the charge to the group is framed awkwardly, deliberative processes are poorly structured, and instructions about interaction with other decision-making bodies are not well defined. The chairman of the group must be chosen with extreme care, since he will be responsible for orchestrating the group's deliberative and decision-making processes.

Members of ad hoc groups must bear in mind that their recommendations are implemented at the pleasure of the appointing authority. They are not considered binding, as are recommendations of policy councils. If, however, many recommendations are not accepted, an appointing authority must be ready to deal with the task force's resentment at having wasted its time, and the issue at stake may be exacerbated. Failure to accept recommendations may quickly become a topic of campus discussion.

If appointment of the chairman of the group and the majority of its members cannot be controlled, then it is wise to be precise in the charge to the group. Expected outcomes and the limits and constraints to be observed must be made explicit. Also to be specified are who should be consulted during deliberations, whether open meetings should be held, what testimony or evidence should be examined, the coordination with other committees or offices that is expected, the person to whom the group is to report, and the sequence and time frame of deliberations.

Composition of ad hoc groups is always open to challenge. Unless all constituencies who have stakes in an issue are consulted from the very beginning of the process of organization, a group may never have a chance to be effective. Constituencies must acquiesce in the concept of an ad hoc group as a means of joint problem solving and must accept the representatives appointed to the group. Otherwise the group may be accused of bias or unfair representation, which may render its decisions void.

Policy Councils. Faculty recommendations on matters such as tenure and curriculum that traditionally are under the faculty's jurisdiction are usually expressed through policy councils. Policy councils are standing bodies, which may operate on a universitywide basis or at the school level. Members of a policy council may be elected by a faculty senate or equivalent body. Administrative appointees may be included, or means may be specified to interrelate policy councils with administrative leaders.

Although deans, as well as university presidents and boards of trustees, may have authority to veto recommendations of policy councils, no administrator can long or often ignore advice from such a source. A president or dean is wise to respond to council recommendations that cannot be implemented with a statement of reasons for his veto. Philosophical, administrative, legal, or financial justification for rejecting the council's advice may be cited. The 1966 joint statement of the AAUP, ACE, and AGB states (Section V) that governing boards and presidents should communicate to faculties their reasons for adversely exercising their powers of review. The joint statement points out that "budgets, manpower limitations, the time elements, and the policies of other groups, bodies, and agencies having jurisdiction over the institution may set limits to realization of faculty advice."

The nature, purposes, and charge of a policy council are usually articulated in a charter. In addition, committees of faculty senates or assemblies may establish rules, procedures, or grounds for subsequent review of rulings. Unfortunately, however, such procedural directives are often ill-defined and are limited only by past practice. Participation, working relations with administrators, and consultation with other councils are also guided primarily by past practice.

A council may be empowered to add members whose particular expertise is needed or to include in its deliberations ex officio, nonvoting persons whose advice can contribute significantly to decision making or to implementation processes. Al-

though charters of many councils may not permit such additions to membership, parent bodies may bless exceptions. An
advantage of representative composition is that faculty members will view policy councils as upholding their values, perspectives, and interests; a disadvantage is that policy councils may
be formed that are wholly lacking in competence to deal with
the problems at hand. Well-intentioned amateurs can learn and
can be of great value, but they should not be saddled with responsibility for deciding important matters beyond their experience. Knowledgeable faculty members should be encouraged to
volunteer to be candidates for policy council positions. The
problem is that faculty members commonly feel overcommitted
and frequently are. Inclusion on policy councils of campus politicians who are no longer active in scholarship or research and
who busy themselves instead by serving on committees is not
necessarily the answer to this dilemma. Being out of touch with
the needs of active scholars, they may recommend policies that
do not meet current requirements. Nevertheless, at some institutions, campus politicians have made exceptional contributions.

Administrators should not try to subvert the representative nature of policy committees by maneuvering behind the
scenes to influence election of members. They must, however,
continually remind faculty members who are unwilling to stir
from their classrooms and laboratories that the decisions of policy committees have constant, direct effects on teaching and research. Faculty members often decide to take turns as representatives when they understand that their personal interests are at
stake.

Because policy councils are usually quite free to establish
their own procedures, routines, agendas, and styles of review,
administrators who are committed to developing positive, fruitful collaborative relationships with policy councils stand a good
chance of being able to do so. Thus, submission of requests or
draft statements to a policy council may yield all the benefits
consultation has to offer. It may, however, have consequences
unforeseen by individuals submitting the material. Having accepted a request or statement into its domain, a policy council
may not be willing to release it until it has explored the issue to

its satisfaction. A suggestion submitted to a policy council should be well considered, since withdrawing it may be no simple affair. Further, a policy council reserves the right not merely to approve, amend, or restructure drafts submitted for its consideration but to prepare from scratch entirely different statements. A naive administrator may submit a draft of a patent policy, for instance, with the intention that the policy council rubber-stamp it. But the council may decide to rewrite the statement and may return to the administrator a product of which he never dreamed. A policy council also reserves the right to refuse to deliberate a problem on jurisdictional grounds.

Agendas and actions of policy councils are usually a matter of public record. This means that submitting a draft document to a policy council gives the draft high visibility. Since the fact that consultation is underway on the council level may be a topic of interest on campus, sensitive matters that cannot be resolved except through the action of a policy council must be carefully handled. The act of sending a draft statement to a policy council has still other implications. The council assumes the right to gather facts pertinent to the issue and to examine relevant documents, some of which certain administrators may prefer to keep unseen. High expectation generally exists that a council's recommendations will be implemented. Having acted on a policy statement, a council reserves the right of review of all subsequent amendments of the statement. A policy council expects to receive progress reports from time to time about implementation of its products and may wish to participate in reevaluation of a policy if complaints about it are made.

Advisory Boards. Advisory boards are of several types. Although none has the scope of authority of a board of trustees, advisory boards serve as vehicles through which opinions of broad ranges of constituencies are solicited. No formal obligation exists to follow advice forwarded by advisory boards, but usually it is wise to be attentive to their concerns.

External advisory boards, such as a board of advisers of a dental or engineering school of a university, often serve several functions. One is to elicit opinions from alumni employed in the profession, from professional and accrediting associations, from businesspersons, and from politicians and other concerned, knowledgeable constituencies. Opinions are sought on planning directions, program changes, and similar future-oriented issues. A second function is to channel not only the opinions of the aforementioned constituencies but their money and their influence to support existing programs and to build new ones. This assists the dean and the president in fund raising, creates a generally favorable public opinion of the school, and solicits political support within and outside the institution. Advisory boards can be used by a president to ease out a recalcitrant dean. They can also be used by a dean to pressure his president into supporting his contention that his school needs a new laboratory or additional faculty members.

The power held by an advisory board depends on the prestige and influence of its members. Relations between the appointing authority and the board tend to be cordial and non-confrontational. An advisory board sees itself as a group constituted to assist an administration, not to cause problems for it. Advisory boards generally operate by deciding major issues by consensus. This means that voting coalitions are rare or are fluid in composition. Both policy and management crises may surface in advisory boards, especially if clients or constituencies become dissatisfied. On an advisory board, interpersonal conflict is rarely expressed as such. It is usually manifested by argument over practices or conflicting principles.

Internal advisory boards have more complex roles than their external counterparts. Some are de facto policy boards, since to ignore their recommendations would lead to unfortunate publicity or to loss of confidence in the administration. Internal advisory boards of this sort may reign over campus newspapers, monitor facilities-planning or development campaigns, or coordinate relations with public school districts or minority communities. Internal advisory boards are often composed of a mixture of concerned constituencies, such as faculty opinion makers, student leaders, responsible administrators, and trustees. Composition and charge are more critical to the success of an advisory group than for most other deliberative bodies. An irascible trustee or an archconservative or ultraliberal faculty member can cause more problems than the advisory board was created to resolve.

An appointing authority should select members with an eye to their expertise, sense of responsibility, and mature judgment. He should not waste time worrying about whether the advisory board will agree with all his opinions or will forward to him only those recommendations that he wishes to receive, because such boards are not controllable under any circumstances. He should be content if deliberations are thoughtful, if recommendations are not unreasonable, and if naive and inexperienced members do not dominate outcomes. If members are to be selected by several appointing authorities (one third by the president, one third by the faculty senate, and one third by the student government, for example), who appoints which parties, and in what sequence? An administrator is wise to await action by all other parties before designating his appointees, so that the best balance of representatives of constituencies and the best blend of expertise, sound judgment, and responsibility can be achieved. Premature action on appointments can deal trump cards to others and thereby predetermine outcomes.

The most important single determinant of success of an advisory body is appointment of the chairman, because he controls agenda and process. Because charge and procedure typically are broadly defined for an advisory body, the appointment of a senior, respected person is essential to management of the group. The chairman can determine with whom the board consults and to whom it circulates its opinions, draft reports and recommendations, appoint subcommittees or study groups, and control meeting times and information flow.

Administrative style in relating to an advisory board must be gauged carefully, relative to the particular charge to the board and how its chairman interprets that charge. If the chairman is reasonably responsive and effective, the administration and faculty should not interfere with his getting on with business. An advisory board is not expected to be counterproductive in its recommendations. But responses to a recommendation that is counterproductive should be to the point, not directed against members of the board, its mode of operation, or other such peripheral matters.

Executive Management Committees. Unlike other types of committees, an executive management committee is intended to represent only the management perspective. All members of such a committee are executives, but they by no means share a unified perspective on issues. Each member represents a different constituency and supports the interests of his group. A vice-president for academic affairs does not have the same interests as a vice-president for business and finance. This does not mean the two officers cannot respect each other's perspectives or work cooperatively for common goals.

A unique situation can occur in executive management committees that can interfere with the cooperative efforts that should result from their deliberations. Some executives tend to be competitive and success-oriented and want their domains to become as strong as possible. These ego needs are often reflected in personal agendas presented to the chief executive of the group for authorization. When personal agendas clash, willingness to compromise is diminished. In a group in which strong personal rivalries exist, discussion becomes more intense and manipulative. Personal flights of fancy of the chief executive officer may be allowed to go unchallenged in efforts to woo his favor. Even so, once a decision is made under such conditions, warring parties tend to comply with the decision and to do so with sophisticated understanding of its impact. If the members of a committee are all professionals, they bring to the arena considerable skill and training in intellectual discourse. They tend to fight hard, to listen well, to understand opponents' viewpoints, and to be critical and manipulative in discussion. They also tend to be outcome-oriented during subsequent implementation, with little tendency to gain revenge against opponents by refusing to cooperate with the majority decision.

If an executive management committee is made up of deputies or assistants of chief executives, as often happens in matrix management, the relative stature and locus in the pecking order of each member's boss are of greater significance than the personal standing of the members themselves. Among themselves, deputies outmaneuver and dominate one another, differ in perspectives, skills, intelligence, and stature, and establish an internal pecking order of their own. As in any group, these factors have some effect on outcomes. Yet, the deputy of the president plays every game with an intrinsically stronger hand than deputies of lower-ranked officials or deans can muster. He can apply this advantage at will, since he has the ear of the person who occupies the most powerful office on campus.

Chances are good that the recommendations of an executive management committee will be implemented, because its recommendations are made by persons with authority or by their deputies. Such participants bring to the decision-making process the best information available. During implementation of decisions, executive management committees expect progress reports because their own staffs are participating. Persistent conflicts that arise during implementation eventually involve participants' supervisors, unless the implementation team agree to keep disagreements to themselves. Deputies inevitably try to arouse their supervisors to oppose the supervisors of rival deputies. Jaded supervisors should remember that sometimes such action is necessary and warranted.

Psychopathology in a member of an executive management committee is particularly hazardous. To an extent unheard of in other committees, aberrant judgment can have great impact on process and outcomes and, of course, on the university community at large. The higher-ranked the person, the greater the impact. Inexperience, a tendency to promote hidden agendas, immaturity, ineptitude, and a habit of placing one's personal interest before the interest of the university are also hazards in high-ranking administrators. Unfortunately, personality defects frequently do not become obvious or incapacitating until responsibility and stress are considerable.

The nature, duration, authority, and charge of executive management committees vary widely. These factors, in turn, determine the composition of the committee, frequency and nature of meetings, and intended outcomes. If the committee is to function as a cabinet that decides universitywide policies, it may meet weekly and include all senior officials. A finance committee may meet intensively only during budget making and only monthly or quarterly thereafter. Many executive management committees are matrix teams appointed to oversee projects or to resolve particular problems. In such cases, each member is chosen by his superior in the hierarchy on the basis of his expertise or current responsibilities. Membership is always appointive and may be of indefinite duration. Persons with knowledge, skills, or connections that could assist the committee may be appointed as needed.

Executive management committees can be extremely effective because they provide a meeting ground for senior officials or their deputies, who bring different perspectives to bear on problems, and try to develop solutions acceptable to all parties. Consumption of so many hours of time of the most expensive and talented persons in the hierarchy can be too high a price to pay, however. Problems brought before executive management committees must be selected carefully on the basis of importance. The appropriateness of executive action in proposing and implementing solutions must also be considered. Other bodies may have formal authority over the issues or be more effective.

The right to designate deputies as substitutes is an important prerogative of members of executive management committees, especially because various executives understandably have differing degrees of interest and investment in the outcomes of particular deliberations. From time to time, topics arise that may be central to the responsibilities or critical to the progress of a particular executive. On certain issues, only a chief executive or vice-president can reach closure. On other issues, however, deputies may be better able to avoid personality conflicts and weigh alternative solutions. When only deputies are in the room, trial balloons may be floated and alternatives tested that could not be broached with bosses present. Controversial or radical ideas can be explored without risking premature reaction by the president that could block a potentially fruitful path to a satisfactory solution. Presidents may have no choice but to ban certain ends because of the means associated with them, but if alternative means to a particular end can be devised in a meeting of deputies, the problem may be solved and the president's dilemma may evaporate. Without compromising either their bosses or the process of negotiation, deputies can return repeatedly to their bosses for instructions and guidance.

Administrators who are tempted to renege on avowed principles when under pressure should remember that they may have to pay a high price in loss of trust and confidence of their staff, subordinates, and constituencies. Thus, senior officials protect themselves from premature public commitment on issues by relying on deputies, who for the sake of resolving problems may engage in bargaining and posturing that their bosses could not dare to do without risking loss of credibility. When a vice-president has taken a stand, compromise may be difficult. When a president has taken a public stand, he may feel compromise is impossible. It may be advisable to avoid premature hardening of positions through early, public commitment.

Because deputies have few ceremonial duties to consume their time or give them public visibility, they are able to investigate issues and engage in consultations. As a result, deputies may be better informed than executives about the issues at hand and about constituencies' attitudes toward the issues. Often their presence is the catalyst and the lubricant that slide negotiations to closure. Owing to these advantages, executive management committees composed of deputies sometimes propose wiser compromises than their bosses, who have less freedom of action.

Governing Boards. Governing boards, like coordinating councils, are usually composed of lay volunteers. Members may be altruistic and service-minded, they may have business interests in the region where the institution is located, or they may be alumni who view board membership as advantageous to their careers. The amount of power each member wields on a board depends largely on his prestige or influence beyond the board. A member may have enough money or authority to stand as an independent power broker, or he may represent the interests of a region, economic sector, or constituent group.

Most board members take their fiduciary responsibilities

very seriously and are eager to hear reports of balanced budgets. Board members are also responsive to problems concerning athletics and pay careful attention to athletic facilities and programs. A third area of intense interest is constituent complaints, including problems in community relations, alumni complaints, and student protests. Seasoned board members refer most such matters to administrators for action. Occasionally, a member will intervene personally in resolving a problem, but for the most part, members want some administrator to take appropriate action to alleviate the problem, if not resolve it. Experienced trustees have no desire to avoid responsibilities assigned to them by charter, but they see no need to become involved in conflicts on most issues.

Boards should never be surprised or pressed for quick decisions on important matters. Administrators should keep board members informed of projects and programs as they develop. Early drafts and progress reports should be circulated among board members for their information and comment, so that when the time comes for official endorsement, any objections will have been laid to rest. Board members should be consulted individually on university matters that fall in their realms of professional competence. Trustees who are lawyers may have particular interest in matters of policy that are brought before them. Often they will confer among themselves, with university counsel, or with external parties before agreeing that a policy statement is fair and appropriate. A board will usually vote to approve legal documents that have passed muster with university counsel and all the lawyers on the board. Similarly, board members with appropriate professional training and experience should be contacted personally when matters involving real estate, facilities planning, or investment are under review. Appointment of trustees to committees should be determined, at least in part, by their backgrounds so that their competencies are used to the fullest.

When reviewing decisions concerning faculty members, boards seek assurance that their institutions are not being compromised, that financial liabilities of alternative solutions are clearly understood, and that due process is being followed.

When tenure decisions are brought before boards for their approval, members rarely overturn recommendations forwarded by faculties through department chairmen, deans, the vice-president for academic affairs, and the president. Instead, boards want assurance that all appropriate parties were consulted, that criteria and standards for awarding of tenure as defined in the faculty handbook were applied, and that no hidden issues exist.

If boards are kept informed of developments and are given opportunities to react to drafts and progress reports well before final projects are submitted for approval, consultation can progress in an orderly and effective fashion. Presidents should encourage their vice-presidents to work closely with chairmen of counterpart committees of the board to develop mutual respect and trust so that issues can be resolved as they are raised. This also produces a sense of continuity and fulfilled responsibility. Boards of trustees are rarely blamed for what they do. More often they are criticized for what they do not do, particularly for not working hard at fund raising or for otherwise not attending to their institution's well-being.

Monitoring programs and requiring administrators to explain and defend policies or issues about which constituencies have raised questions are appropriate functions of a board of trustees. Deeper involvement in university affairs would mean taking over executive functions, a state of affairs that trustees and administrators alike generally wish to avoid. Boards of some state-supported institutions have statutory responsibility to elect faculty members, to confer tenure, and to authorize budget amendments in detail. Under such circumstances, boards are particularly insistent that appropriate administrators carry out all preparatory analyses and draft recommendations for special action. They tend to amend administrative drafts only in their own areas of professional competence, such as law, finance, real estate, or investment. They expect administrators to play ministerial roles, acting as if they were empowered to proceed, and seeking board approval before or after they have acted. For example, when a board is empowered to elect faculty, department chairmen must still organize faculty recruitment procedures, and vice-presidents for academic affairs must still prepare letters of appointment, even though all appointments are subject to board approval. No board would undertake to conduct a search for a faculty member to fill a vacancy, although from time to time a board member may ask a vice-president for academic affairs or a dean whether an opening exists for which a friend might qualify.

Boards of trustees hold a public trust and have final authority over most areas of university decision making. Schenkel (1971, p. 9) states: "As a body, the governing board of a public university can . . . be either a defender or a censor of the university, depending on the political climate in which individuals are appointed to board membership." Responsible boards learn when to question or challenge decisions for the good of the institution and when, instead, to protect their university or its administration from improper outside pressures. Administrators are the losers if they fail to keep board members informed or fail to consult them routinely on appropriate issues.

State Coordinating Councils. In 1976 coordinating structures existed in all but two states (Glenny, 1976, p. 37). At the beginning of the 1970s, supporters of centralized control sought to expand access to education while maintaining quality. By the mid 1970s, cost-effectiveness had become the driving consideration. The recommendation by the Carnegie Commission on Higher Education (1974, pp. 332–333) that strong state agencies be established may have been a factor in the expansion of the authority of such agencies during the 1970s. The commission recommended specifically, however, that state agencies confine themselves to exercising control over establishment of new institutions, new campuses, and new degree programs. Some state agencies have acquired broader powers that far exceed the limits recommended by the commission.

Minimum powers of regulatory coordinating boards have been defined by Glenny and others (1971, p. 7). Mortimer and McConnell (1978) summarized these powers: "(1) To engage in continual short-range and long-range planning. (2) To acquire information from all postsecondary institutions by means of statewide data systems. (3) To review and approve new and existing degree programs, new campuses, extension centers, and departments and centers of all public institutions and of private institutions receiving substantial state aid. (4) To make recommendations on all facets of both operating and capital budgets and, when requested by state authorities, to present a consolidated budget for the entire system. (5) To administer directly or have under its coordinating powers all state scholarship and grant programs to students, grant programs to private institutions, and state-administered federal grant and aid programs" (p. 223).

Diminishing finances constitute one of the most critical stresses on universities during the last decades of the century. Mortimer and McConnell state: "The overriding problem has become how to use limited resources more effectively. To this end, some form of effective coordination has become needed even more than ever to minimize duplication of educational offerings, overambitious educational plans by institutions and faculty entrepreneurs, and inefficiency" (p. 230). In undertaking such efforts, coordinating boards should be attentive to three main issues. First, not every school should try to become a research-oriented, doctorate-granting multiversity. Mortimer and McConnell claim, very rightly, that "less diversity means a reduction of educational opportunity" (p. 231). Schools must define their missions in terms of their traditions and the publics that they serve, while bearing in mind the missions of other schools in the system. The tendency of administrators and faculty members to try to mold their colleges into more prestigious institutions, combined with the tendency of coordinating boards to standardize all schools under their supervision, can produce a homogeneous product that does not adequately meet the full range of public needs.

Regional coordination is a second issue to be considered in efforts to utilize resources more efficiently. In some cases, coordination may be more effective if conducted not on a statewide basis but with smaller groups of institutions that serve populations of particular areas. Program coordination of institutions by category is also necessary to prevent inappropriate duplication of services among state universities, among state colleges, and among community colleges. Such analysis gives institutions a chance to differentiate missions and programs to mutual advantage.

A third issue to be borne in mind in resource allocation and planning is the fact that the central coordinating body should not unnecessarily substitute its judgment for that of individual campuses when the competency to make necessary decisions resides at the campus level. However, Mortimer and McConnell cite a problem of decentralization—namely, that "organizations generally have an almost inherent tendency to displace, modify, and expand their original goals so that the result is very different from the original intent" (p. 245). Consultation helps to contain this tendency. Mortimer and McConnell join Selznick (1957, p. 115), who advocates, at an institutional level, "collaborative development of plans and policies by as many levels of the organization as possible, so that a unified view, or at least understanding of the controlling viewpoint, will be achieved." Collaborative development of plans and policies by institutions within a statewide system is no less important.

A state coordinating council may consist of persons appointed by the governor, may be empowered by the legislature to perform certain reviews, and may have full delegated authority over approval of degree programs and distribution of resources among state institutions. Members of such councils commonly serve the state system part-time while working full-time on their own careers. The bulk of the council's work, therefore, may fall to a paid staff. If the staff director has high credibility with state political leaders or with members of the coordinating council, he may become the most influential figure in higher education in the state.

Attitudes of staffs of state coordinating councils are shaped by a variety of influences, among which are the opinions of political leaders in the executive branch or the legislature. If a council staff perceives that key leaders are currently stressing quality, then council guidelines, statements, and approvals of new programs will reflect such considerations. Occasionally, staffs misinterpret signals and move in directions that political leadership did not intend them to take. Because staff of a coordinating council may function in an advisory capacity to appropriations committees as well as to the executive branch, they are very sensitive to the state budget cycle and to the priorities and special interests articulated therein. They are by no means insulated from the political process, and to make their recommendations more acceptable politically, they may routinely adjust formulas that govern building construction or numbers of faculty and staff members at institutions. Otherwise, the formulas themselves might be abolished, or the usefulness of the council might be compromised. By protecting both formulas and council, council staff depoliticize allocation of resources somewhat, although perhaps not as much as their creators intended.

In states with single statewide governing boards rather than coordinating councils, examples of decisions that may be made at the central level of the state system include facilities planning, major program directions for the future, allocation of faculty positions among schools, and fundamental policies on tenure and retrenchment. This does not mean that deliberation on these issues must originate centrally or that outcomes should be implemented there. Often, all that is required is that proposals be approved by officials of the system.

For most issues of this type, planning frequently begins at the department or school level with ideas advanced by faculty members, rather than being imposed from the center outward. At some institutions, redirection of programs can be shaped only by faculty members of schools, since no central officials have knowledge of the field sufficient to propose appropriate plans. Similarly, on large campuses, detailed planning efforts cannot be imposed by the central office but can emerge only from planning committees at the department and the school levels. A statewide council or board may elect, however, to influence statewide program planning decisions, such as whether more engineering programs are needed or whether teacher-training programs should be scaled back. Strategies for implementation should always be developed by cooperative action among the central authority and the units. A central authority may indicate that a certain level of productivity will be attained (measured by cost figures or by student-credit-hour production or student-faculty ratios). At the school or department level, each discipline or profession may have a particular means of reaching its goals that makes the best sense for that unit.

From the point of view of government agencies, centralization, routinization, and consistency are virtues. This value system contradicts a fundamental premise of university operations—that intellectual progress is facilitated in a climate of intellectual freedom. Excessive centralization and regulation can also impede, rather than facilitate, both cost-effectiveness and success of efforts to meet social needs. To sustain intelligent balances between centralization and decentralization, consultation is essential between central offices and component units. At each unit, process and means of implementation should be decentralized to an extent that violates neither the prerogatives of the central office nor those of the institution. Whatever economic or pedagogic logic is involved, outcomes cannot be successful if opposed vehemently by powerful constituencies.

A consultive component exists not only in the ground rules that govern working relationships between a state council or board and its staff and the institutions it regulates but also in the procedures through which institutions seek approval to add new personnel, buildings, equipment, degree programs, or centers. Information flows in both directions between the council and each institution as questions are raised, discussion ensues, and information and suggestions for mutually agreeable solutions are exchanged. In some cases, institutions may retain certain prerogatives in dictating the terms of a solution and may have access to an established, formal channel of appeals. Even so, extensive gray areas exist in each dealing that a university has with its state council. Such areas must be examined through consultation to determine the authority and responsibility borne by each side in the matter at hand.

Possibilities for profound disagreement are innumerable, given the desire of institutions to defend whatever autonomy and freedom of action they possess. A consultive process involving a half-dozen negotiating sessions may be required before a council authorizes an institution to add a new degree to its repertory. Studies by expert consultants hired by the council and an institution and extended negotiations over a period of many months may be required to gain approval to establish a new off-campus site. Discussion may proceed for years over the building programs that an institution hopes the council will endorse. Consultation may fail if not conducted with patience, toughness, and sensitivity, and relations may degenerate into a less productive, adversarial mode.

Consultation can influence decision making by state councils or boards on a number of levels. Starting consultation very early, as soon as an institutional goal is conceived, can persuade members of a council staff not to object to directions that are being taken. Staff may be presented with a succession of draft statements to give them a chance to shape the final product from the beginning, to understand the need underlying the effort and why the institution regards some outcomes as more favorable than others, to learn the benefits and costs involved, and to weigh the political implications of offering and of withholding approval. Similar approaches for similar reasons might be made to members of the state council or board, a secretary of education, a budget secretary, a director of state computer services, or other directors of central staff offices. Consultation with state legislators can also be effective, although finding out from legislators or their financial backers or sponsors which legislation they will or will not find it worth their while to support can be difficult.

The need for extensive consultation becomes particularly important when budgets must be reduced. A state coordinating council or board can use rational formulas to determine appropriate target levels of budget reduction for institutions, but in order to minimize damage, it must allow institutions substantial freedom in achieving those targets, since institutional and regional needs, budget flexibility, and plans for the future differ greatly from institution to institution. Some may be able to reduce the size of their faculties, depending on their stages of development, traditions, and goals and on current demand for select programs. Others may prefer to reduce their numbers of nonfaculty employees, while still others may decide to terminate entire programs and their staffs. Each alternative may be correct for a particular institution in a particular budget cycle.

In West Virginia, consultation with several major constituencies has been established by statute. West Virginia has a single board of regents, which acts as the sole governing board over the sixteen colleges and universities in the system. It has responsibility for approving programs, policy planning, and management of all the institutions. It approaches the legislature for funds and distributes the state allocation to the colleges and universities in the system.

To ensure consultation with key constituent groups, the West Virginia legislature established, by legislative act (West Virginia Code 18-26), advisory councils of faculty, of students, and of staff, as well as an advisory council for each institution. The Advisory Council of Faculty, for instance, is composed of sixteen faculty members, one from each institution, each elected by the faculty of that institution. Its charge is, in essence, to consider matters of importance to faculty and to advise the board of regents about them. A parallel Advisory Council of Students and an Advisory Council of Staff (nonfaculty classified employees) also exist. This unusual, legally established structure ensures direct communication with the regents for major campus constituencies.

Chancellor Robert R. Ramsey gives each council opportunities to examine and to make recommendations about any significant programmatic or policy item that will affect that constituency. Matters brought to various councils include, for example, drafts of proposals that the board of regents may take to the West Virginia legislature to obtain salary increases or increased fringe benefits, and policies that the regents might approve that affect campus life, tenure, programs, or related issues. The advisory function of the councils to the board of regents is further facilitated by having the chairmen of the Advisory Council of Faculty and the Advisory Council of Students sit as voting ex officio members of the board of regents itself. Communication links are improved by this interaction, and the central system staff need not always be the conveyor or interpreter of faculty and student requests.

Each council operates by its own rules, which include seeking consensus on recommendations when possible. Each elects its own chairman and controls its own agenda and minutes. Meetings of each council with staff of the board of regents are scheduled regularly. To further facilitate board/constituency consultation, one central staff officer is assigned to each council to conduct studies and to maintain flow of information, to coordinate preparation and distribution of policy documents, and to interpret the logic, implementation, and/or language of administration or systemwide policy or practice. In addition to the consultive structures required by statute, other advisory groups have been created, including an advisory council of presidents and another of academic vice-presidents or deans.

The system that has evolved is effective, though not perfect. Since it isolates each constituency in its own committee, it does not accommodate the need for representatives of different constituencies to meet face to face to discuss particular issues, and, therefore, task forces are still needed for such purposes. Communication, interpretation of needs and positions, mediation, and compromise must be conducted by intermediaries from the central staff. Furthermore, an inherent inequality exists among members of advisory councils. One faculty representative may, for example, represent several thousand faculty members of a large university, while another may represent a hundred faculty members at a community college. Interests also vary among representatives according to their institutional affiliations. Fortunately, individual self-restraint and common sense keep voting blocs from forming that could diminish the effectiveness of the group. If the groups became politicized, most likely the board would be less attentive to their advice.

Educating and Coordinating Roles of Administrators

Consultation occurs through an extended network of interconnections among individuals and deliberative bodies that permeates all constituencies of a university community. Although this description of the process is written from the administrator's point of view, it must not be forgotten that consultation occurs in all directions through the network. To an administrator, the portion of the network that links him with influential individuals and with representative deliberative bodies may seem most important. He should remember, however, that all constituencies are constantly in touch with all other constituencies. The portion of the network that he can tap into is only the tip of the iceberg, and it is precisely because the rest of the network is so complex that effects of certain of his actions can be felt throughout the institution.

An administrator plays important educating and coordinating roles *vis-à-vis* representative deliberative bodies. No administrator who neglects either of these roles is able to utilize an institutional consultive network to its fullest. In his educating role, an administrator informs deliberative bodies of actual conditions and facts pertinent to the issues they are examining, clarifies institutional needs, and describes probable consequences of alternative decisions. He may inform new members of a board of trustees of their duties, he may restate a charge to a meandering task force, or he may point out to an executive management committee that it must direct policy to the typical or general case, not tailor policy to control particular individuals.

In his coordinating role, an administrator identifies potential and newly formed problems as they are surfacing and decides whether to call them to the attention of deliberative bodies as policy questions or to nip them in the bud by administrative action. An administrator also facilitates information flow within and among deliberative bodies by recommending that contacts be made or reports be written on particular issues. He watches over decision making to make sure proper representation and fair processes are observed and may step in with suggestions to break impasses or encourage slow-moving deliberations. He oversees implementation of policies and reports on results to the deliberative groups responsible for the decisions. His job is to orchestrate the whole, to keep all portions of the network in synchrony with all others. He cannot give orders to deliberative bodies, but he is free to exert his full range of authority, influence, and persuasiveness in trying to persuade them to undertake particular efforts or to resolve particular problems.

Conversely, deliberative bodies are not the final authority in resolution of most significant campus issues. Whether the issues involve tenure, curriculum, or program planning, deliberative bodies can only recommend appropriate means of resolving the issues to a provost, a president, or a board of trustees. The consultive process cannot displace the final authority of these officials, who must take into account a larger range of consequences of particular outcomes than an appeals panel or other deliberative body must. Members of deliberative bodies must clearly understand their role and its limits and subsequent reviews of their recommendations that may be necessary. They should not assume that their group has the power to cause change unilaterally without concurrence of the president and the board of trustees or that resources will automatically be forthcoming to implement their recommendations. Executives and governing boards have legal authority and responsibility that they cannot abdicate. They may be held legally liable for certain of their decisions if they do not discharge their responsibilities properly. Members of consultive groups escape such constraints.

If the advice of a deliberative body cannot be followed, a written statement listing reasons for overruling recommendations should be distributed to all parties. This may be necessary not only because a deliberative body did not understand the full impact of its recommendations but also because it did not perform its deliberations properly. Faculty members serving on deliberative bodies are often reluctant to rule against colleagues when they are guilty of wrongdoing. Other arbitrary assumptions that may influence decisions of deliberative bodies are that large institutions or systems are probably at fault, that the issues at hand may have arisen in natural reaction to unfair decision-making practices, or that administrators involved are not to be trusted.

Simply telling people what to do can be a good deal faster than consulting, but authoritarianism is usually less effective because only in rare cases is speed the crucial overriding element of major decisions. The other side of the coin is, of course, that coordinating consultation can be akin to grabbing a tiger by the tail. Anyone who asks for opinions on a major issue will receive quantities of them, often strongly presented. An administrator must be capable of holding the good of the institution above all other interests, or he will not survive the barrage. Occasionally, an administrator may find himself in a situation in which majority opinion overwhelmingly supports an outcome that he knows will harm the institution. Consultive networks may arouse significant pressure under such circumstances, and majority opinion may make him fear that he has no choice but to move with the tide. In such a case, the very networks that alerted him to the support that exists for the faulty solution may be used to identify a more satisfactory outcome and win support for the new measure. To accomplish this, a leader promotes new rounds of consultation on the issue and educates participants on the broader implications of each potential solution. He also tries to redirect emotion associated with the issue into constructive efforts to find a sound solution. Having to begin consultation anew can be frustrating, but dealing with the negative consequences of the faulty solution would be worse.

4

Specific Issues
Handled by Consultive
Decision Making

Distinguishing among issues that can be resolved effectively by use of the consultive process and those that cannot is critical. Furthermore, issues that require broad consultation must be distinguished from those that can be dealt with most fairly and effectively if consultation is selective. Many issues can best be resolved by informal consultation; others lend themselves to consultation only under strict procedural rules. In the latter case, development of rules should involve broad consultation.

Policy matters that affect large numbers of people are suitable for review by established governance organs in accordance with rules and traditions of the organs. When applying policies to individuals, however, allowing broad participation in the decision-making process is often not appropriate. A supervisor evaluating a subordinate's performance, for example, may discuss the problem with colleagues in order to gather as much information as possible, but he should not sidestep the responsibility of making the decision to reassign the subordinate by referring the matter to an advisory committee. Considering the appeal of a faculty member who has been denied tenure is a matter in which consultation can be extremely helpful in reaching a fair decision, but in such cases, those consulted must be selected according to preagreed plan, and strict guidelines must be followed to ensure confidentiality and due process. Under these conditions, consultation is a formal process, quite different in ritual from the informal approach a supervisor may use in seeking further information about an unproductive employee. Not only the breadth and formality of the process but the constituencies that can and must be consulted must be gauged carefully.

Consultation with a review committee can produce situations in which administrators are forced to deny the committee's recommendations for promotion or awarding of tenure because committee members did not take the goals and welfare of the institution into account in the decision-making process. Alternatively, administrators may make rulings from selfish motives, denying promotions or tenure to faculty members who have voiced criticism of their policies. In either case, administrators may be challenged by embittered faculty members. A point to remember is that reactions of constituent groups often occur not in response to actions themselves but to the way they were performed. Presenting an action in a dictatorial manner is nearly always less effective, no matter how necessary to the well-being of the institution the action may be. Constituencies should remain aware, however, that actions having extremely restrictive consequences can be presented by dictatorial administrators in an open, low-key fashion—a wolf in sheep's clothing approach.

Examples of general areas of decision making in which consultation is not particularly useful include settlement of problems that have traditional solutions established by the academic culture or problems that are resolved according to generally accepted routines (which may have evolved through consultation). Situations that involve compliance with state or federal law are not matters to be dealt with through consultation, although an institution may devise through consultation policies to guide compliance. Management of endowment, facilities maintenance, and accounting and other business management procedures are examples of particular types of decisions in which consultation is not useful. In general, consultation is not appropriate in a decision-making area if particular professional expertise is required to make sound decisions and the results of the decisions do not affect faculty members directly. Some areas of decision making in which consultation is particularly important are discussed in the following sections.

Structural-Functional Relationships

Distribution of functions among structures, change in distribution of functions over time, and location and relocation of effective power are topics that may deserve substantial consultation. Often they receive the wrong sort of attention or none whatever. Employees of a university understand that its schools perform teaching, research, and service functions, and they are familiar with such institutional structures as deans' offices, departments, centers, and institutes. Relatively few employees, however, fully understand total universitywide structure or can explain how functions are distributed among units in the institution's structure and which offices or staff have effective power on particular issues.

The structure of a university as represented by an organizational chart shows the president at the top, suggesting that he has major power to make decisions affecting units below. But the key functions of determining curriculum, hiring faculty and staff, and establishing degree programs are carried out not by the president but essentially at the department or school level. At many universities, the president's veto power over major curricular change is rarely exercised. The president also exercises virtually no authority over course content, refinements of curriculum, admissions and grading, or recruitment, retention, and promotion of faculty, except, perhaps, for approving tenure awards.

However, a president or vice-president may have virtually sole authority over budget, space allocation, and new programs or centers and, through effective power over these matters, may retain sufficient control over department- and school-level activities to consider himself in charge. Commonly, effective power over faculty appointments and promotion is divided, with power of initial review and recommendation residing with faculty members in units and power of final approval residing with the president. Other relationships among structures may be more ambiguous, with functions and power loci determined more by personalities and interests than by inherent structures. A willful director of a physical-plant office can keep a department from expanding or adding new missions and programs. Presidents have often delegated to budget offices de facto power over academic program. Vice-presidents of academic affairs may delegate to deans all significant decisions concerning program development and recruitment of faculty. Under such circumstances, low correlation exists between function and structure, and loci of effective decision making may be displaced from apparent loci of authority. Deans usually control a greater proportion of university functions than is commonly acknowledged, and presidents control less. Relationships tend to evolve over time as changes in personnel or style occur. Such changes in relationships are rarely authorized by charter and are often so subtle as to escape detection by most constituencies.

Disturbances of existing structural-functional relationships are rarely resolved by consultation with constituencies unless protests are made. Administrators are accustomed to subtle shifts in power and structure-function relationships as colleagues with differing strengths, weaknesses, and interests enter and leave the institutional power structure. In the face of overall institutional changes, an administrator usually does not rely on consultation to defend his role and power base but will use other means, such as attacking budget allocations for rival programs. Consultation is resorted to, for the most part, only when an unhappy constituency raises an alarm.

The extent of consultation and the mode of consultation that is followed depend on the level of paranoia surrounding an issue and whose ox is being gored. An example of a controversial issue is reorganization or merger of a department or school. Any action related to such an issue may be perceived as threatening by faculty members and perhaps by students or alumni as well. When proposing centralization of semiautonomous units such as branch libraries, multiple admissions offices, or placement services to create new universitywide systems, extensive consultation through existing councils or special task forces or study groups is common practice. Under such circumstances, the goal is to accomplish structural change in a cost-effective fashion while addressing objections and fears of concerned and vocal constituencies. Usually, only superficial attention is given to proposed additions of structure or subtle changes in function. But overreaction and excessive consultation far beyond the level a topic deserves can occur on elimination of a structure, merger of structures, or substantial change in function.

Program Planning and Budget

The planning process is usually the responsibility of one or more planning or academic officers. To make valid planning decisions, these officers must seek information about desirable outcomes and costs over time from expert faculty members, often chairmen of departments. At some institutions, goal definition and planning can be accomplished without serious objection from the university community by establishing a planning committee that includes faculty members, deans, and students. At larger institutions, particularly those with multiple missions and diverse schools, a multistage process has been found more useful. The first stage may consist of asking each departmental unit to define its goals and aspirations and to propose a plan for a period of five years or longer. In a separate stage, various unit plans may be synthesized into a universitywide plan and endorsed by the planning committee, the president, and the trustees or state agency. In any case, according to Cleveland (1982), " 'Planning' has to be dynamic improvisation by the many on a general sense of direction which is announced by 'leaders' only after genuine consultation with those who will have to improvise on it." Cleveland adds, "Maybe that is the updated definition of democracy" (p. 12).

In the 1960s, a university's long-term building plan was often called its master plan. In the 1970s, attention turned to academic program planning. Planning in the 1980s became a budget process, with program evaluation and retrenchment as

integral components at many institutions. To deal with the anxiety generated by evaluation and threatened reductions in programs and terminations, consultation is needed at present far
more than in previous periods of growth. Reductions in programs and services must not be allowed to propel institutions
back into an authoritarian mode of decision making. Hatchet
men are often granted control during periods of retrenchment,
not because they are capable of sound judgment but because
they are willing to endure the turmoil surrounding the difficult
and unpopular decisions that must be made. Not surprisingly,
they often make faulty decisions that cause far more discom-
fort than is involved in a more open decision-making process,
disturbing though the process may be when it is underway.

Definition of limits within which planning can be effective is fundamental to the planning process. Major trends and
externally imposed conditions that will control development of
the institution in the near future must be identified, including
prospects for financial support, personnel needs, demographic
trends, and markets for graduates. Willingness of faculty members to address such issues varies enormously, and only occasionally can knowledgeable persons who are both informed and
objective be identified. Planners are urged to go beyond consultation with knowledgeable faculty members and look at available information from disinterested public and private sources,
as well as from sources external to education, when identifying
planning parameters. A faculty task force on trends and parameters can define some interesting issues and assist the planner,
but professional analysts can usually provide more objective and
useful operational conclusions. Consultation with faculty members is most productive when focused narrowly on objectives of
particular programs and selection of planning directions for the
departments in which they are located. A wealth of insight can
also be gained at the school level by consultation with faculty.
Unfortunately, to undertake the process may be to raise expectations that cannot be met.

In discussing expansion, it does little good to point out to
faculty members in a department that increasing their staff to
the extent they recommend would require reducing appoint-

ments elsewhere in the university. When contraction is on the agenda, faculty members always agree that some university program or other should be abolished, as long as it is not their own. But even when their units are not threatened, and when they agree when questioned that some units must be abolished and have strong opinions about which units should be dissolved, very few faculty members will endorse administrative action to abolish a unit or tolerate termination of colleagues. Likewise, faculty groups may resolve to cut resources in other units to allow their own to develop, but when the time actually comes to take action, indecision and philosophizing run rampant. Often decisions are deflected by timely recommendations that substantial cuts in administration or support services be made instead.

Some institutions begin a major planning effort by convening an alternative-futures group, which is charged with examining institutional development projections and constructing a set of alternative scenarios of the future. Using different combinations of variables that must be integral to whatever finally does come to pass, such a group can develop three or four plausible views of what the institution may be a decade or two hence. The great advantage of this sort of exercise is that it teaches everyone involved in the process to think in terms of the long-term implications of everyday decisions. Interdependence of variables becomes clear.

Alternative scenarios can portray what an institution will look like in the future, the scope and scale of facilities, how programs will differ, characteristics of student bodies, and related concerns. The futures group can then define the changes in staffing patterns, programs, resources, or any other forms of intervention that would be required to make each of the scenarios come true. Since most of the key variables in each scenario are resource-limited, the group can obtain quantifiable information about them. On university campuses, sometimes a need for decisiveness exceeds even the need for resources. Tough decisions can be made through the consultive process once members of a central planning committee have understood each alternative scenario and how each integral decision will affect it and have committed themselves to making certain preconditions become realities. If the group is appropriately constructed, it will be able to convince the constituencies it represents that sound decisions are being made. This kind of planning can be effective, but it is not possible without extensive, mutually supportive contemplation and analysis. "Best case/probable case/worst case" strategic planning is an option preferred by some as more precise than alternative-scenarios planning. Consultation in strategic planning should be undertaken exactly as in alternative-scenarios planning.

On completion of a planning process, which has already involved extensive consultation among faculty members, senates, departments, colleges, and, as appropriate, administrators and the board of trustees, the time arrives to seek endorsements of parts of the plan by parent councils. If bylaws or charters of groups require it, a planning document may be submitted to the board of trustees, faculty senate, collegiate councils, or other groups. In each case, the representatives on the central planning committee from that particular constituency group can present the plan to the group and lead discussion of it. This simple expedient helps to assure a faculty senate and other groups that their interests were represented, their needs were protected, and their values were not compromised. If a summary of the key policy issues in the plan is circulated before presentation to various groups, their endorsement is more easily secured.

Leadership by administrators must be demonstrated throughout the planning process by constant work in coordination and facilitation of deliberative processes. Final and official expression of leadership should occur only when a plan can be announced as a product of extensive consultation. The president may announce a plan, but he should not claim entire credit for the plan. He shares the stage with the chairman of the planning committee and representatives of all campus constituencies to ensure their continued support and endorsement as implementation of the plan begins.

Planning as a Budget Process. Needs for consultation, deliberation, and self-determination grow more acute when financial tensions increase in the university environment. When paying utility bills and giving salary increases must be of first priority in program-planning and budget processes, establishment of policies centrally is of overriding importance. Universitywide councils develop guidelines that ensure that whatever resources are available are applied according to priorities. At school and department levels, consensus building is the most constructive approach in deciding budget matters, for it is here that particular decisions and changes have impact on individuals. Having given schools their budget targets, encouraging them to develop their own objectives and invent strategies for implementing budget reductions tends to produce the healthiest possible attitudes toward accommodation to necessary changes. Each faculty member is expected to share in the common burden of instruction and budget cuts according to demand for programs and the priorities and needs of his school.

Consultive processes that are used in times of universitywide change vary according to the traditions of the institution and the extent to which its mission is being altered. If only minor program revisions and modest reallocations of resources are required, changes may be made through ordinary deliberative bodies in a routine fashion. Where a major transformation of mission is required and traumatic accommodations must be made by faculty members and administrators, a broadly representative, existing budget committee is preferable, since recommendations of a well-established and influential task force are viewed as informed and legitimate by most constituencies. If a budget committee does not exist, or if the existing committee is not respected, and faculty members expect budget decisions to be made by their deans, then a task force of deans, elected faculty representatives, and key budget administrators may be viewed as the best-informed and most legitimate group. In either case, the group can assess as accurately as possible the full extent of the changes that can be expected and set institutionwide budget reduction strategies. The group may recommend freezing existing vacant positions, reducing travel, truncating planned renovations, reducing library expenditures, or other measures. The group may also discuss the dollar value or percentage reduction that should be required of each school or division.

Decisions about the details of such reductions are best

made, however, by individual schools, divisions, and departments. Nonrenewal of nontenured faculty, elimination of graduate assistantships, and reduction of staff positions are examples
of school-level decisions that cannot reasonably be made centrally. A central administration and a universitywide budget
committee have insufficient information and understanding of
consequences of particular budget reduction measures to do
more than determine targets for units. Nevertheless, if this core
group is staffed with appropriate experts from the central office
of institutional analysis and advised by experienced, paid external consultants who have gone through the process at other institutions, the product of its deliberations can be essential to
the success of the entire effort. Each representative takes back
to his or her constituency a plan for action that has been recommended by all members of the task force. These plans play a
key role in educating implementers of the plans regarding need
for change, universitywide impact of the overall plan, and relative stringency and impact of measures to be taken by their
units. The plans are also important in sustaining morale and
maintaining perspective and in developing support for required
changes.

How well such groups work is partly a function of presidential involvement of two types—that is, whether the president
chooses to direct the proceedings, perhaps silencing those who
disagree with his opinions, or whether he accepts and imple-
ments the collective wisdom of the group. An authoritarian
president can produce a façade of consultation by dominating
the group and ignoring its conclusions. By contrast, a consultive
president may be a receptive listener and facilitator or may even
absent himself from group deliberations and have staff attend
instead to assist the consultive process, provide information, and
forward his proposals. A president should not feel he must attend all budget sessions, foreclosing exchange of views and accommodation by competing factions. The consultive process
does not weaken leadership of the budget process but changes
the manner in which leadership is exercised. A president who
explores budget matters in depth, is capable of suggesting efficient solutions, and then has the courage of his convictions to

organize universitywide analysis and discussion of his proposals, rather than requiring unquestioning obedience to his directives, can lead with effectiveness and grace that an authoritarian administrator cannot match.

Administrators know that thoughtful budget planning requires hard labor and that the effort needed to make a plan a success does not end when the last recommendation for action has been written. Recommendations are rarely implemented by the groups that make them. Oversight of the process by senior administrators is required to develop precise policy guidelines and action agendas. Implementation can fail at this stage without careful attention. If implementation requires centralized development of guidelines and agendas, the consultation that is needed centrally must be carefully orchestrated. Examples of issues that may require centralized policy development and implementation are changes in faculty appointments and tenure policies, changes in distribution of faculty members among schools, facilities planning, major program changes or deletions, and administrative reorganization. Data-reporting requirements and overall performance goals for workload and curriculum management may also be established centrally. When such an issue is being addressed, options should be provided to units for their deliberations and comment. Other categories of issues may be referred to decentralized consultive bodies. Most curriculum change, for example, should be referred to the faculty members or the curriculum committee of a single school. Implementation of workload and class assignments should be decentralized as a matter for departmental deliberation.

The central objective of such procedures is to enable an institution to revise its budget to accommodate the future. Careful planning may determine whether it remains an economically viable and intellectually and educationally sound institution. A second objective is to modify policies and programs to meet future demands. Pain always accompanies change, but an institution is better able to weather change if appropriate plans have been made. The third objective is to preserve the institution's academic community as a productive group of scholars, with good morale, a coherent view of what lies ahead, and a capacity to get on with the work to be done without unnecessary distractions or wasted energy. Finally, constituents at every level, including faculty members in each department, must feel that they have helped to shape their destiny, that their opinions have had an impact on outcomes. When ad hoc governance processes and structures are phased out and traditional structures and processes follow through on revised policies and programs, those structures generally emerge stronger as a result.

Evaluation and Retrenchment. * Consultation is important not only in development but in evaluation of programs and policies. Evaluation may be undertaken for many reasons, and the consultive process must reflect the particular reasons for an evaluation and the specific regulations governing it. When an evaluation occurs as part of required and periodic assessment, an orderly and regularized format and approach for consultation are provided. Faculty councils are usually involved in the design of evaluating mechanisms and criteria, and faculty members in the unit being evaluated play a role, often by doing a self-study that includes descriptive statistics, a statement of mission, and plans for future development. Advice of faculty members is sought in selecting an evaluation team and identifying external experts to serve as consultants. Evaluations can also be undertaken to redirect the missions or energies of a unit or to regain administrative authority or constituent influence over a unit that is not performing well *vis-à-vis* other structures of the institution. Often in such cases, external consultants are called in, and the extent of consultation is expanded or limited according to the nature of their charge. Consultants are frequently appointed to facilitate consultive processes as well as to synthesize results into coherent, useful recommendations.

If a unique, summative or formative, nonrepetitive evaluation is being conducted—as when a unit is dysfunctional, of low quality, or a candidate for termination—every aspect of the evaluation procedure must be designed to incorporate extensive consultation. This is necessary to legitimize the evaluation pro-

---

*This section was adapted from David R. Powers, "Reducing the Pain of Retrenchment," *Educational Record*, 1982, 63(3), 8-12.

cess in the minds of all constituencies. Otherwise, emotion generated by the changes required to remedy the situation can be deflected to the evaluation process itself and damage or destroy its effectiveness. A decision by a group of faculty members to terminate a part of their own program is given passing notice, if any, by the rest of a university. At the same time, should any hint surface that administrative action is contemplated to terminate a program for which faculty members had other plans, almost insurmountable resistance will instantly appear. Advisory councils of every governance structure will place the matter on their agendas. Calls will be made for justification, additional data, and further evaluation, for task forces, and for outside examiners, no matter how rational and necessary the proposal to disband the unit may be in terms of the overall well-being of the institution. Pressure may also be brought to bear by accrediting agencies and professional guilds. In the face of such uproar, administrative resolve may wither. When pressures that can be mounted by legislators and citizens' groups are added to this vignette, it becomes clear why few branch campuses of publicly supported institutions of higher education have been closed, although a number have been merged.

The extent and effectiveness of consultation involved in evaluation of programs depend on (1) whether evaluative processes are institutionalized and understood by all parties, (2) whether a particular unit is being singled out for evaluation or systemwide evaluation is being undertaken, (3) whether all criteria and standards of the evaluation process are considered legitimate by affected parties, and (4) whether expected outcomes are serious, such as termination of programs. Levels of paranoia concerning real or imagined administrative objectives may run high. Advice that results from consultation on program changes depends to a considerable extent on the self-interests of involved parties and on their perceptions of outcomes. If affected faculty members do not raise an alarm, broad-based consultation may be inappropriate. But termination of programs always raises alarms, and the jury is still out regarding whether any faculty group will ever vote to abolish programs of its members against those members' wishes. In cases of program termination, therefore, consultation must be broad-based to gain support for the move in administrative sectors and to convince faculty members of the wisdom of the move. Many faculty members who cannot bring themselves to support termination of a program can be persuaded not to oppose it.

As in ordinary planning processes, the first step in retrenchment must be to forecast as accurately as possible the situation in which a university will have to operate and to define clearly the implications of that situation for the institution. Trend analysis, alternative futures, or scenarios of best case/ worst case/probable case can be undertaken, and the planning required to respond to various alternatives can be explored. Involving faculty experts in this process can increase accuracy and make the alternative that is selected appear legitimate to constituencies.

Once future prospects are analyzed, the second step involves thorough familiarization with the programs of the institution. This can be a formidable task, which requires extensive consultation. Some understanding can be gained through data collection and analysis. Universities should employ specialists in institutional analysis and evaluation to provide information to administrators, whose knowledge of the university outside their own academic specialties is often limited. Professional and accrediting associations, especially state or regional divisions, often provide useful insights concerning demand for professional programs. Potential employers should also be consulted.

Criteria for making decisions on termination of programs should then be developed. Consensus should be sought, if possible, regarding these criteria. The University of Pittsburgh has used the following list of criteria in evaluation of programs and planning.

1. *Centrality*. Centrality of a program to the mission of the institution must be determined. The extent to which the program is essential or is necessary to support other, vital programs must be determined.
2. *Quality*. Quality of the program must be estimated in relation to similar efforts nationwide and to comparable programs within the institution.

3. *Cost.* Cost of the program must be determined relative to the cost of comparable programs, both at other schools and within the parent institution. Determining the relative degree of economic self-sufficiency and benefit to the university in terms of revenues produced or support provided to other, crucial programs is part of the evaluation process.

4. *Potential redistribution of resources.* Effects of redistribution of the resources that will be available as a result of termination of a program must be weighed against costs, lost income, and other negative effects of the cutback.

5. *Timeliness.* Decisions to terminate programs should take into account proper timing. A vacancy in the leadership of a program, faculty vacancies resulting from an unusual pattern of retirements, resignations, or nonrenewals, and a significant decrease in enrollment or in revenues are critical factors in retrenchment decisions.

6. *Demand for program services.* Applicant flow rates and number and quality of acceptances, services performed by the program in support of other programs, prospective market for graduates, and general public need must be considered in determining demand for program services.

A two-stage process can be used when deciding which programs to terminate. First, all programs are examined only to the extent needed to identify the ones that appear of high cost, low productivity, low demand, or questionable value and thus warrant further review when considered in light of the six factors just mentioned. Separating the vulnerable programs from the top-quality, essential, or workhorse service programs makes a far-reaching evaluation more manageable. Next, programs singled out are subjected to more careful scrutiny during the second stage. Each of the six factors should be used in assessing the merits of every program. Changes in each factor expected to occur over time must be taken into account. Characteristics and needs of programs under examination must also be compared with those of other programs of the institution. The good of the institution as a whole is always the final goal and the basic criterion of judgment. Recommendations for termination may emerge from this analysis. Examination may reveal that the quality of the unit could be improved, but only if other units were deprived of necessary resources. Furthermore, the level of quality that could be attained might be no higher than that which could be realized by another unit, given a more reasonable investment.

Some institutions have prepared a formal statement that defines the course of the review process and who has final authority over adding or terminating programs. Final decisions about a degree program may rest with a state coordinating council or with a board of trustees. In other situations, the president or dean has full authority to make final decisions. At some institutions, a vote by the faculty of the school in which the programs are located or by the faculty senate may be required. In all cases, the decision-making process must be carefully designed and clearly articulated. It should reflect rationality, sensitivity, fairness, and humanity.

The process must specify who should be consulted and on precisely what issues when examining various levels of a program. For example, the charter of a graduate council may require it to be consulted in phasing out degrees but not specialty tracks within degree programs. Who must rule on merging or reorganizing faculties must also be determined. If the program review process has not been codified, past practice could be identified and used as the starting point in the codification process. Under such a circumstance, who must approve the codification process? Faculty senate action may not be enough if the charter or tradition of the board of trustees requires it to play a role in approving policy documents.

When a program is under scrutiny and, therefore, jeopardized, the most common cry of protest is that correct process is not being followed. Critics often charge that a necessary step was omitted or that a procedural flaw existed. Programs selected for evaluation usually have some obvious and incontestable defects. Unable to challenge the substance of the charges against the program, its defenders will attack the review and evaluation process and sometimes the evaluators as well. For this reason, when process guidelines are being prepared, great care must be taken to specify levels and scope of review, proper sequence of review, and time schedules to be followed. The process should then be carried out exactly as written. The best defense against an attack on a review and evaluation proceedings is a spotless record of adherence to proper process.

In specifying steps in an evaluation process, many details must be spelled out precisely. For example, a proper way must be defined by which a dean or provost may initiate a proposal to terminate a program or department. He should make the proposal in writing and simultaneously present copies to specified personnel. Further, all persons to be invited to comment before any action is taken must be identified for the faculty members who will be affected by the action.

A time line for an evaluation process should allow faculty members of the school in which the department is located, the graduate council, and the senate to make recommendations or, if required, to authorize action without haste. If each of the steps in the process described herein were allowed sixty days for completion, the process could continue for an entire year. After a decision has been reached, a year's notice may be required before substantive action can be taken. Because a properly conducted evaluation procedure is so time-consuming, it cannot be undertaken lightly.

A few generalizations on the subject of retrenchment apply both to institutions in which modest budget reductions must be made and to institutions having severe financial difficulty:

1. Retrenchment procedures should be developed through consultation with faculty leaders and formally adopted before they are needed. Ad hoc processes developed in the heat of battle are open to challenge as faulty, prejudiced, or inadequate. Ideally, both the faculty senate and the board of trustees will endorse or accept a procedures document.

2. Often, a party to a disagreement over termination of a program who cannot win by evidence or logic will try to win by proving that the process being followed is flawed. Therefore, planners should anticipate confrontations and prepare a document that explains the procedures clearly and precisely in plain English. Protecting approved retrenchment procedures to ensure

their survival can be more important than any particular decision about termination of a program.

3. If the driving force behind retrenchment is reduction in state subsidies or declining enrollments, that message must reach all constituencies. They must be advised that every effort has been made to avoid retrenchment, including organized lobbying, mobilization of donors, and recruitment of more students. Only by addressing all options can those involved convince more adamant supporters that program termination is necessary.

4. The highest level of authority required to approve programs—which may be a state coordinating council, president, or board of trustees—must be promptly informed of a decision to initiate program termination proceedings. The authority must be warned that constituent, press, or public outcry may occur regarding the proceedings. He or she must be armed with information for an effective response to protests and supported by assistance from senior officials, who can answer questions and challenges or attend meetings of unhappy constituencies. Members should not be asked to become experts on the program being terminated or its problems.

5. Faculty members and administrators must share responsibility for ensuring that a retrenchment process is not arbitrary, capricious, or punitive. Faculty members who would never vote against execution of a colleague's position or program can, even so, assume a responsible role in the retrenchment process by being called on to ratify necessary retrenchment guidelines.

6. In a complex, highly politicized environment, how one acts often determines whether one can act. Administrative leadership style is the key to successful implementation of retrenchment decisions. Elements of effective style include encouraging all constituencies to express their opinions and playing the role of patient, informed, and accessible guide and counselor.

Van Gieson and Zirkel (1981) reported the conditions under which courts have accepted the concept of financial exigency and how policies governing termination of non-tenure-stream faculty members may be applied to tenured faculty members. The burden rests on the institution to prove that termination was actually due to financial exigency and that the process by which particular programs and faculty members were selected for termination was not arbitrary or capricious. If institutional process is not merely a matter of following past practice but has been developed in written form, usually the courts have found it acceptable. That faculties of a university were consulted in devising a retrenchment program and in establishing the criteria and standards that were followed in a decision to terminate may influence the judge's ruling.

No rewards—only pain—come to administrators who must cut budgets. As many are discovering, budget cutting is a lonely occupation indeed. When a decision to terminate a program has been reached, faculty members often engage in a ritual of public protest, even while privately affirming that the decision is wise and appropriate. When facing a common problem, administrators too often turn on one another, each arguing that someone else's ox should be gored or impugning the integrity of colleagues. Trying times should bring out the best in academic leaders that their education and professionalism have prepared them to deliver. Patience, sound process, and careful analysis can lead to solvency, flexibility, and coherence in programs.

Appellate Procedures

Consultation with faculty members has a long-standing, well-established role in appellate procedures. One of the most fundamental and most jealously guarded elements of self-governance by faculties is the right of peer review in appointment, promotion, and awarding of tenure. Peer review in denial of tenure or removal for cause is a corollary right. Personnel decisions regarding faculty members are initiated at the department or school level. At virtually all institutions, concurrence with such decisions by the dean, vice-president for academic affairs, and president is required. In some cases, trustee action is necessary to confer tenure. Increasingly, the role of faculties in the review of appointments and in the appeal of unfavorable decisions is being codified, and in many cases it has been made part of an institution's bylaws.

Faculty members also play a major role in determining punishment for student behavior and in ruling on appeals. The traditional *in loco parentis* role of deans of students has disappeared during the past two decades as courts have shown increasing concern for due process and the exercise of adult rights and responsibilities by students aged eighteen or older. A dean of students now should have on hand a formal statement defining improper student behavior. The statement must make clear which behaviors constitute actionable offenses under the student code. Because due process and peer review provide a sense of objectivity, universities usually establish panels or juries to hear cases. The level of consultation undertaken varies, but a typical panel may consist of half faculty and half students, with all members elected or drawn from an elected pool. In every disciplinary action, faculty and student consultation must proceed according to an agreed-on method with fixed ground rules and legitimized participation. Such a procedure must also be followed when appeals of administrative decisions on disciplinary matters are being considered.

Not all codes of conduct consist of rules banning disruptive behaviors. Recently, codes of conduct identifying constructive behaviors have begun to come into fashion. Honor codes, involving pledges not to cheat and to report those who do, have become widely violated and unenforceable in recent decades. In their place have evolved statements of academic responsibilities of students and explicit lists of violations of academic integrity, complete with provisions for due process appeal. An example is the University of Pittsburgh's *Guidelines on Academic Integrity and Statement on Faculty Responsibilities* (1974), which was developed at the direction of Chancellor Wesley W. Posvar. This statement reviews faculty responsibilities toward students in a classroom setting and specifies procedures through which students may protest misbehavior of teachers who do not meet the stated responsibilities. Although these procedures do not allow a student to penalize a faculty member, they do guarantee that student grievances will be heard. They also make it possible for injuries to student morale to be redressed and steps to be taken to prevent recurrence of problems. Consultation with both faculty members and students is usually required in academic integrity cases. When a faculty member brings charges against a student for cheating, a review panel or jury may consist mostly of students. When a charge of unfairness is brought against a faculty member, redress is often mediated by other faculty members, in an approved fashion, but usually not according to fixed procedures. In general, consultation with students and faculty is required whenever abuse of authority or violation of academic integrity has been alleged by a complainant.

Consultation with faculty members is a vital component of particular review or appeals cases concerning faculty appointments. More widespread consultation must be undertaken when developing statements of responsibility, due process, and rights to appeal if codes or statements are to be regarded as legitimate, objective, and acceptable to all parties. An example is development of policy and process statements under which individual cases are to be reviewed or appealed. Policies governing appointment of faculty members and awarding of tenure, and concomitant appeals systems, are usually developed through extensive consultation with faculty senate committees. Because these policies are of fundamental importance to faculty interests, a year or more may be spent in developing, refining, and editing successive drafts of the documents.

When administrators are not viewed as objective or sensitive, policies they impose without extensive consultation may be suspect, and outcomes of individual cases settled according to such policies may also be viewed with suspicion. Lack of trust can become a difficult problem when a case achieves notoriety. Development of policies that directly affect the lives of individual faculty members and students requires utmost patience in consulting as widely as possible to legitimize any administrative act that may be taken in accordance with the policies.

Grievance Procedures. In 1981 McCarthy and Ladimer of the Center for Mediation in Higher Education produced a monograph, *Resolving Faculty Disputes,* in which they outlined with admirable clarity the key elements of comprehensive formal grievance procedures. The authors state (pp. 2, 11): "Broad judicial intrusion in higher education is widely viewed as a threat to institutional autonomy. The development of responsible and responsive complaint procedures is one important way in which higher education can resolve disputes equitably and at the same time maintain the essentially autonomous nature of academic institutions. . . . For the institution, mediation, with its emphasis on cooperative problem solving, fosters collegiality and a professional environment that is conducive to the educational process. A successfully mediated solution, in which the parties themselves formulate the outcome, provides a timely resolution that is tailored to the needs of the parties."

If a university has no grievance procedures, McCarthy and Ladimer recommend that a committee to design procedures be appointed that includes representatives from every segment of the faculty, plus appropriate administrators. Consultation not only should be involved in designing the procedures but should be incorporated into the procedures themselves at crucial points. According to the McCarthy model, for example, review committees should be representative, and hearing officers may be appointed from a list approved by the faculty senate. A "faculty relations administrator" may be appointed who receives complaints and directs them through the mechanics of the complaints process but holds no authority over it. The McCarthy model is broad in scope, and both universities with authoritarian hierarchies and universities that are seeking to improve involvement of constituencies in decisions that affect them will find many of the suggestions in the monograph helpful in designing and operating suitable grievance procedures. For many institutions, the price of continued absence of grievance procedures or reliance on inferior procedures includes angry and frustrated faculty members and costly court battles.

Miracles should not be expected from appeals panels, however, even when grievance procedures are well defined. Most faculty members shun unpopular roles or causes and seek compromises or negotiated settlements, although such alternatives may be antithetical to the duties with which their groups have been charged and to their personal values. An appeals panel may have to be reminded, at intervals throughout its deliberations, of its charge and of the range of outcomes that are acceptable under approved guidelines. These reminders are most effective if given in writing. Lists of approved outcomes should be developed to be referred to when needed. Otherwise, an outcome that seems fair in all respects might in fact exceed the authority of the panel. If such a list is not available, an appeals panel should prepare one and give it to all parties concerned before hearing testimony. This not only serves to control disputants but clarifies the thinking of the appeals panel itself as it deliberates its decisions.

Solutions to some issues are black and white, such as awarding or not awarding tenure. But if the possible solutions to an issue include not only these clear-cut alternatives, for example, but a restricted appointment outside the tenure stream of negotiable length, salary, and duties or some other special settlement outside the charge of an appeals panel, then the body is wise to recess at the request of both parties to enable a mutually agreeable mediation committee to negotiate the matter. Normally an appeals panel cannot function in a negotiating mode without violating its charge. An appeals panel operates according to judicial processes and hands down decisions. A mediating committee operates according to flexible negotiation processes and announces settlements. Both groups play important roles, but care must be taken to bring before them only cases of the types they are designed to handle.

Court Action. Most faculties are eager to uphold the principle of self-regulation and protect academic freedom, and many try to minimize external intervention from the courts or outside agencies. In the opinion of many persons who have been fired or not hired, however, internal appeals or administrative remedies no longer have final authority. Because of the precedent-setting character of court decisions and their ability to shape policies and practices of universities across the country, institutions have been spending increasing sums to retain legal counsel, and they now regard the courts as another influential constituency.

A university acquires a reputation for behaving responsibly, irresponsibly, compassionately, leniently, or implacably on such issues as tenure, damage suits, discrimination, and retrenchment. Management of internal affairs, availability of due process appeals, and willingness to fight to protect institutional prerogatives or educational traditions are factors that contribute to a university's reputation. This reputation becomes known to potential plaintiffs and to local lawyers and judges. Unless a judge wishes to set precedents in his rulings and is willing to have his court tied up for prolonged periods, and unless a grievant is willing to invest time and legal fees in his case beyond reasonable returns, they must evaluate carefully the nature and duration of the battle in which they are about to engage. Universities that are willing to be persistent and dispassionate in arguing their cases are often able to ward off court intervention in their affairs and maintain their autonomy.

Behavior in courts and interactions among administrators and lawyers can also have significant long-term effects. The process of deciding which cases to fight and which to settle out of court should lead to refinement of internal policies and practices. Bad cases not only make bad law but may have unfortunate consequences for years to come, not only for the university that was charged but for other institutions in similar situations. Conversely, cases that involve improvement of principles are worth pursuing, especially when the alternative for universities is to allow courts to make certain categories of decisions for them.

Fortunately, most judges are reluctant to overturn the results of proceedings internal to a university if the plaintiff's rights were protected and due process was observed. Judges have repeatedly ruled that they should not decide which particular individuals should be tenured or admitted as students by a university. They have affirmed that certain principles should be adhered to in compliance with federal law. Seeking legal advice at early stages in the development of policies and procedures may be an excellent investment because precedence in court rulings can be as binding as law.

Administrators throughout an institution must be aware

that procedures and processes developed in consultation with professional groups, such as faculty senates, are looked on kindly by the courts, and if they are found to represent consensus of the professionals involved, they more than likely will be allowed to stand. Lawyers should be consulted in development of policies which stand a good chance of being tested someday in court or which have implications that may not be fully understood by the faculty structures and administrators involved in their development. Although consultation is improper once court action has begun, it remains the most effective means available for institutions to avoid going to court. Once a case is in court, well-established rules drive the process, and departing from those rules is foolish, except on advice of counsel or on encouragement by a judge to negotiate a settlement.

Extrauniversity Consultation

Major Changes in Physical Plant or Programs. For some issues, consultation on campus among university constituents can be less critical than consultation among external constituents. Such issues may include change in physical plant as campus development occurs, change in programs requiring approval of external authorities or bodies, and effects of program changes on nearby institutions. Expanding the physical plant may require extensive consultation with the neighboring community, city planning department, local zoning board, mayor and city council, and, conceivably, utility companies, police and fire departments, and environmental safety agencies. If campus growth is frowned on by the surrounding neighborhood, and if the issue of expansion should arise in an election year, an amazing number of proposals can be tabled, and a surprising number of agencies may decide to request more information before granting approvals. Plans for expansion should be made public when political leaders are not facing reelection. Plans should be exhaustively reviewed and refined during early and extensive discussion with community leaders, city planners, and major political figures.

Major changes in programs may require approval by accrediting bodies, state coordinating councils, professional associations, and alumni. A series of informal meetings held early in the planning stage for discussion of concept papers or initial drafts can prevent many problems. Often, difficulties that arise are not related to proposed changes in programs so much as to lack of consultation with particular groups. When many interest groups exist, how and to whom a program change is presented may be far more significant than the substance of the change.

Many institutions base their range and scale of programs on their perceptions of regional markets for their graduates. Undergraduates' estimates of the market for graduates can determine the financial viability and even survival of many private colleges. Under such circumstances, program changes that may affect the market or enhance another institution's recruitment efforts must be examined with extreme care. For instance, a decision by a liberal arts college to add a popular new business major may be devastating to a nearby private college. Program decisions that will seriously affect the market or services of a marginally healthy neighboring institution should be preceded by extensive consultation with its administrators for reasons that are not entirely altruistic. Well-connected trustees of a tiny college can exert amazing leverage on political power networks if a big institution threatens their survival. Enough legislators can be mobilized to make a major university reconsider and perhaps even reverse its plans if a significant deleterious impact on the smaller institution is forecast.

Sometimes consultation cannot entirely prevent escalation of emotions, but usually the plans of each institution can be modified so that neither is so seriously damaged by the struggle that a peace treaty cannot be worked out. Compromises reached in such cases have included articulation agreements limiting enrollment or the program scope of each institution, the territory to be served, and sometimes procedures to be followed in sharing faculty or facilities.

University/Industry Collaboration. Some years ago, Harlan Cleveland made the point that the boundary between public and private enterprise is no longer distinct: "Bigness and complexity are already blurring the traditional line between 'public' and 'private.' The managers of private enterprise, profit or non-profit, will move further toward the concept that they are responsible to people in general and thereby bring the government more into their affairs. At the same time the government will farm out to the 'private sector' a growing proportion of the public business. No large organization, whatever its formal ownership, will be able to escape its public responsibility" (1973, p. 13).

Universities have been experiencing comparable blurring of their boundaries for several decades. The challenge is not to redefine the boundaries sharply but to find new ways to accommodate to government, industry, and other new partners in mutually satisfactory fashions. Japan is a classic example in which government, industry, and research institutes have developed ways of working together toward common goals. In contrast, the adversarial relations that have evolved between government and industry in the United States, and the distrust that both display toward academe, will complicate relations that will develop in the future. Nevertheless, future trends in industry and technology must be explored to assist program planning. Out of such consultation can come not only better-informed administrative decisions but a variety of opportunities ranging from contractual research projects to work-study opportunities for undergraduate and graduate students to offers to faculty members to serve as consultants. The desire of faculty members for financial rewards from their research in advanced-technology fields such as genetic engineering, robotics, and computer and information systems is another driving force that must be taken into consideration.

These trends pose challenges to certain traditions of higher education and to the individual missions of institutions. Debates over academic freedom, rights to publish results of research without undue delay or violation of rights governing proprietary information or patents, and potential conflict of interest by faculty members or universities that hold equity in profit-making research and development corporations are examples of issues that require extensive consultation for resolution. Institutions respond differently to these challenges. Some see them as insignificant and, because of their particular traditions and practices, accommodate rather easily to partnerships marked by contractual ground rules that are acceptable to all parties. Other institutions struggle mightily because they view proposed changes as having philosophical implications that threaten their very purposes and those of the professions whose skills they teach. As university/industry relations develop, it becomes increasingly clear that universities are not alike, that industries are not alike, that some relationships are more beneficial and productive than others, and that certain types of partnerships stand better chances of success.

Councils, committees, and task forces, either *pro tem* or standing, are appropriate vehicles for ensuring sound consultation on ordinary topics. When new issues emerge, however, consideration of whether traditional structures and processes provide adequate responses is appropriate. If necessary, new relationships must be defined or new structures must be tailor-made to respond to the issues. University/industry collaboration is an example of a topic that requires expanded involvement of external constituencies and development of multilayered processes for consultation whereby three or four separate councils take part in deliberations. This requires that fine points of jurisdiction be taken seriously to prevent problems. Appointment of an advisory board or coordination or planning group may be required, members of which are representatives of existing councils and committees. The purpose of such a structure is to coordinate work of traditional councils with that of newly developed, often disparate groups and to make symmetrical consultation with groups that are inherently asymmetrical.

Each representative of a coordinating body must serve as ambassador of his parent council, company, or department. Authority of a faculty senate is not displaced by having the chairman of its faculty matters committee serve on a coordinating body. The faculty senate's charter, operating rules, and jurisdiction still remain, and drafts of policy statements that originated with or were approved by the coordinating body or any other structure must survive senate review. A department chairman who agrees to serve on a coordinating body must continue to seek the usual endorsements by his faculty members, dean, and other administrative officers for new policies that he helps to develop as a member of the coordinating body to accommodate university and faculty needs as well as individual opportunities.

Special attention must be paid to consultation with researchers who are working on projects in collaboration with scientists from private industry or who are members of research teams associated with corporations in which the university holds equity. Policies must be developed to ensure that special needs or contractual obligations encountered by such researchers will be met. Since only a small proportion of university faculty members are likely to be involved in research in conjunction with private industry, it may be wise to locate them in special facilities and to write special policies that define clearly how their needs and interests will be met. Policies devised for the more traditional academic community must not be violated by agreements with researchers who have accepted contractual obligations; yet, to comply with contracts, reasonable exceptions must be allowed.

As collaborative research becomes more common, a new class of faculty members may be created who are identified primarily with joint university/industry projects. Policies suited to a simpler era would be strained under such circumstances, as would collegial governance, which is rooted in a sense of common purpose and shared interests. A sense of commitment to the institution must be protected without denying the benefits of collaborative endeavors. Striking a balance is possible, but it requires responsible behavior of all involved to minimize tensions and to maximize benefits.

If a university decides to assist in the development of a "high technology" research park, chairmen of departments of science and technological disciplines must be involved in planning and development sessions with county planners, industrial representatives, and perhaps even state or regional development authorities. In such a case, creation of an umbrella advisory board or coordinating council would be essential. Membership might include chairmen of faculty senate committees, the chairman of the state government's economic development authority, members of local or county regional development authorities, chairmen of departments that would be affected by the results of deliberations, and vice-presidents whose jurisdictions include academic and public affairs. Composition of an umbrella board or council would probably include persons who hold positions at differing levels in their organizations with differing authority and responsibilities.

Unusual advisory bodies having broad spectra of members should rarely be given authority to reach closure on issues. Except in carefully defined areas, their duties should be confined to discussing issues and forwarding recommendations on them. Establishment of a coordinating council does not involve major changes in the way business is conducted in jurisdictions of areas or structures that are represented. Groups seek accommodation with each other only on issues of common concern.

Task forces devoted to special problem areas might report to the umbrella coordinating council. In the current example, task forces might be organized to study subjects such as compensating faculty, facilities design, research programs, and financing requirements. Each task force may be chaired by a member of the council, but members must be chosen on the basis of expertise, and not merely be representative either of the membership of the council or the constituencies it includes.

As compound, multilayered consultation becomes more common and familiar, participants learn that members must frequently request adjournment to consult with their parent bodies or the constituent groups they represent. Department chairs, for example, will have extremely limited authority to make commitments. A chair is bound by decisions of faculty members in his department, by his dean's plans for the school, and by the routines of the university's director of grants and contracts. Apart from formal constraints, he must also be guided by the counsel of the president, reactions of legislators in the districts in which the university, the industrial park, and involved industries are located, and other parties.

In addition, the faculty senate will require evidence that involvement in such a project will not compromise academic freedom or the mission of the university. The budget office will worry that appropriated funds not be diverted to support industrial research. Faculty members will have to be reassured that curricula and their freedom to set their own workloads above departmental requirements and to select their own areas of research will not be affected adversely. Participants must understand one another's complex needs and interests. Each must realize that the assumptions, prejudices, values, and pertinent experience of other parties arise, for the most part, from the organizations they represent and the places they occupy in larger systems.

Special Considerations

Faculty Unions. Emergence of faculty unions has not resulted from unity of opinions or support. Some faculty members favor unionization as a device through which to lobby for larger shares of state revenues. Others support a particular union to prevent their institution from being captured by another union having a less professional orientation. Collective bargaining arrangements may also be supported at some institutions because autocratic leaders and inadequate governance mechanisms have produced an imbalance of power on campus issues. Substitution of an adversarial mode of governance for the collegial mode is a fundamental alteration in decision-making processes. Even if unions confine themselves to settling issues of terms and conditions of employment by negotiation and arbitration, coexistence of union activities with traditional collegial resolution of program and policy questions can be difficult to maintain. In addition, their presence on campus can lead to loss of autonomy, through external intervention by courts and off-campus agencies. Mayhew (1977, p. 253) summarized the problems inherent in unionization in a passage that he identified as derived from Kemerer and Baldridge (1975):

> The adversarial relationship that is fundamental to unionized faculty may lead to intense polarization of administrators and may thus destroy the collegial sharing of academic values. Detailed

contracts may assign disproportionate power to unions, which, when combined with power that already had evolved to statewide governance agencies, could leave a campus executive powerless to govern. Unionization in state systems clearly leads toward centralization of authority, and it does introduce new bureaucratic factors to governance itself. First there are the complexities of the union, and second there is the ripple effect of increased bureaucratic activity up and down the line of a state system. By complicating dismissal procedures, the unionization of a campus could limit the qualitative strengthening of a faculty. Also, increased procedural complexity could seriously hamper institutional innovation and change. And there is the very real but as yet unanswered question as to what effect unionism will have on that important but somewhat abstract factor called *quality of education*.

Some observers do not agree that unions and collegiality cannot coexist. Adler (1977, p. 32) quotes a vice-president for academic affairs of an institution that had been unionized for over four years: "The faculty senate is increasingly sharing power with the administration and the administration with it. Generally problems here are now examined in a collegial atmosphere. This is a great change from earlier years when confrontation and polarization were the rules of this campus." This positive attitude is echoed by Douglas, who says, "The state of the art of collective bargaining has developed a lot over the last decade. Today, there is less conflict and more cooperation between the administration and the union. They have a much more mature relationship. The adversarial model may be dying off" ("State Laws . . . ," 1982, p. 6).

On campuses where decisions are made in a climate of heated, adversarial relations, senates tend to be weakened, according to Mortimer and McConnell (1978, p. 85). It may be presumed that collegiality and consultation likewise would suffer. Mortimer and McConnell also point out that "the viability of senate influence under collective bargaining is directly related to its viability before bargaining." Thus, in mature institutions where senates were viable before the advent of unions, they may survive. Likewise, in institutions in which consultive processes are well established, unions need not be expected to destroy cooperative decision making. The point underlying these speculations is that the ability of a campus to operate in a cooperative mode does not depend only on whether it is unionized. If the scope of union negotiations is limited to a few items, preferably concerned with compensation, sustaining a cooperative atmosphere concerning curriculum and program development, and decisions on hiring and tenure may be feasible. Collegiality is a fragile creature, however, which withers in an adversarial climate that discourages free communication and problem solving. On many unionized campuses, consultation would lead a precarious existence.

Faculty Participation in Consultive Processes. The major problem with participative governance is, of course, that it requires people to participate. Many faculty members are not willing to take the time to do so. They ignore the point that to improve their institutions is to improve the opportunities and advantages available to them. As a result, consultation may be charged with being too unwieldy to be effective because persuading people to take part is too difficult.

Certain topics are of ongoing interest to faculty members, however. The 1966 AAUP/ACE/AGB joint "Statement on Government of Colleges and Universities" affirms that faculties traditionally play a dominant role in deciding content of curricula and programs, criteria for admission of students, and requirements for graduation. Faculties also retain initial jurisdiction, if not final authority, over selection, retention, and promotion of their members. It is generally accepted that matters that affect academic freedom, policies that set standards of professional performance for faculty members, and policies that govern academic performance of students are under faculty purview. For administrators to neglect to consult faculties or seek their approval on such matters would constitute a serious breach of authority.

Some issues that are not traditionally under faculty control nevertheless have such direct impact on the capacity of faculty members to act as independent teachers and researchers that administrators should seek their advice and consent when the issues arise. Such issues include policies governing welfare of graduate assistants and research staff, use and development of library collections, operation of computer centers and their processing priorities, design of new academic facilities, organization and reorganization of schools, departments and centers, use of human subjects, and radiation safety, for example. Even on administrative or business matters that clearly seem beyond faculty jurisdiction, excluding faculty members from discussion and planning may be a serious error. Energy conservation plans, book-center practices, and relations with corporations and government sectors can have significant impact on the work of faculty members as teachers and scholars. Appropriate faculty structures should be invited to participate in policy development or to comment on contemplated changes in policies or on problems encountered in matters that seem likely to affect faculty members. An issue that is not of interest to the faculty at large may be of great urgency to particular individuals. For instance, researchers who must maintain cell-culture temperatures or power input to a particle accelerator are very likely to show interest in the provisions for emergency power that their institution develops.

Who among a faculty participates in governance of a university, and who most affects the consultive process? Above all, faculty participation involves self-selection based on individual interest and is open to all who are willing to devote time and effort to it. Nearly an entire faculty may become involved in some issues, but over the long run only a small percentage of a faculty is likely to choose continuing involvement. The nature of that small percentage defies simple analysis and may reflect personal concerns rather than ideological principles. Faculty members may be inattentive to governance during years in which extensive research commitments or outside obligations make unusual demands. Many persons are independent by nature or are not articulate and so are not elected to participate in consultive processes. For the most part, faculty members who participate are tenured educational traditionalists. In a national survey of social science faculty, Lazarsfeld and Thielens found that conservatives are more likely to be involved in campus affairs regardless of age (1958, p. 443). As McConnell notes, untenured faculty members participate actively on select issues, but not on an ongoing basis (1971, p. 103). Taking part in governance may be useful in building a balanced record to attain promotion, tenure, or an administrative post, but it cannot be allowed to interfere with research, publication, and teaching activities that are crucial to building an academic career.

Administrative action is required to engage many faculty members who could make significant contributions to consultation. Appointment of persons not normally active in governance can broaden the consultive process and draw in experts whose opinions contribute to sound decisions but who would not participate on their own initiative. Appointment of representatives can also provide some voice for the large faculty group that constitutes the silent majority. Obtaining representative opinions by other means is difficult. Many faculty members will not become involved in the governance process even to the extent of returning ballots or questionnaires. Most will not bother to read position papers or even news announcements. Only by direct, personal solicitation can reasonably accurate estimates of faculty opinion be obtained.

From issue to issue, faculty members fall into ever-changing, widely diverse coalitions that can have significant effects on decision making of any kind at any level where faculty involvement in the process is appropriate. To view faculty as an employment classification might be more accurate than to consider faculty members a cohesive group of persons with similar interests, values, and goals. It seems to be a law of academic affairs that academic policy matters (and perhaps administrative policy as well) repeat themselves cyclically. Perhaps the best way to categorize faculty members—or administrators—as progressive versus traditional would be by determining whether they are inclined to speed up or slow down the periodicity of the cycle. As far as curriculum is concerned, yesterday's progressive tends to become a traditionalist after he has been through the curriculum reform cycle once or twice.

The vast majority of faculty members are deeply committed to their teaching and research duties. It is understandable that they feel too busy to be involved in consultation except when protecting their own activities becomes necessary. It is also understandable that often busy administrators would prefer not to bother with consultation but to make decisions on the spot and get on with business. Indeed, if faculty members do not make it clear that they wish to be consulted, they will probably not be. Engaging faculty members in consultive processes has liabilities as well as advantages. It slows decision making. It consumes busy people's time. It encourages discussion of issues over which differences of opinions or priorities exist, and it may lead to confrontations that might have been avoided if no opportunities for discussion had been provided. Faculty members do not have deeply held opinions on many issues of campus governance, but once they become involved in and informed about issues, they will be far more distressed if their preferred outcomes are rejected by an administration than they would have been if they had never been asked. Rejections must be carefully handled so that constituencies are not alienated either from consultive processes or from the administration that issues the final decisions.

Faculty members are acting in their best interests if they maintain the balance of authority by retaining their right to voice opinions, rather than delegating to professional administrators authority to make all decisions of significance to the institution. Faculty involvement in governance is not an activity that should be delimited by written regulations. It must remain a matter of individual interest and responsibility. But maintaining balance of authority remains a crucial goal if authoritarianism and lack of leadership are to be avoided.

Consultive processes intended to facilitate faculty involvement in decision making should not be confined to single channels. It is a mistake to try to design governance councils with the broadest possible powers to accomplish every possible purpose. An institution is better off living in the state of ambiguity that accompanies division of responsibility and decentralization of jurisdiction. Many employees must be educated to accept dispersion of consultation, decision making, and rights of review. Persons involved in university governance are apt to try to simplify matters that cannot be simplified, to charter governance bodies with sweeping jurisdictions, and to be overly sensitive to apparent breaches in involvement in decisions. But tidiness of a governance structure is not an indicator of its effectiveness, a broad mandate may not produce the wisest outcomes in particular situations, and involvement in decision making is not effective if carried out strictly on a more-the-merrier basis without careful selection of the most qualified representatives. Participants in governance who have become aware of these facts often become more willing to share advisory or decision-making authority with others who have greater technical expertise or immediate experience with particular issues.

5

Keys to Successful Participatory Management

Consultive processes must be administered, staffed, provided with accurate information, and led. Because of the nature of the processes, consultive administrators are not in sole charge of most activities that are involved; nonetheless, they provide leadership by initiating and coordinating various phases of consultation. They must take the initiative in opening consultation on significant topics with appropriate individuals as needed, in proposing issues to councils for deliberation, and in drafting documents or statements to foment discussion and move processes along. By lending their persons and positions to processes, they help to legitimize them. Wisdom and sensitivity displayed by administrators in leadership roles greatly affect outcomes. Taking part in, administering, and leading consultation in institutional decision making are activities that can be learned. Attitudes and skills needed for success grow out of appreciation of institutional objectives and the differing roles played by constituencies, including administrators, in governance processes.

Elements of Leadership

Balance of Authority. Understanding the loci and balance of authority in a university is essential to learning to play an effective leadership role. The 1966 joint statement (Section II) affirms the principle of shared authority by three groups: trustees, administrators, and faculty members. The board of trustees, which Clark (1961) calls the "holders of the public trust," has legal authority on some issues. On many matters of resources, authorizations, and capacity to enter into binding contracts, the administration has "bureaucratic authority" by delegation of the board. A university faculty holds enormous "colleague authority" over many spheres. For good or ill, faculty authority is usually a conservative force directed toward maintaining the status quo in programs, academic policies, and other such matters.

Changes in the financial situation of universities have great impact on the balance of power among constituencies and on their behavior. Budgets can become so driven by personnel expenses and fixed costs that little leeway for discretionary decisions remains. Administrators who must deal with funding crises, enrollment declines, and recalcitrant state authorities may be tempted to become more dictatorial, to challenge the principle of collegial authority for the sake of balancing the budget. Some faculty members do not realize that delegation of authority to administrators to exercise broader control lies within the power of the board of trustees.

Furthermore, an administration is in the fortunate position of being able to call attention to the traditional authority of the faculty over teaching and research when facing a threatening board of trustees or a state council of education and then being able to call attention to the traditional authority of those bodies over fiduciary matters and goals of the institution when facing rebellious faculty groups. Being on the high ground between the faculty and the sponsors of the institution gives administrators an advantage. It also obliges them to be responsive to demands of both groups, which can be a difficult position for administrators who are not sufficiently adept to cope with challenges in meetings, criticism in the media, votes of no confidence, and continued harassment concerning their competence, values, and judgment.

If one believed that philosopher-kings could exist, one might argue in favor of all authority being invested in a single element of Clark's triumvirate—in the board of trustees, in the administration, or in the faculty. Each element has interests and limited perspectives, however, that prevent it from being impartial. No one person or group should hold all power in a university, because perceptions of issues and wisdom of judgments are too strongly influenced by position in the system. It is not surprising that individuals and groups do not understand, and in many cases have not even heard of, problems facing individuals and groups elsewhere in their institution. Balance of power has survived as an operating premise of Western universities for many years. The fact that it has survived so long may be the strongest possible argument for continuing to rely on it. Slight alterations in balance of power by alteration of roles or redefinition of boundaries of authority occur from time to time as part of slow evolution in response to changing dynamics. This is natural and should not be suppressed by administrators with a tendency to overcontrol.

A major attribute of consultation is its effectiveness as a preventive in heading off crises. Crises that could result from extreme, abrupt changes in an institution's power balance can be averted, for example, by relying on consultation to keep Clark's authority-bearing groups in touch with one another, instead of allowing them to act independently, prematurely taking public, hard-line stances on issues or assuming adversarial positions toward one another that make problem solving nearly impossible. Administrators must constantly bring constituencies together, formally or informally, to share information and explore alternative outcomes. Attention must be directed away from internecine warfare to getting on with business. Because trustees and faculty members have duties other than university governance that are their prime concerns, responsibility for sustaining consultation falls on administrators.

Conditions currently exist on many campuses that could contribute to opportunities for administrators to assume roles on a universitywide basis that could seriously disturb the balance of power by posing threats to collegial governance. In addition to the power that accrues from being charged with coordination of activities of institutions that are exceedingly complex, at least three other readily identifiable elements are involved. The first element arose as faculties became more interested in investigating energy sources, the environment, gerontology, and other subjects that lie on interfaces between disciplines previously regarded as discrete. As this movement continues, administrators must assume further coordinating roles among schools and departments, which will give them increasing influence over curricular matters.

Second, availability in computerized data banks of facts about all segments of multiversities and the interrelations among components has increased greatly the potential power of administrators. They are able to examine budgets, faculty workloads, details of expenditures, and activities of programs and departments and, most important, offer interpretations of the comparisons and weigh them against others. Most faculty members do not have a universitywide perspective and often must capitulate to administrators on issues because they have no choice but to assume that the administrators know what they are doing and are acting in the best interests of all. With the addition of a third factor, authority to plan and to budget, the potential power of the administrative hierarchy becomes considerable. In times of restricted funding, balancing the budget becomes the dominant administrative activity. Operating on a shrinking financial base further complicates the always-complex business of managing a university and increases the control that administrators are delegated or may assume of their own accord over staffing at the departmental level and coordination of teaching and research. A need to make tough decisions inevitably strengthens hierarchies and alters the balance of power.

It is to be hoped that few university administrators will be inclined to take full advantage of this situation. The hand of those who decide to do so is strengthened even further by faculty members' traditional lack of interest in participating in governance. Devoting oneself entirely to teaching and research may seem ideal, but if over time such behavior transfers to administrators undue authority over those very same teaching and research activities, a significant error has been made.

The challenge is to enable structures of university governance to function in a way that preserves collegiality to the fullest extent possible while ensuring simultaneously that decision-making authority is assigned clearly, that urgent needs are not allowed to steal attention from important needs, and that parties affected by outcomes are included in decision processes. An administrator who relies on consultive processes to meet these goals may encounter a problem that may be exacerbated by the tensions associated with budget reductions and program cuts. That is, sometimes an appearance of authoritarian command may persist even though the broadest possible consultive participation in making a particular decision occurred and the outcome that was agreed on differed markedly from the solution that the administrative hierarchy would have preferred. This impression arises because many decisions arrived at through consultation must be given final approval by administrators who have the legal authority required to render binding edicts. Letters about budget reductions, termination of appointments, and other actions must be signed by such administrators, usually presidents or vice-presidents, under authority delegated to them by their boards of trustees. A signature on a document may be misinterpreted even when it represents only the capstone of a process of wide consultation with faculty members, who shared in the decision under their collegial authority. The answer is to publicize widely not only administrative commitment to the practice of consultation but each and every consultive process as it occurs.

In seeking to offset growing administrative authority, activist faculty members should not make the mistake of demanding that the collegial role of faculty in consultive processes be fully codified. Codification would increase faculty power only within areas that thereafter would be carefully delineated, at the expense of crippling forever the potential that currently exists for exerting influence across nearly all arenas of university decision making. If a list is to be developed of the exact topics on which faculty members are to be consulted through particular councils, certain considerations must be borne in mind. Administrators should point out these considerations to faculty members who are not aware of them.

First, because many faculty councils already have numerous issues entirely under their jurisdiction, including those issues on a list of subjects appropriate for consultation with administrators would not increase faculty power but instead would subtly increase administrative influence over the issues.

Second, no list can be all-inclusive. If a topic is not included in a faculty jurisdiction list, it may appear that by default it has to fall under administrative control. All lists that are prepared should be structured as examples only of issues requiring faculty consultation. They should be preceded by statements reaffirming traditional faculty authority over academic programs, over matters that affect the welfare of the faculty, and over issues that are important to the entire academic community and to the educational process.

Third, the consultive process should not be overloaded by requiring administrators to consult on every detail of every problem that arises. Whenever formal agreements to consult are drawn up, the implication seems to be that formal consultation thereafter is required. Of course, administrators must consult constantly with faculty, and vice versa. But consultive councils must not be overburdened, and administrators must not be hampered by being forced to comply with consultation codes that overprescribe rather than facilitate.

Motivation. According to Blake, Mouton, and Williams's academic administrator grid (1981), administrative style can be described by rating an individual on two scales, each ranging from 1 to 9. One scale measures concern for institutional performance, the other concern for people. Blake and associates characterize persons with a 9,9 orientation as using a team administration approach. They state, "A 9,9 orientation involves an integration of concerns: a high concern for institutional performance combined with a high concern for people. This integration is carried out in ways that encourage subordinates to achieve the highest possible performance in terms of quality, quantity, and personal satisfaction. The consequences of 9,9-oriented administration are that subordinates develop a personal commitment to organizational achievement" (p. 15).

Consultation may be viewed as a practice or technique by

which outcomes can be accomplished in a fashion that reflects the dual concerns of the 9,9-oriented leader. Administrators who lead through consultation are simultaneously task- and people-oriented. They rely on behavioral science principles in dealing with people because, as Blake and associates point out, such an approach "sets forth a value system or conceptual basis that permits institutional members to see and develop sound methods for interaction and for resolution of differences" (p. 324). Sound methods for interaction and for resolution of differences lead to improvement in the organization, which Blake, Mouton, and Williams measure by four criteria: productivity, satisfaction, creativity, and physical and mental health (pp. 332–333).

Administrators of 9,9 orientation approach their work in a fashion that makes them particularly effective in conducting consultive processes. Blake, Mouton, and Williams describe their approach:

> The positive motivation of a 9,9-oriented administrator is the desire to make a difference by contribution, while the negative motivation is to avoid administrative action that might betray the trust of others. . . . Planning is a key attribute of a 9,9 orientation because it provides a way of anticipating the future and of taking administrative actions that are consistent with long-range plans. This means utilizing the resources of others and doing this by making sure that those who implement actions also have a voice in planning them. . . . Directing is a matter of setting clearly identified goals that are consistent with plans and ensuring that those who are responsible for achieving goals understand them. Controlling places reliance on feedback for ensuring that performance is consistent with goals as set and for creating the conditions under which goals that have ceased being relevant and appropriate are revised. . . .
> A concern with the stated mission is at the core of a 9,9 orientation to administration. . . . Resources are allocated in a way as to support activities that contribute to the completion of the

institution's stated mission. . . . Decisions are reached after those who are capable of contributing to them have been consulted. Convictions are strongly held, but a 9,9-oriented administrator feels no contradiction in changing his or her mind in the light of new information [pp. 274–276].

General attitude toward fellow human beings is a crucial factor in administrative performance. Administrators should be concerned with individual well-being, tolerant of individual differences, and optimistic about the potential for growth of individuals through sharing facts and perspectives. If administrators lack faith in the positive effects of encouraging communication and group problem solving, the consultive process will fail because of lack of confidence that outcomes are sound, even if they are. Ouchi (1981), in describing decision making in Japanese organizations, makes a related point about outcomes that are the result of group effort: "When an important decision needs to be made in a Japanese organization, everyone who will feel its impact is involved in making it. . . . Once a decision is reached, everyone affected by it will be likely to support it. Understanding and support may supersede the actual content of the decision, since the five or six competing alternatives may be equally good or bad. What is important is not the decision itself but rather how committed and informed people are. The 'best' decisions can be bungled just as 'worst' decisions can work just fine" (p. 37).

Also crucial to administrative performance is a conviction that education is of vital importance to society and that universities are performing a service to society. Because the world is full of people who take themselves seriously, instead of taking what they do seriously, administrators must believe wholeheartedly that what their institutions do is important. Any reservations will affect their ability to be patient and persistent in carrying out the tiresome, exasperating, and frustrating tasks that often fill their days. University administration has always attracted the pompous and the power-hungry. Fortunately, it also attracts quite a few tough, pragmatic idealists as well.

Leaders of consultive processes must also be convinced that attitudes and contributions of individuals can affect the institution as a whole. This conviction is expressed by the value they place on individual perspectives, by their willingness to listen to controversial or undeveloped arguments, by their insistence in meetings that all who wish to speak on an issue shall be heard, and by their commitment to the principle that although upholding a policy may be necessary to the good of the institution, needs of individuals are also important, and justified exceptions to policies are always permissible.

Superficial commitment to consultation does not provide sufficient motivation to stir an administrator to oversee the process properly. An administrator must believe in the wisdom of the outcomes of the process. If consultation is undertaken merely as a device to relieve potentially explosive tensions among constituencies, that alone may make engaging in the process worthwhile. If consultation is undertaken, however, with manipulative intent or with a conviction that one's own position is irrefutably superior to any other that may be suggested, such a perspective will eventually become apparent and will fail to elicit the best collective wisdom of the group.

Administrative Functions. Of course, an administrator who wishes to lead via consultive processes not only must understand the balance of authority of his institution and how to maintain it and be properly motivated, he must be competent to perform certain functions that all administrators must perform. Hickman (1968, pp. 61-62) developed a list of functions to summarize the duties of administrators in addition to routine business management. These functions are—

1. To provide overall leadership concerning institutional objectives.
2. To coordinate operations of the elements of an institution.
3. To provide leadership in planning and innovation.
4. To help oversee maintenance of the quality standards of the institution.
5. To serve as a mediator or buffer between the faculty and the public.

These functions must be performed by authoritarian and consultive administrators alike, according to their differing styles.

Although only the first and third functions mention leadership explicitly, it is required of administrators in performing all of them. Consultive leaders exert influence regarding institutional objectives by orchestrating institutionwide deliberations to identify factors that seem to be making some kind of change inevitable, followed by determination of exactly what change would be appropriate. In coordinating elements of the day-to-day operation of their institutions, consultive administrators also initiate extensive universitywide consultation that involves not only horizontal and vertical deliberations but multiple diagonal contacts. Use of consultation even when apparently mundane issues are at stake is not inappropriate, since relatively minor matters such as parking difficulties or weekend library hours can irritate large numbers of people. Sometimes a particular solution arrived at is less important than hearing opinions, asking advice, and assuring complainants that any errors of judgment or irrational practices that may have caused the problem need not continue.

When budgets are restricted, participative leaders can be especially effective in providing leadership in planning and innovation. They may call discussion sessions and make site visits across the university, asking researchers in various departments about current projects and ferreting out hidden interests, talents, and resources that might be developed at little additional expense into programs that would meet public needs, attract additional students and increase tuition revenues. Consultation is essential in evaluating programs and personnel, which is at the heart of the fourth function of administrators—that is, overseeing maintenance of quality standards. As far as serving as a buffer against the outside world is concerned, administrators consult extensively with members of their boards of trustees, with local, state, and government officials, and with representatives of unions, industries, and accrediting associations to settle matters of common interest or concern.

Skill in Orchestrating Consultive Processes. To be successful, consultive administrators must have the knowledge and skills required to orchestrate a number of factors:

1. *Goals or objectives.* A leader must perceive clearly the goals or objectives that are being sought, must be able to define them in charges to deliberative bodies, and must have alternative guidelines and parameters in mind in case those that seem to have maximum potential are rejected by conferees.

2. *Participants.* A leader must be able to identify persons or groups of constituents who should participate in the consultive process. Participants may be (1) constitutionally required to participate, (2) leaders of constituencies, (3) opinion makers for important clienteles, (4) representatives of a mission of the institution, (5) knowledgeable about the topic under examination and therefore needed to implement the outcome of the process, (6) needed to oversee support services essential to the outcome, and/or (7) representatives of an existing structure or line of authority that may be modified or affected in some way to accommodate the outcome.

In the consultive process, as in any form of governance, an effective leader must be able to identify strengths and weaknesses of personnel and to try to match characteristics of individuals with tasks that must be accomplished. An administrator who does not wish a suggested measure to be adopted need not necessarily speak against it. Choosing as representatives of constituencies persons who are prone to emotional outbursts, who are chronically illogical or prejudiced, or who are otherwise unfit to contribute positively to a consultive process can be sufficient to kill the measure. Principled administrators, by contrast, appoint as representatives of constituencies persons who are trusted and respected. They make balanced selections that tend to block domination of deliberative bodies by strong-minded individuals or factions with special interests. They place on committees experts who are able to persuade people to heed their advice and assign to production of policy drafts assistants who understand the problems that must be dealt with and the needs they must meet. An alternative to the latter approach is to adopt a custom, practiced in Japan, of assigning an energetic but less well-informed junior person to do background research, draft an initial position paper, and circulate it among constituencies to determine reactions. A junior person is motivated to succeed, and his or her lack of identity with any particular special-interest group helps to avoid premature solidifying of positions to resist alternatives favored by competitors.

Understanding participants in consultive processes is a function of understanding the constituencies they represent. Constituencies represented in consultive processes may include parties internal to the institution, such as the faculty, board of trustees, administration, bureaucracy, student body, or alumni, or external parties connected in some way to the institution, such as the local community, state government (including the state coordinating council), the federal government, prospective employers, and accrediting agencies. Understanding the characteristic needs, interests, and salient traits of these groups is necessary to resolve problems that arise among them, whether the process used is consultation, mediation, or some other technique. In orchestrating consultive processes, certain conflicts can be expected to arise, as, for example, when faculty members who are concerned with quality teaching and research disagree violently with certain decisions made by budget directors whose prime concern is cost-effectiveness. The point of consultation is not to suppress or avoid such conflict, which would be impossible and counterproductive, but to try to reach solutions that are satisfactory to all sides.

3. *Oversight of process.* To oversee a consultive process effectively, a leader must be able to provide background information and resource data so that conferees share a common fund of information. Issues that require examination must be clearly drawn and must be maintained as foci of group attention throughout the process. Experts must be invited to speak to decision-making bodies as needed to provide explanations of problems to be solved or to explore implications of proposed solutions. Agendas must be designed and controlled so that issues are brought to the attention of people who can affect outcomes. Issues must be included on agendas in an order that will not prematurely bring closure and circumvent desired outcomes. Constituencies must not be made to feel that outcomes are predetermined or that they have been manipu-

lated. All alternative outcomes must be reviewed, and the feasibility of implementing them must be explored.

An administrator must never stop learning about his institution, its people, and its programs. He should be familiar with the common analytic approaches and methodologies of various disciplines of his university, since an integral function of administrators in coordinating consultive processes is to recognize the conceptual, analytic, and methodological bases from which various parties to problems are speaking and to act as interpreter and mediator among them. For example, parties may have to be reminded that solutions that they personally find appealing may be unacceptable to other members of the group, not because the solutions as such are unacceptable, but because they were selected by opinion poll rather than by examination of conditions, or vice versa. More parochial group members may have to be taught that attitudes other than those with which they are familiar and solutions other than the type usually adapted for the kind of problems being considered may be not only valid but preferable.

In overseeing consultive processes, unspoken agendas of constituencies must be recognized, and a spirit of cooperation and open communication must be maintained. Individual needs and ambitions must be met to some degree. Otherwise, groups lose motivation and cohesiveness and cannot reach consensus on issues. Individuals should never be pressed to admit they were mistaken in some of the things they said during the course of discussions; nor should they be asked to recant formally positions they had taken earlier. Scoring points or ideological conversion of opponents is not a goal of consultive processes. The Socratic method may be a tradition in education, but its value in consultive processes is limited. Anyone acting as devil's advocate can be interpreted too easily as attacking *ad hominem*, serving his own ego, or scoring debate points at the expense of group goals. A consultive process is a common endeavor, not a contest.

A leader of a constituency, however, must be treated with some forbearance. He must be allowed opportunities to state the fundamental interests of the group he represents, and he cannot be expected to go on record supporting any measure that might undermine these interests. Sometimes he may find it necessary to deliver himself of rhetoric to make it clear that his allegiance to these interests is not affected by his willingness to abide by a particular compromise. For leaders of constituencies, particularly external constituencies such as the state or local government, reelection is often of top priority. Having members of deliberative bodies playing to the galleries and the press may be unpleasant, but accepting it as a fact of life may be necessary to sustain the consultive process. In short, the consultive process, the deliberative body, and each individual member must always be respected. Impatience, scorn, or arrogant behavior by leaders leaves deep scars and renders unworkable a process that is entirely dependent on trust and mutual respect.

4. *Outcomes of process.* A leader does not relinquish his role until a product of group deliberations has been shaped. Synthesis by the leader of disparate and apparently unconnected ideas that bear on the recommendations being developed by the group is often necessary to shape an outcome. The leader must also be able to prepare successive drafts of position papers sensitive to the ambitions, needs, and egos of individuals involved and to the special interests or agendas of constituent groups. Amendments or recommendations of members of the working group must be worked into subsequent iterations by a group's leader. A leader must also contact influential opinion makers or key administrators outside the working group who should review the drafts before adoption and make suggestions so that the report can be accepted and acted on without delay. Recommendations and other outcomes are presented orally and in writing by a leader to the legitimizing councils, governing bodies, or administrators whose approval is essential for implementation.

5. *Implementation.* A leader must provide whatever is needed to effect outcomes, including preparation of memoranda to authorize specific steps of the procedures that are required to implement changes in policy. Resources needed to implement policies, such as funds, space, and staff, must be ob-

tained and allocated properly. Because a common problem in the implementation stage is failure to secure cooperation of key persons who can oversee the process, one of the most important duties of a leader is to appoint policy executors. An appropriate advisory body—consisting, perhaps, of the original working group—must be established. Functions of the group will be mixed. The group will counsel, endorse, guide, and evaluate to ensure that implementation is consistent with the intent of the approved policy and fulfills the goals that the projected outcomes were designed to embody. Means should be provided for amending the original policy or program, if necessary, after a year of trial.

A leader of a consultive process should understand the functions of the service offices that keep the institution in operation. If he thinks of members of the support staff as perhaps not worthy of much attention because they belong to the bureaucracy of the institution, he is making a serious error. Projects can be stonewalled by uncooperative budget officers, deadlines can be missed because computer services employees are uncaring, and coordination of the consultive process can be impossible if administrative assistants and executive secretaries feel no responsibility to transmit information to constituencies or communicate with one another informally. Through staff contacts, an administrator can monitor implementation of many decisions reached through consultation that otherwise might die the natural death that is the fate at universities of many good intentions. Decisions may not be implemented because faculty members forget to do so, or because bureaucrats have not done things that way before, or because administrators are afraid they would have to give up some of their personal power if they changed their approaches.

Yukl's Review of the Literature on Leader Effectiveness

A brief look at Yukl's (1981) review of the literature on leader effectiveness may help to put into perspective the information on leadership that has been discussed. As Yukl points out, definitions of leadership and leadership effectiveness have varied from theorist to theorist. Yukl's summary of the ways leadership effectiveness has been studied lends coherence to the diverse and numerous studies that have been performed. He groups research on leadership effectiveness in four categories:

1. *Power/influence approach.* According to the power/influence approach, leader effectiveness can be explained in terms of (1) the amount of power available to a leader, (2) its sources, and (3) how he exerts it over followers. A dominant theory in this approach has been social-exchange theory, which tries to explain the processes by which leaders influence followers and by which followers influence leaders and to use these interaction processes to explain behavior in groups. Versions of social-exchange theory concerned with leadership have been proposed by Hollender (1979) and Jacobs (1970).

The types of power that may be brought to bear in interactions include referent, expert, legitimate, reward, and coercive power. Yukl points out that various types of power do not directly affect outcomes (which he calls "end-result variables") but instead affect leader influence over intervening variables that are concerned with group performance. These intervening variables may affect outcomes directly. Yukl believes that the amount of power that is required for a leader to be effective is a function, in part, of the situation (p. 63). Studies by Bachman, Smith, and Slesinger (1966) and by Smith and Tannenbaum (1963) provide evidence that reciprocal influence of followers over leaders as well as leaders over followers is characteristic of organizations that are most effective.

2. *Traits/skills approach.* Studies of leadership traits have been conducted since the turn of the century. In 1948 Stogdill reviewed 124 trait studies conducted from 1904 to 1948, and in 1974 he reviewed 163 trait studies conducted from 1949 to 1970. These studies showed that although certain traits are conducive to effective leadership, none is absolutely necessary. Miner (1965, 1978), McClelland (1975), and McClelland and Burnham (1976) found leader motivation to be useful in predicting effectiveness. Another useful predictor of leadership effectiveness is ability as measured in skills. Katz

(1955) and Mann (1965) proposed typologies in which three skill categories were defined as essential to effective management: technical skills, human relations skills, and conceptual (analytic and problem-solving) skills. Yukl points out that importance of both traits and skills to leadership effectiveness depends on the situation (pp. 70, 87).

3. *Behavior approach.* The behavior approach attempts to distinguish between effective and ineffective leaders on the basis of differences in behavior patterns. Mintzberg (1973) developed a set of ten underlying managerial roles that account for the activities performed by managers, since activities by themselves are of little value in explaining what managers actually accomplish unless they are examined in a context such as a role. Other ways of studying manager behavior have included the "critical incidents" method, which involves descriptions by managers of events and behavior they consider crucial; leader behavior questionnaires, such as those used in the Ohio State leadership studies to relate "consideration" and "initiating structure" categories of leadership behavior to leader effectiveness; and field studies, such as those used in the Michigan State leadership studies, which utilized interviews and questionnaires to discover relations between patterns of leader behavior and effective group performance.

Likert's (1961, 1967) work was based on the Michigan studies. He argued that management effectiveness is improved by certain practices, which include supportive behavior, supervision through group meetings, setting high performance goals, and performing "linking pin" functions that depend on maintaining influential relationships with bosses and with other subunits in the organization. Likert's model placed "intervening" variables (for example, attitudes toward leader; subordinate motivation) as an element in the causative chain between "causal" (leadership-associated) variables and "end-result" (productivity, quality of work) variables. Bowers and Seashore (1966) based their theory of leadership effectiveness on both the early Michigan and the Ohio State studies but emphasized the importance of leadership functions being assumed by subordinates. Throughout his discussion of the behavior approach,

Yukl emphasizes that situational variables are extremely important in studying leadership effectiveness (pp. 103, 105, 113, 119).

Yukl and Nemeroff (1979) identified nineteen categories of leadership behavior that were not only measurable but meaningful in the sense that they were descriptive of many kinds of leaders in a wide range of situations. Their nineteen categories were performance emphasis, consideration, inspiration, praise-recognition, structuring reward contingencies, decision participation, autonomy-delegation, role clarification, goal setting, training-coaching, information dissemination, problem solving, planning, coordinating, work facilitation, representation, interaction facilitation, conflict management, and criticism-discipline.

4. *Situational approach.* Yukl discusses several situational theories of leadership effectiveness, which are sometimes called "contingency" theories because they presume that the effects of leaders on subordinates are contingent on situational "moderator" variables. Situational variables include such factors as the nature of the task performed by a group, the leader's authority and discretion to act, and role expectations of superiors, peers, and subordinates. Relevance of leader traits, skills, and behavior is determined by situational variables.

Fiedler's contingency model (1964, 1967) was the earliest and best-known situational theory. A leader is asked by questionnaire to select his "least preferred coworker" (LPC) and rate him in various situations. Leaders who achieve high LPC scores are more lenient and value interpersonal success over task success. Such leaders supposedly are more effective in situations with intermediate situational control. Leaders with low LPC scores supposedly are more effective in situations with either high or low situational control.

Hersey and Blanchard's situational leadership theory (1977) is an extension of Blake and Mouton's managerial grid (1964, 1969). A single situational moderator variable, follower "maturity," is the focus of the model. This variable has two components: "job" maturity (task-relevant ability) and "psychological" maturity (self-confidence). To achieve optimal outcomes, subordinates with high maturity in one or both areas should be treated differently by superiors as the situation changes than subordinates with low maturity.

House's path-goal theory of leadership (House, 1971; House and Dessler, 1974, House and Mitchell, 1974) presumes that leaders motivate subordinates by increasing personal payoffs and making it easier for subordinates to attain them. This theory involves intervening variables used in expectancy theory (Georgopoulos, Mahoney, and Jones, 1957; Vroom, 1964), which assumes that motivation is a result of a rational choice process in which workers decide (on the basis of desirability and likelihood of goal attainment) how much effort to devote to trying to achieve possible outcomes. Situational moderator variables such as characteristics of the subordinate doing the evaluating, the task, and the environment affect intervening variables (subordinate expectancies).

Yukl's Multiple-Linkage Model of Leader Effectiveness

Yukl strongly advocates increased emphasis on situational variables in research on leader effectiveness. He blames the fact that few studies take situational variables into account for the mixed results obtained in many studies of the effects of participation in which satisfaction was improved but productivity was not affected significantly. He also states, "A major limitation on participation has been the conception of participation as a general management style rather than as a set of specific decision procedures that differ from each other as well as from autocratic procedures. . . . Most of the correlational studies define participation as the overall amount of influence allowed subordinates in decision making, without any concern for the particular mix of decision procedures used by each leader. . . . The experimental studies also show little concern for comparing differing participative procedures. . . . In some studies, participation means consultation, whereas in other studies it means a group decision or delegation" (1981, p. 219).

In an effort to lead the way in resolving some of these

difficulties, Yukl has refined a theory he first proposed in 1971 that uses situational moderator variables and intervening variables simultaneously to explain leadership effectiveness. Yukl defines intervening variables in his model as "group characteristics and individual subordinate characteristics that influence group performance" (p. 153). He identifies seven intervening variables: (1) subordinate effort, (2) subordinate role clarity, (3) subordinate task skills, (4) resources and support services, (5) task/role organization, (6) group cohesiveness and teamwork, and (7) leader/subordinate relations.

Situational variables are of three types. The first type indirectly affects group performance by directly affecting one or more intervening variables. As examples of this kind of situational influence, Yukl mentions (1) the formal reward system of an organization and (2) the intrinsic motivating potential of subordinate tasks (p. 155). He describes a second type of situational variable as "any aspect of the situation that determines the relative importance of intervening variables as determinants of group performance" (p. 157). The relative importance of each intervening variable changes from situation to situation, but some have greater effect than others regardless of the situation. Yukl gives an example of the effect of the situation on the intervening variable of subordinate task skill. He states, "The relative importance of subordinate task skill is reduced in situations where the technology and design of the job simplify the work, reduce skill requirements, and minimize the adverse consequences of subordinate errors" (p. 157). The third type of situational variable in the multiple-linkage model consists of "organizational constraints on leader actions to directly alter the intervening variables" (p. 158). A leader's position, power, and authority dictate the limits of his ability to act in the short run to improve intervening variables that affect outcomes.

Yukl mentions action strategies that leaders can use to improve the intervening variables he has defined. Subordinate effort can be improved by goal setting, positive reinforcement, job enrichment, delegation, and decision participation. Subordinate role clarity can be improved by meetings with leaders to agree on duties and by goal assignment. Subordinate task skills can be improved by instruction. Task/role organization can be improved by planning, as can quality and availability of resources and support services. Group cohesiveness can be improved by rewards for group performance, "team building" activities, and conflict management. Leader/subordinate relations can be improved by leader consideration. Yukl gives two basic, general propositions of the multiple-linkage model:

1. In the short run, the effectiveness of a leader depends on his ability to act to correct deficiencies in intervening variables.
2. Over the long run, leaders can make the situation more favorable by changing situational variables.

The importance of Yukl's model for consultive leadership is twofold: First, as Yukl points out, it provides a way to stop treating participative leadership merely as a style and, instead, to analyze participative decision processes to determine when and how effective leaders exert influence. Second, the model provides expanded opportunities for future studies comparing the relative effectiveness of participative and consultive leadership and authoritarian leadership.

Leader as Initiator

In much of what he does, an administrator must rely on policy and principles that are not captured in bylaws of boards, faculty handbooks, senate resolutions, or administrative guidebooks. Where feasible, however, his actions should be guided by recommendations resulting from consultive processes specifically tailored to meet categories of issues that he must confront. An administrator is the key communicator and coordinator among the three communities of authority identified by Clark. He must identify areas where policy or planning is inadequate, seek guidance in improving policy, and oversee its implementation.

In carrying out the function of managing policy change,

a consultive leader can merely preside over the consultive process, or he can be proactive. Much of this book describes the consultive leader who believes in a noninterventionist mode. Such a consultive leader involves as many other people as practical in every step of consultive processes, including proposing ideas, drafting position papers, and seeking approval of agreed-on measures from appropriate authorities. He takes the initiative, as a leader must, in beginning the process and moving it along from step to step, but he may decide not to play an active role in performing any of the tasks associated with particular steps. During various phases of consultive processes undertaken *vis-à-vis* many types of issues, however, being proactive may be necessary to induce needed changes within a reasonable time frame. If necessary, an entire consultive process can be managed by a single energetic person, who seeks out opinions, engages in factfinding, drafts and redrafts position papers on his own, and carries out singlehandedly other elements of consultation up to the point in the process at which formal consultation through established structures is required.

A proactive leader of consultive processes may run with the action through the early steps of a consultive process without violating the basic tenets of consultation, even though he may rarely talk to more than one person at a time. Typically, such an effort would begin with a series of telephone conversations with leaders of key constituencies asking whether they have perceived a problem the consultive leader has himself perceived (or has been assigned to pursue by a superior) and, if so, how they would define it. This is followed by careful research of the facts of the case. In the course of research, conversations occur with people who are knowledgeable about the problem or about alternative solutions or who would be affected by proposed changes in the current policy. A list of feasible alternative solutions is prepared and revised as more information is gathered about accepted practice elsewhere and about the type and extent of change that would probably be accepted by constituencies. In light of this information, a proactive leader may pose yet another round of questions on the topic, orally or in writing, to knowledgeable or affected individuals and groups that may or may not have official standing. The purpose is to refine his understanding of the problem, to reveal feasible alternative solutions, and to discover what approaches were tried in the past and whether they succeeded. He may also ask members of the board of trustees, the president, or other authorities whose signatures would be required for approval of any measure that may result whether any constraints or objections exist to any of the alternatives.

At this stage, a proactive leader may personally prepare a draft of a position paper or revised policy. Such a document may not only include the policy revisions but identify the authority under which the policy was originally developed or which is currently empowered legally to approve revisions, state the expected route of formal consultation that will be undertaken in presenting the draft policy to various established councils, and articulate any fixed parameters that must be observed, such as costs, which limit choice of alternatives. The draft should also include a clear statement of the problem or opportunity, a summary of background information, a statement of past practice, a description of models successful elsewhere, and a succinct list of feasible alternatives. At this stage, the draft may or may not explore in detail the advantages and disadvantages of each alternative or actively support the alternative that seems likely to have the greatest payoff. Politics of consultive councils may require that evaluation and recommendation be left entirely in their hands. An enthusiastic author may be able to gain support for the alternative he prefers by speaking before a consultive council, but including the same comments in his position paper could be less helpful.

Before forwarding a draft to appropriate policy councils, it may be shown individually to the leaders of councils and constituencies. They may improve it by removing or revising statements to which they know the members they represent will object, and they may give excellent advice on how best to route the draft through the list of consultive bodies that should see it in its developmental stage. The revised draft is then circulated to appropriate councils authorized to make recommendations on such documents. Usually the order of this circulation has been established by a combination of charter and past practice.

A proactive leader who has the right by virtue of his position to speak before the councils considering the policy change he has drafted may choose to do so to defend the product of his labors. A presiding leader of consultive processes would probably not try to influence publicly the opinions of members of policy councils, although he might speak to them behind the scenes. Whether a consultive leader is proactive or presiding in a given instance depends on his position, the issue, his personal style, how busy he is at the moment with other responsibilities, whether others are more knowledgeable and should be in the forefront in a particular case, who traditionally has overseen a particular kind of issue, and any number of other such considerations.

A leader, however, is always expected to have his own ideas on how to solve problems, as well as personal prejudices and dreams, which he should not hesitate to reveal, when appropriate, during the course of consultive processes. Although he should not dominate consultations or foreclose communication by overemphasizing his position, he must check constantly to make sure that consultation actually is occurring as appropriate within the areas under his jurisdiction and must initiate and facilitate consultation among these areas with other jurisdictions. He also must not allow himself to become a cipher. From time to time, he should argue for values he supports and argue for objectives he favors, even though he prefers a presiding to a proactive role. He has to be pragmatic about how effective alternative outcomes will be in achieving those objectives. Although he may wish to play a less active role on occasion during consultation, he must always stand ready to help advisory groups understand why particular outcomes matter in terms of their relations to stated objectives of a broader nature. He must plan ahead to allow time for consultation on crucial issues, and he must constantly educate members of the university community about the importance of participation. All these actions involve taking the initiative, one of the marks of a leader, regardless of his style—proactive or presiding, authoritarian or participative.

Leaders of consultive processes must also accept that disapproving and being denied approval are part of the routine. No matter how personally inclined toward an alternative an administrator may be, if it has not been recommended through proper process, if it does not serve the mission of the university, if it is too costly, or if it duplicates or interferes with efforts of other units, he should not approve it. A proactive consultive leader may experience some difficulty in learning the hard lessons that come from doing weeks of work on his own on a problem long in need of solution, only to have his position paper rejected when previewed by an approving authority or submitted to a deliberative body. This may occur because he did not appreciate certain consequences of the course of action he recommended. Occasionally, in light of new evidence, he may even be forced to reverse his position entirely, which may make him feel foolish but actually is a wise move under the circumstances. A proactive leader should be prepared to withdraw voluntarily from meetings of deliberative bodies to allow uninhibited discussion of his position paper and/or to propose a compromise alternative that falls somewhere between the alternative he prefers and the alternative his superiors would rather approve. This may not please him if he has invested great time in developing his position paper and truly believes no alternative can be as satisfactory as the one he has selected. If he is closely identified with an alternative, however, and that alternative is adopted but subsequently fails to be effective, then he alone will have to bear the consequences.

More Elements of Style

Because administrators of colleges and universities generally move into administration from faculty positions, they tend to be well acquainted with academic traditions. Their loyalties and values and their ideas of how administrators function have been shaped by impressions they acquired while teaching. As administrators become experienced, they tend to become increasingly mission-oriented. Their focus shifts from the effects decisions will have immediately on particular individuals to the effects that will be felt by entire constituencies over the long run.

Experienced, central administrators typically develop a degree of cynicism about faculty responsibility, not only in traditionally neglected duties such as governance but in teaching, research, and professional behavior. This, of course, is due to the nature of the duties of administrators at the presidential or vice-presidential level, among which are to hear complaints and settle problems that for various reasons could not be brought to satisfactory conclusions at the department or school level. Sympathy for faculty needs and interests is also leavened by knowledge of the impact on budget that proposed changes in policies and programs will have, the priorities that will be set, and the actual purposes that will be served, which often turn out to be individual priorities disguised as being in the best interests of the university. Nevertheless, administrators typically continue to assess their own behavior and management style according to faculty values. They develop confidence in their judgment by dealing with ever-widening ranges of problems that affect not only individual faculty members but the entire university community.

Most academic administrators assume their positions without training. Often, before starting work, they are under the impression that they will have authority to change policies and programs at will and that they will be supported in everything they do by all the friends they have made over the years throughout their universities. They underestimate the requirements and stresses of their jobs and the amount they must learn about their institutions and the interrelationships among programs. They do not realize how difficult it is to retain the loyalty and support of various faculty factions when initiating needed changes. Often they develop appreciation for their predecessors' skills and achievements, which seemed unremarkable until they tried to do it themselves. Because constituencies who benefit from policy revisions usually take improvements for granted, and those who feel put upon complain loudly and bitterly, administrators soon stop expecting praise. They realize that the greatest compliment they will ever be paid is a low incidence of complaints. Whatever praise they receive usually comes from spouses and administrative colleagues.

Experienced senior administrators have discovered that at least half a faculty always initially opposes any proposed change. They have learned that the concepts of equity and justice are easy to advocate but difficult to define and to implement. They know that their labors may lead not to substantial change in policy but to exhaustion. Compromise is a standard, necessary process. Every administrator favors autonomy and flexibility for himself but strict regulation of others. As a result, disagreements about territory and authority occur constantly. Unfortunately, most work done by administrators is caused by other administrators, and much of this work is not done in service to the university but is devoted to self-serving ends. The problem can be so pervasive that it constitutes a sociopathology within an institution. When a Byzantine court is allowed to develop around a high-ranking administrator, a large percentage of the time of those involved may be devoted to protecting themselves by leaving "paper trails" to prove legitimacy of their actions or show culpability of others or to enhance their images by doing harm to others or by increasing their empires in staff, budget, or power.

A senior academic administrator tends to view himself as advocate and savior of the university mission. He quite literally is the man in the middle, attempting to protect faculty members and students from the effects of tight budgets and from requirements of other administrators or of legislators who do not understand the operating premises of academe. Although he values faculty judgments, he understands that few problems admit of single, clear, correct answers. In his effort to avoid being narrow-minded, prejudiced, or not open to new information or opposing opinions, he may err in the direction of trying to be a partisan of all points of view. This will probably earn him a reputation of being indecisive and timid, rather than broad-minded, impartial, and open to new ideas.

Finding solutions that strike balances is essential but very difficult, given financial constraints and competing needs of numerous constituencies. He must consult constantly on every issue that arises, not trying to be perfect, but doing the best he can.

Persons who are appointed to administrative positions have dramatically different characteristics. Many are selected for reasons unrelated to the qualities that are required for adequate performance in particular positions at particular institutions. Some administrators who are successful deans would be wholly miscast as presidents. Many presidents would be failures as vice-presidents for finance and budget. The particular moment in the life of an institution is another factor that must be considered in institution/administrator matches. The same person who was a huge success as a president or dean of faculty in a growth stage of an institution might be an abysmal failure during a retrenchment stage. An institution may need a builder and planner at one stage and an implementer and consolidator in the next stage. It may not be able to afford two high-risk visionaries in a row.

To be effective, a leader of consultive processes must be articulate and persuasive. A touch of charisma as a public speaker and an attractive style in small-group settings are helpful in making anyone a more effective communicator. Of course, a leader must also have something to communicate. He must do his homework to prepare himself for meetings, or he will become an attractively packaged nonentity. A successful leader must have energy and stamina sufficient to wear down the most dedicated negotiator. He must be able to concentrate on primary issues and not be diverted from them by secondary goals. This means that he must be able to suppress even his ego needs and personal interests for the sake of the process and its outcomes. To do this requires a tough, independent spirit that can sharply separate personal needs, desires, friendships, loyalties, and sympathies from making policy and applying it. Although innate stability is probably needed to function dispassionately and consistently, self-control and emotional detachment are skills that improve with practice.

Because unprejudiced coordination and mediation among diverse constituencies are a primary function of a leader of consultive processes, he is barred from the common administrators' practice of building political coalitions, cadres of supporters, and mutual-protection associations. He tries to gain instead a reputation throughout the university of being fair, reasonable, and impartial, in the hope that it will offset his lack of coalitions of supporters. Having to rule against friends and supporters on occasion, and in favor of critics and past opponents, is the price of such independence. To remain impartial, identifying with the goals of the institution rather than with a particular outcome of an issue or with one's personal needs or the needs of one's friends, is essential.

An additional tension is suffered by all consultive administrators that arises from a desire for ease and speed of problem solving plus constant pressure to get on to the next problem, set against the responsibility to consult. Thus, consultive administrators can find themselves in the no-win situation of having to choose between efficiency of administration and democracy. Decentralization of leadership is one answer to this problem, in the sense of sharing with others the responsibility to consult that each leader bears. In an efficient consultive system, individuals should be leading miniconsultive processes on subtopics within subunits throughout the system at every level. Passing up through the hierarchy the results of these deliberations can ease the burden on the high-level leaders and also achieve great improvements in participation and information flow. One of the greatest services a consultive leader can perform for his institution is not necessarily to conduct consultive processes himself but to ensure that they are conducted by others at every possible level throughout the organization.

When a problem is of great importance, and when the process of reaching a solution is drawn out and involves much informal, confidential consultation, the role of the leader of a consultive process can become highly stressful and very lonely. Cravings for understanding, sympathy, recognition, and honors frequently occur but are rarely satisfied. An administrator who coordinates consultive processes cannot lust after recognition. A key to successful consultation is always to give all credit for sound decisions to the constituencies that gave good advice. Rewarding their behavior is the best encouragement to them to continue it. An administrator also must not attract too much attention when he enters groups, or he will disrupt their function. He must be respected, but he must maintain a low profile to avoid becoming the target of group concerns or reactions.

Rewards must come from successful completion of tasks or from institutional service. Over long periods, sincere and enduring support from colleagues throughout a university may be generated, which can be far more satisfying than awards or other visible indicators of popularity. Both Bennis (1976) and Townsend (1970) quote Lao-tzu on the rewards of leadership: "As for the best leaders, the people do not notice their existence. The next best, the people honor and praise. The next, the people fear; and the next, the people hate. . . . When the best leader's work is done, the people say, 'We did it ourselves' " (Townsend, p. 99).

Especially in times of crisis, dedication to the success of the consultive process can be so demanding that it weakens an administrator's relations with his family, starves friendships, makes leisure an unknown commodity, harms his academic career by leaving him without psychic energy to engage in creative thought that is unrelated to consultation, and over time even affects his health. Establishing consultive processes in a university is an exhausting experience that should not be undertaken without acquiescence, if not support, from the highest quarters. As consultation becomes accepted in an institution, the strains on an innovator decrease to some extent, and the results can be worth the effort. Particular outcomes often appear similar to those that would have resulted from edicts from an authoritarian system. However, an authoritarian system cannot provide the sense of accomplishment and feeling of control over one's own activities that a consultive process can confer on each participant.

A certain competitiveness can be found among the personality traits of leaders of consultive processes. Perhaps individuals drawn to consultation need to prove that they are self-sufficient and are able to rise above the squabbles of their fellow humans. Any person in charge of a consultive process must clearly understand his abilities and limits and know when and when not to delegate assignments. He must be able to adjust to odd work cycles and to devote himself single-mindedly and intensely to tasks for short periods, as required. He must know when his efficiency is so reduced that he must rest and when a task should be assigned to someone else because that person can do it better than he can. He must have confidence both in the consultive process and in his own abilities. Lacking such confidence, he is likely to falter, promote outcomes for no other reason than that they are preferred by his superior, and politicize issues by turning to coalitions for support.

Above all, consultation requires integrity in administrators, consistency of values, goals, and actions, coherence of words and deeds. Superhuman insight, competence, or expertise is not required to lead consultive processes. Hard work and honesty are necessary factors, and intelligence, compassion, generosity of spirit, and objectivity can be of great help, as they are in all cooperative endeavors. Listing the qualities that a leader of consultive processes should possess does not explain how he does what he does or predict with any degree of reliability how effective he will be. Such a list, however, can serve as a good indicator of whether he has the endurance and the instincts that are required to be effective in such a role.

Some administrators simply lack the skills and traits required for successful consultation. If a president or other administrator is ill suited to playing a full-fledged consultive leadership role, a vice-president can stand in for him on committees and task forces without displacing the final decision-making authority of the office of the president or disrupting consultation. Deputies of other key administrators can play comparable roles. Administrative teams must be built with care to include a mix of complementary interests, personalities, and skills. A double error of logic that administrators make too frequently is to assume that because they themselves are uninclined toward or incapable of playing a certain role, no one else is either, and that role, therefore, must not be important. A president learns that heterogeneity of skills is essential among administrators playing different roles and does not appoint only carbon copies of himself to the diverse range of positions he oversees. Search committees should seek out or promote persons who have demonstrated skills that the committee perceives to be lacking in the present team and vigorously recruit those who have shown sensitivity and integrity in conducting consultive processes.

The role of an administrator during the coming decades will not be to dictate or to berate in the style of his predecessors. Instead, his role will be to lead by initiating, convincing, and orchestrating. He will give up none of his decision-making authority, but he will not exercise it without seeking appropriate advice. He will perform his leadership role most effectively in an institution that is staffed by task-oriented professionals who expect to bear responsibility for activities and development in their areas. In universities in which faculties and staff are less sophisticated, paternalistic and evangelical styles of administrative leadership will be replaced more slowly.

Consultive, not authoritarian, leaders are needed to bring into being recommendations made in a long-range planning study done at the University of Maryland under a grant from the Carnegie Foundation: "Two key changes are needed for university leadership of the future: a shift from a relatively passive administrative style to a more active management approach, and a move from hierarchical authority to shared authority with differentiated functions. . . . The trick in the 1980s will be to avoid a more assertive management imposing its will on the faculty and staff and instead build new structures that allow a more self-conscious university leadership and a more influential and executive faculty to impose their strategies and will in partnership on the institution they both wish to see flourish. The new management of our universities should be a shared management, especially in academic matters" (University of Maryland, 1981, pp. 250-251).

6

Providing Ethical
Administration

A modern campus is a world of specialists, and discussion of morals and ethics in academe is generally confined to faculty committees and to courses particularly designed for that purpose. A problem with this system of compartmentalization is, of course, that some matters that are intrinsically of campus-wide concern, including not only morals and ethics but governance, literacy standards, and other topics, cannot be made the responsibility of particular units but require attention from everyone. Unfortunately, subjects that are everybody's responsibility often end up being nobody's responsibility. As a result, they may receive less attention by far than they warrant.

Occasionally, administrators become involved in facilitating the development of a new code of behavior or a grievance or appeals procedure, but for the most part they are concerned primarily with any liability the institution may have to bear as a result of the misbehavior of its employees, not with moral or ethical dimensions of that misbehavior. Although administrators are no longer called on to sit in judgment on the personal behavior of faculty members and students, as they were in an earlier era, they continue to face innumerable moral dilemmas in the decisions they make daily involving personnel and programs.

148

They must approve tenure and salary decisions, plan new buildings and allocate space in existing ones, and design new programs and terminate out-of-date programs. Their duties are as widely varied as are the activities of their universities and the needs of employees of their institutions. In many of their decisions, granting something to one person, unit, or program means denying it to others.

Certain moral values are common to authoritarian administrators and to administrators who rely on consultation in decision making. Both, for example, supposedly operate in accordance with the principle that the decisions they make are those that promise to yield maximum benefit to the institutions that employ them. As has been pointed out, however, other principles distinguish consultive decision making from authoritarian governance, including the principle that members of university communities should play a role in making decisions that affect them, rather than being subject always to decisions made unilaterally by administrators. Therefore, maintaining a system that balances access to decision making and to power is of prime importance in consultation.

It may be dangerous to claim that a moral choice is involved in deciding between consultation and other administrative techniques that allow collegial governance the fullest possible rein and authoritarian techniques that stifle it, since such a claim may make many people turn away from the issue. Arguing moral issues, which, by their nature, cannot be resolved by observation or logic, is considered by many a waste of time. But to treat the choice between consultation and authoritarianism as a mere practical choice that can be settled by empirical studies of relative efficiency overlooks aspects of the issue that are vital to the traditions of university life and the people who have adopted that life as their own.

In a remarkable book entitled *After Virtue* (1981), Alasdair MacIntyre presents a moral theory in the context of which calling the decision between consultation and authoritarianism a moral choice becomes understandable and defensible. As a professor of ethics, MacIntyre does not speak directly to administration in any detail, but he does use what he calls a "manager" as a key figure in illustrating many of his major points. The theory he presents is broad in scope and, to yield full benefits, must be studied in more depth than is possible by merely reading the brief summary presented herein. MacIntyre's moral theory will be neither criticized nor defended here but will be used to stimulate thought on the subject of what it is to be an ethical administrator.

MacIntyre's Ethical Theory

MacIntyre begins his book with a serious claim. The fact that his claim will probably not strike many people as particularly important may be a good indicator of how serious it is. MacIntyre claims: "We have—very largely, if not entirely—lost our comprehension, both theoretical and practical, of morality" (p. 2). To understand how this state of affairs came about, he says, we cannot turn to philosophical analysis. Instead, we must study philosophical history.

MacIntyre points out that it was not until the late seventeenth and early eighteenth centuries that it became commonplace to think of moral rules as being separate from theological, legal, or esthetic principles. Before that, in European culture, morality was commonly justified theologically, as being in accordance wth God's law. During the eighteenth-century Enlightenment, philosophers tried to construct independent, rational justifications of morality. Hume tried to provide a foundation for moral choice by appealing to the passions, and Kant tried to provide a rational justification of morality based on reason. Since for the first time morality was being thought of as separate from other kinds of principles, it was presumed that rational justification was necessary. Otherwise, being moral would make no sense.

In 1842 Kierkegaard put an end to the long effort to construct a rational justification of morality by pointing out the essential arbitrariness of moral debate. MacIntyre says that by that stage in the development of European culture, moral debate had become a "confrontation between incompatible and incommensurable moral premises" (p. 38). Moral commitment consisted in choosing between these incompatible and incommensurable moral premises. Moral choice had to be made in the absence of criteria or standards because the premises being chosen among could not be compared. This kind of choice Kierkegaard called "radical choice." It is ultimate choice—that is, choice for which justification cannot be given.

In discovering the concept of radical choice, as MacIntyre points out, Kierkegaard also broke a connection between authority and reason. Until Kierkegaard, reason and authority had been intimately linked concepts. Reason embodied authority. In post-Kierkegaard modern life, however, the concept of authority is used extensively in two senses. We say that we turn to the authority of reason for guidance. We also say that we turn to authority when reason fails. Because we often carry the separation between reason and authority to the limit, appeals to authority frequently carry the connotation of being irrational and arbitrary. Understanding that authority and reason are so often used as distinct concepts is essential to understanding later pieces of MacIntyre's thesis.

Kierkegaard's observation that debate about moral issues is arbitrary shocked nineteenth-century society. MacIntyre states, "The project of providing a rational vindication of morality had decisively failed; and from henceforward the morality of our predecessor culture—and subsequently our own—lacked any public, shared rationale or justification. In a world of secular rationality, religion could no longer provide such a shared background and foundation for moral discourse and action" (p. 48). MacIntyre explains in detail how failure of the Enlightenment was inevitable and traces the effects of Kierkegaard's work on present-day beliefs and attitudes.

By early in the twentieth century, MacIntyre claims, the doctrine of emotivism had become prevalent in our culture. He states a fundamental tenet of emotivism as follows: "There are and can be *no* valid rational justification for any claims that objective and impersonal moral standards exist and hence . . . there are no such standards" (p. 18). Since no justifiable moral standards can exist, each person must serve as his own moral agent. Location of moral agency in the individual self is called the "democratization" of moral agency. As a result, "all evaluative judgments and more specifically all moral judgments are *nothing but* expressions of preference, expressions of attitude or feeling, insofar as they are moral or evaluative in character" (p. 11).

MacIntyre describes the Nietzschean "great man," the *Übermensch,* as "the man who transcends, finds his good nowhere in the social world to date, but only in himself which dictates his own new law and his own new table of the virtues" (p. 239). As an alternative to emotivism and to Nietzsche's thesis, which, he admits, has a "terrible plausibility," MacIntyre suggests a return to the moral tradition that grew out of Aristotle's teachings about the virtues. The Aristotelian moral tradition differs from the morality of rules that Enlightenment philosophers tried so hard (and failed) to justify rationally in that in it virtues are transcendent, not moral rules. In the Aristotelian scheme of things, the self had a social identity; that is, a person identified himself and was identified by others in terms of the relationships he bore to kin, to servants, to others in his village, to his tribe, and so forth. In the Nietzschean view of the human state, all this is stripped away. But MacIntyre contends that the price paid for freedom from shared activity is high: "It is the isolation and self-absorption of 'the great man' which thrust upon him the burden of being his own self-sufficient moral authority. For if the conception of the good has to be expounded in terms of such actions as those of a practice, of the narrative unity of a human life, and of a moral tradition, then goods, and with them the only grounds for the authority of laws and virtues, can only be discovered by entering into those relationships which constitute communities whose central bond is a shared vision of and understanding of goods. To cut oneself off from shared activity in which one has initially to learn obediently as an apprentice learns, to isolate oneself from the communities which find their point and purpose in such activities, will be to debar oneself from finding any good outside of oneself" (p. 240).

The foregoing passage contains a number of terms that must be understood in order to understand MacIntyre's ethical theory. These are *virtues, practice, good, narrative unity,* and *tradition.* Since the first term on this list is Aristotelian in origin, in the sense in which MacIntyre develops and uses the concept, it cannot be understood or applied except in the context of social and moral life. MacIntyre develops the concept of a virtue in three successive stages and in each stage relates the concept to other key concepts of his moral theory. The first stage in this development of the concept of virtue relates the concept to what MacIntyre calls a "practice." A practice is defined as "any coherent and complex form of socially established cooperative human activity through which goods internal to that form of activity are realized in the course of trying to achieve those standards of excellence which are appropriate to, and partially definitive of, that form of activity" (p. 175). MacIntyre explains that the range of practices is wide, including "creation and sustaining of human communities . . . arts, sciences, games . . . making and sustaining of family life" (p. 175).

In other words, an important characteristic of every practice is that it has "goods" internal to it that can be obtained only by trying to achieve the standards of excellence integral to that practice. A practice not only involves standards of excellence, but obedience to rules. One must accept the standards and be obedient to the rules as part of the process of being initiated into a practice. MacIntyre offers an initial definition of a virtue in relation to a practice: "A virtue is an acquired human quality the possession and exercise of which tends to enable us to achieve those goods which are internal to practices and the lack of which effectively prevents us from achieving any such goods" (p. 178). Any practice, says MacIntyre, must involve as necessary components the virtues of justice, courage, and honesty. Practices also require technical skills. But the technical skills required by a practice and its internal goods or goals are constantly changed by the performance of the practice. Thus, every practice has a history. Another characteristic of practices is that they are so intimately associated with institutions that if the virtues are not exercised, practices may be corrupted by institutional competitiveness.

MacIntyre presents a second-stage definition of a virtue in

relation to what he calls the "narrative order" of a human life. The tendency of modern students of human behavior is to examine particular actions in isolation from other behavior and to try to understand those actions in terms of their components. MacIntyre believes that instead of being atomistic, we must "begin to understand how a life may be more than a sequence of individual actions and episodes" (p. 190). The idea of "unity of the self" that MacIntyre defines is not a self separated from its social roles, as Sartre and the existentialists would have it. But neither is that self defined entirely through its social roles, for this "allows no scope for the exercise of dispositions which could genuinely be accounted virtues in any sense remotely Aristotelian" (p. 191). When a particular action is examined, it can be understood only in a dual context: (1) by placing the agent's intentions in causal and temporal order *vis-à-vis* their agent's history and (2) by placing the agent's intentions in causal and temporal order *vis-à-vis* the history of their setting. The emphasis is not on "individuating" human actions, which is the common approach to understanding them; on the contrary, the emphasis is on interpreting them in the broader contexts of which they are vital elements.

The point of MacIntyre's first-stage description of virtues is to define their relation to practices. The point of his second-stage description of virtues is to define them in relation to the good life for human beings, and it is toward that end that he argues for the unity of the self. MacIntyre states, "The unity of a human life is the unity of a narrative quest" (p. 203). He continues:

> The virtues therefore are to be understood as those dispositions which will not only sustain practices and enable us to achieve the goods internal to practices, but which will also sustain us in the relevant kind of quest for the good, by enabling us to overcome the harms, dangers, temptations, and distractions which we encounter, and which will furnish us with increasing self-knowledge and increasing knowledge of the good. The catalogue of the virtues will therefore include the virtues required to

sustain the kind of households and the kind of political communities in which men and women can
seek for the good together and the virtues necessary for philosophical enquiry about the character
of the good. We have then arrived at a provisional
conclusion about the good life for man: the good
life for man, and the virtues necessary for the seeking, are those which will enable us to understand
what more and what else the good life for man is
[p. 204].

MacIntyre's third-stage description of virtues is to define
them in terms of traditions. He defines a "living" tradition as
"an historically extended, socially embodied argument, and an
argument precisely in part about the goods which constitute
that tradition. . . . So when an institution—a university, say, or a
farm, or a hospital—is the bearer of a tradition of practice or
practices, its common life will be partly, but in a centrally important way, constituted by a continuous argument as to what a
university is and ought to be or what good farming is or what
good medicine is. Traditions, when vital, embody continuities
of conflict" (pp. 206, 207).

Out of all this, MacIntyre presents a summary definition
of the virtues: "The virtues find their point and purpose not
only in sustaining those relationships necessary if the variety of
goods internal to practices are to be achieved and not only in
sustaining the form of an individual life in which that individual
may seek out his or her good as the good of his or her whole
life, but also in sustaining those traditions which provide both
practices and individual lives with their necessary historical context" (p. 207).

University as Community

MacIntyre believes that the negative consequences of
emotivism have been extreme and will become even more extreme in the future. He concludes his book with this gloomy
prophecy: "What matters at this stage is the constriction of
local forms of community within which civility and the intellec-

tual and moral life can be sustained through the new dark ages that are already upon us. And if the tradition of the virtues was able to survive the horrors of the last dark ages, we are not entirely without grounds for hope. This time, however, the barbarians are not waiting beyond the frontiers; they have already been governing us for some time. And it is our lack of consciousness of this that constitutes part of our predicament" (p. 245).

It is to be hoped that modern society need not be as MacIntyre describes it—"a collection of strangers, each pursuing his or her own interests under minimal constraints" (p. 233). MacIntyre may be correct in his assessment that emotivism can be countered by developing more communities in which civility and intellectual and moral life can be sustained. Parallels between the traditional university community and MacIntyre's concept of community are striking. University communities can allow that peculiar combination of individual development and contribution to the community that MacIntyre believes makes up the "good life." They can also embody the various elements that are intrinsic to communities according to MacIntyre's moral theory. In university communities, principles are rooted in virtues, and virtues are expressed through practices, individual development, and traditions. Academic practices include, of course, the academic disciplines, the professions, and, if the point of view of this book is accepted, academic administration. Neophytes enter training in academic disciplines or professions not only to learn relevant skills but also to become imbued with the traditions of their disciplines or professions. They also learn about and accept the authority of the standards of the practices.

Academic administration can be defined as a practice if a distinction is made in the goals of administrators between maintenance of their institutions and maintenance of their university communities. Maintenance of their institutions constitutes pursuit of what MacIntyre calls an external good because it involves acquiring money from outside sources and distributing money, power, and status within the institutions. But even institutional maintenance can be considered a practice under a particular condition, according to MacIntyre, in spite of the tendency to

corrupt that is inherent in institutions owing to their brokerage
in money and power. That is, if maintenance of an institution
is entailed by making a community, which is a practice in its
own right, then institutional maintenance can also be a practice.

An academic administrator who is dedicated to governance through consultation is engaged in a practice in a second,
stronger sense because he is pursuing an internal good—maintenance of a university as community. Whereas other members of
the university community may be devoted, to varying degrees
and in varying combinations, to maintenance of their institutions or some part thereof, to furthering their individual development, and to engaging in practices and carrying on university
traditions, administrators should be involved in an additional
pursuit. They are responsible for maintaining the structures and
processes that make a university a community in the fullest
sense. To foster practices and traditions and development of individual members, a community cannot be a mere collective of
activities and interests; it must function in ways that provide
internal networks of support for all members in each area of endeavor to sustain them in all necessary ways while they undertake their tasks. It is with the development and maintenance of
these networks that persons who regard administration as a
practice concern themselves.

University communities also have traditions of many
types. Some are trivial and only peripherally connected to the
preservation, transmission, and pursuit of knowledge, which are
the fundamental goals of all universities. Others are local, important to the integrity, identity, or morale of single institutions, but not compelling to other universities. Traditions of
significance transcend any one school or any one system—they
are held in common esteem by all. Among the most important
of these are the structure by discipline of institutions, the professor as both teacher and researcher, academic freedom and
tenure, and collegial governance. It is possible to move from one
university community to another across the country and find
common traditions everywhere, from Ivy League schools to
community colleges to land-grant universities. Differences in

endowment, date of establishment, snobbishness or defensiveness in attitudes, quality of faculty and programs, or missions should not be allowed to cloud the fact that all institutions are fellows under the skin. When a harmful precedent is set at one school, all may be harmed.

University communities also provide a milieu in which individual members can exercise the dispositions that MacIntyre calls virtues and can spend good lives in quest of the good life. Exercise of virtues sustains practices, traditions, and pursuit of the good life, and the most important of the virtues, according to MacIntyre, are justice, truthfulness, and courage. Few would argue that these virtues are unessential to traditional university life. He also mentions an important underlying virtue—constancy—which was of great importance in Jane Austen's novels, and certain "relevant intellectual virtues" that may be less obvious, such as the ability to recognize a tradition when one sees one.

In *The Academic Revolution* (1968), Jencks and Riesman made the now familiar observation that research-oriented faculty members have shifted their primary loyalties from their institutions to their disciplines. This increase in independence was possible because of the availability after World War II of significant amounts of federal money for research, which gave researchers funding bases that were independent of their institutions. In addition, the postwar baby boom created a need for teachers that lasted for decades and increased teacher mobility. A shift in loyalty of such magnitude was bound to have significant effects on the stability of common university traditions. These effects were both positive and negative. On the one hand, faculty members moving from one institution to another expected traditions to be in place and protected wherever they went, and they complained if they were not. This tended to strengthen traditions and make them more uniform from school to school. On the other hand, mobile faculty members cast off responsibility for maintaining local and common traditions alike. In the case of local traditions, usually little harm was done. If faculty members lost interest in supporting a particular tradition, it was either picked up by another constituency or allowed to die.

In the case of common traditions, conditions for significant potential damage have been building for some time, as faculty members not only have become more profession-oriented
and less institution-oriented, as Jencks and Riesman suggest, but
have become more self-oriented and less community-oriented,
as MacIntyre believes. Instead of feeling responsible for supporting the academic communities that are supporting them, many
faculty members have turned inward and focused on their own
pursuits, career goals, and needs. Administrators have been
hired as faculty surrogates to guard traditions and practices.
Many of these administrators were appointed at the campus
level; others have served at the state system level or as members
of professorial, professional, or regional accrediting associations.

This pervasive shift in emphasis holds the potential for
producing damaging situations on some campuses should certain
combinations of circumstances arise. Three conditions in particular could contribute significantly. The first condition is a need
to make budget cuts because of decreasing enrollments and/or
decreasing revenues from other sources, unfortunately a common state of affairs since the mid 1970s. Against this backdrop
must be placed the second factor—namely, administrators who
are less concerned with guarding traditions than they should be
because they are under extreme pressure from the financial
squeeze of the moment. Many administrators become despots
even during peaceful times because authoritarianism can be
gratifying, especially to the inexperienced or immature, and it is
easier than alternative modes of governance. In addition, budget
problems are an example of conditions that can be so stressful
that extreme measures seem necessary. Having taken control, an
autocrat may proceed to make sweeping, unilateral decisions
that may change the course of his institution for decades to
come. In the process he may trample on traditions and practices
alike.

A third and last factor is the inactive faculty member
who, through his lack of interest, allows despotic administrators
to continue in power. Unfortunately, guarding universal traditions is not done primarily through brief service on blue-ribbon,
specially appointed AAUP committees that propose guidelines
on significant matters. Most often, guarding universal traditions

is manifested through service on little committees in departments or schools of particular campuses. Meetings often seem interminable, although, depending on the issue, they also on occasion can be more lively than members expect when they agree to serve. Faculty members who do not involve themselves in the day-to-day work of maintaining traditions often do not understand what particular traditions actually amount to and what constitutes violations of them. They may not appreciate how much work goes into the routines that must go on constantly to maintain traditions, and they may not have any notion of the magnitude of the battles that may be fought behind the scenes by involved faculty members, administrators, funding agencies, and other parties on issues that affect traditions. To some extent, faculty members must be like Rudyard Kipling's jungle cat, who "walked by himself, and all places were alike to him." They need peace and freedom to do their work. But they must also know the traditions that preserve that peace and freedom, and they must do their part in maintaining those traditions. Tenured full professors bear special responsibility, since their jobs are secure and their promotions are not in question. Unless one has experienced a situation in which senior faculty members have shirked this responsibility and have chosen to remain silent in the face of massive violations of basic traditions by high-ranking administrators, perhaps one cannot comprehend the profound, campuswide malaise that can result. Courage is, as MacIntyre states, one of the most fundamental virtues.

MacIntyre mentions, in the passage that introduced this section, another virtue, that of civility, but he does not discuss it in detail in his book. This omission is odd because, in a sense, concern for others and one's community in balance with concern for oneself—as opposed to single-minded concern only for oneself—is at the root of the differences between Aristotelian and Nietzschean ethics. Good manners may seem to be a subject that is too effete to be included in a discussion of moral theory; yet, in the absence of civil behavior, nurturing a spirit of cooperation and mutual respect may be impossible. Incivility and bad manners are an extremely effective means of indicating the relative strengths of one's concern for one's own interests and one's concern for the interests of others.

Good manners are essential to administration as a practice. Good manners do not include *pro forma* civility under cover of which scheming and violations of rights occur. They do involve respect for all fellow human beings as such and for their rights. This respect must be built into all decisions and acts that administrators or faculty members make. Consultive decision making can bring civility to governance to an extent that authoritarianism can never achieve, because the latter is rooted in subjugation rather than in respect for others. Exercise of good manners is an indication of good will, which allows much to be accomplished even under the most severe circumstances.

If we are lucky, Professor MacIntyre's belief that we are entering a new dark age will prove to be melodramatic. It is to be hoped that the citizens of his adoptive country have retained the fortitude to prove him wrong, as undoubtedly he wishes to be. We Americans have in our heritage dual traditions—of being rugged individualists and of building communities from disparate elements. For decades, our educational system has been compared with systems in various European countries and has been found wanting. Instead of being criticized, it should have been praised for the massive numbers of students from widely disparate backgrounds that it has educated and for the incredible technological advances of the twentieth century that could not have been accomplished without such training. Similarly, regarding the doctrine of emotivism, it is important to look at the other side of the issue and note that millions upon millions of Americans continue to try to help others and avoid violating their rights.

Traditional bastions of authoritarianism have fallen. Fathers are no longer kings of their families and households, as they were in Victorian days. On the job, workers increasingly expect and get responsibility to share in decision making. People do not accept the edicts of priests and ministers without question but try to think through dilemmas for themselves. It seems far better that human beings come together in communities knowing what they are doing and why than to have no choice in the matter. Emotivism may be only a way station, a stage through which each of us must pass in the process of learning independence. Even as we become aware that each of us may be stronger than we realized, we must recognize that none of us can hope to survive alone.

MacIntyre's Theory and University Administration

MacIntyre portrays the bureaucrat or manager as what he calls a "character"—that is, a "moral representative" of our culture. His personal view of managers is negative, and his discussion of their functions would not be considered accurate in every detail by experts in the field. Nevertheless, his moral theory is extremely useful in examining the crucial role of moral behavior in administration. For the purposes of this discussion, the term *management* is used in a broad sense to include administration.

The major charges that MacIntyre makes against managers are two. He argues, first, that emotivism not only democratizes moral agency but also obliterates the distinction between manipulative and nonmanipulative social relations. Second, he claims that emotivism turns managerial expertise into an "elitist monopoly." MacIntyre draws these ideas from Max Weber's theory of bureaucracy. He states: "Weber's account of bureaucracy notoriously has many flaws. But in his insistence that the rationality of adjusting means to ends in the most economical and efficient way is the central task of the bureaucrat and that therefore the appropriate mode of justification of his activity by the bureaucrat lies in the appeal of his (or later her) ability to display a body of scientific and above all social scientific knowledge, organized in terms of and understood as comprising a set of universal lawlike generalizations, Weber provided the key to much of the modern age" (p. 82).

Emotivism obliterates the distinction between manipulative and nonmanipulative social relations by allowing each person to be his own moral agent. In a society that holds that moral principles cannot be justified rationally, each person is free to follow in his personal life whatever moral principles he chooses. The ordinary person is self-serving; he follows those principles that allow him to get what he wants. If, in the course of striving to attain such ends, means must be used that involve manipulation of others, then so be it. The moral principle that manipulative behavior is wrong cannot be justified rationally; therefore, there is no reason not to be manipulative. On the contrary, for managers in particular, every reason exists to be manipulative. As MacIntyre points out, "On Weber's view no type of authority can appeal to rational criteria to vindicate itself except that type of bureaucratic authority which appeals precisely to its own *effectiveness*. And what this appeal reveals is that bureaucratic authority is nothing other than successful power" (p. 25).

On the job, ends also are not available for rational examination because they are preset, fixed by the employer institution and the managers it employs. Thus, not only in his personal life but in the social context of the workplace, the worker is manipulated. Because in our society each person is his own moral agent, managers are free to choose to pursue with single-minded persistence the goal of financial gain for their employers. According to MacIntyre, they view their function simply as increasing efficiency. And because it is the responsibility of managers to direct human resources as well as other types of resources possessed by their organizations to be maximally productive, no method of dealing with the human resources of an organization, no matter how manipulative, need be considered improper. MacIntyre claims: "There are only two alternative modes of social life open to us, one in which the free and arbitrary choices of individuals are sovereign and one in which the bureaucracy is sovereign, precisely so that it may limit the free and arbitrary choices of individuals" (p. 33).

But the Weberian justification of adjusting means to ends is not the most fundamental defense that managers use for being manipulative, according to MacIntyre. They claim that effectiveness is a morally neutral value. As MacIntyre puts it, "Managers themselves and most writers about management conceive of themselves as morally neutral characters whose skills enable them to devise the most efficient means of achieving what end is proposed. Whether a given manager is effective or not is not on the dominant view a quite different question from that of the morality of the ends which his effectiveness serves or fails to serve" (p. 71). Managers also claim expertise, knowledge that enables them to take charge of situations. They "enjoy their status in virtue of their membership within hierarchies of imputed skill and knowledge" (p. 30). MacIntyre continues:

> The claim that the manager makes to effectiveness rests of course on the further claim to possess a stock of knowledge by means of which organizations and social structures can be molded. Such knowledge would have to include a set of factual lawlike generalizations which would enable the manager to predict that, if an event or state of affairs of a certain type were to occur or to be brought about, some other event or state of affairs of a specific kind would result. For only such lawlike generalizations could yield those particular causal explanations and predictions by means of which the manager could mold, influence, and control the social environment.
>
> There are thus two points to the manager's claim to justified authority. One concerns the existence of a domain of morally neutral fact about which the manager is to be expert. The other concerns the lawlike generalizations and their applications to particular cases derived from the study of this domain. Both claims mirror claims made by the natural sciences. [p. 74].

Having accused managers of claiming expertise and moral neutrality, MacIntyre then attacks them on both counts, calling effectiveness a "masquerade of social control." He argues that since lawlike generalizations do not exist in the social sciences, managers cannot lay claim to being any better than anyone else at predicting outcomes. He also argues that managers are not morally neutral, as they claim to be, because they do not have access to a realm of value-free facts, as they have pretended. Facts cannot be value-free because theory is required to support observation, just as observation is required to support theory.

MacIntyre's attack on managers is, however, not so detached as this extremely brief summary might indicate. He has no use for the breed, apparently. He states:

The concept of managerial effectiveness is
after all one more contemporary moral fiction and
perhaps the most important of them all . . . the
manager as *character* is other than he at first sight
seems to be: the social world of everyday hardheaded practical pragmatic no-nonsense realism
which is the environment of management is one
which depends for its sustained existence on the
systematic perpetuation of misunderstanding and
of belief in fictions. . . . For it follows from my
whole argument that the realm of managerial expertise is one in which what purport to be objec-
tively grounded claims function in fact as expressions of arbitrary, but disguised, will and preference
. . . in the social world of corporations and governments private preferences are advanced under the
cover of identifying the presence or absence of the
findings of experts. . . . The effects of eighteenth-
century prophecy have been to produce *not* scien-
tifically managed social control, but a skillful dra-
matic imitation of such control. It is histrionic
success which gives power and authority to our culture. The most effective bureaucrat is the best ac-
tor [pp. 101-102].

Ethical Administration

In short, according to MacIntyre, an administrator who
wishes to be ethical would not subscribe to emotivism, would
not claim an elitist monopoly over administrative practice, and
would not be manipulative in dealing with other university employees. What are some of the major administrative functions
through which the virtues may be exercised to foster practices,
traditions, and opportunities for individual development within
a university? An administrator performs the following basic
services for his institution:

1. *Information system.* Administrators serve as human
data bases and information retrieval systems. They are expected
to understand university structures and their functions and to
know whom to contact to acquire detailed and accurate information about particular areas as needed. They are supposed to

understand the goals of the university, the goals of all units, and how these goals mesh and support one another, as well as the strengths, weaknesses, and needs of all units and how changes in one unit will affect the others. They must also be familiar with university policies and practices, past, present, and planned, and have an idea of how well each policy or practice worked in the past and the circumstances under which it was invoked, both at the home institution and at other schools. In sum, every administrator must know a good deal about the "culture" of his institution, its goals, history, and traditions, its practices, its formal and informal systems and processes, its constituencies and their interests, the strengths and weaknesses of its faculty members and programs, the problems it faces, and how well it measures up against peer institutions.

Without such detailed knowledge, administrators cannot perform any of their responsibilities effectively. They must know when university structures, programs, practices, processes, traditions, and personnel are functioning properly so that they can recognize problems when they occur, propose solutions, understand effects throughout the system that various alternatives will have, recognize costs as well as benefits of solutions, and understand how to implement solutions and how to evaluate their success. Administrators are not behaving morally if they impose their wills on their institutions in ways that cause them to deviate radically from the traditions and practices that are at the heart of university communities or to stifle the peculiar opportunities for individual development that such communities can afford. They also are not behaving morally if they assume that their broad knowledge of their institution qualifies them to make unilateral decisions about what is best for the institution and all who are associated with it. They are not behaving morally if they fail to provide information at their command to individuals or deliberative bodies responsible for determining solutions to problems.

Administrators should understand fully the past out of which their communities evolved, their present states and conditions, and the futures for which foundations are presently being laid. MacIntyre makes a profound point when he labels the quality of recognizing traditions a virtue. He calls this virtue "one whose importance is perhaps most obvious when it is least present" (p. 207). He continues, "An adequate sense of tradition manifests itself in a grasp of those future possibilities which the past has made available to the present" (p. 207). Administrators must also be familiar with the mechanics of how traditions remain alive, which may be rather indirect and not immediately obvious to untutored observers of campus life. It is not an uncommon failing in university administrators to believe wholeheartedly in traditions such as academic freedom but to fail to recognize developing situations as being threatening to those traditions.

University communities are what cooperative activity over centuries has made them, and they should be respected as such. Although they have strong traditions, they are constantly changing, as individual institutions and as a genre. Changes are manifested through constant, ongoing conflict among members of communities who are determined to play roles in producing and directing change. Administrators may take the lead in suggesting and implementing changes, but at the same time they must always remain responsible for facilitating their universities' basic functions of increasing and transmitting knowledge. To balance these roles of instituting change and protecting tradition, administrators must thoroughly understand the operation of their institutions so that they can perceive the implications not only of changes but of continuing to maintain the status quo.

Information availability is a crucial element in sound decision making, but it is not the only important factor; nor are the best decisions always those that are based on the most impeccable logic. Decisions must also be acceptable to those who must implement them, or they will not be implemented. The success of an administrator may not depend on his decision making as such, but on his ability to encourage and coordinate implementation by disparate constituencies.

2. *Buffer against external stresses.* Administrators must deal with the world beyond the campus to perform many support functions. They obtain funds from outside sources that in-

clude government, industry, foundations, and private donors and, in areas where it is necessary, secure state approval of programs. They protect their institutions from political influences and other external factors. They are the prime interface between their institutions and the public, the community, alumni, parents, and the press. An important element in the practice of administration is to maintain the ivory towers within which university communities live while securing outside support for the continuation of those communities and seeing to it, in return, that public needs that can and should be met by universities are met. The public has a right to expect much of its universities, but it does not have the right to subvert their missions, traditions, or practices to serve political ends or the whims of the powerful.

3. *Program planner and allocator of resources.* One of the most important aspects of the practice of university administration is program planning and allocation of resources. Even when the budget of a unit seems large, all but modest amounts is devoted to fixed costs, such as salaries. Creative use of the amount that remains can be a prime incentive in encouraging faculty and staff members to continue the constant evaluation and development of programs and research foci that are the marks of healthy units. When funds are tight, every nuance of support, financial or otherwise, is analyzed by units, anxious to determine what their futures hold. In allocating resources, the intimate interdependence of many units within and among university communities must be borne in mind, because this interdependence is centrally important to the ability of any university to achieve its goals. Few institutions can afford not to have sharply defined goals in this era of scarce resources. University administrators are paid to allocate available resources in ways that meet these goals most efficiently. At the same time, sharply defined goals must not become a straitjacket that stifles free inquiry and continued program evolution. One mark of a successful administrator in the 1980s and 1990s will be whether he can allocate scarce resources to meet defined goals in ways that foster on campus a sense of constant renewal, interest, and excitement.

4. *Governance nanny.* An activity integral to the practice of administration is that of governance "nanny." As MacIntyre points out (p. 235), Marx was correct in his assertion that conflict, not consensus, is at the heart of the modern social structure. Conflict is also at the heart of the social structure of healthy university communities. Through institutional structures and processes, conflict can be directed to maintain and improve communities, rather than contribute to their destruction. University administrators tend these structures and processes. They make sure that a balance of power is maintained by encouraging consultation of appropriate constituencies in decision making. Since faculty members commonly do not consider governance as important as their own career goals, administrators often must nudge them into accepting their responsibilities and block opportunistic administrators from moving into power vacuums created by incompetent administrators or by passive faculty members.

An administrator should not act as a governance nanny by lecturing on the sin of noninvolvement. This has the effect of discouraging everyone from ever playing any role in governance. Instead, his *modus operandi* is to set in motion appropriate, established processes, encourage faculty members to take part in them, and let the processes achieve the effects they were designed to accomplish. Likewise, although administrators keep an eye on governance processes, looking for active violations, they generally should not have to discipline offenders except by invoking the existing procedures that provide checks and balances within the system. Ideally, every administrator should work constantly to make his governance-nanny role superfluous; that is, after developing through broad consultation the processes that are needed, he should try to educate his community about standard processes and involve constituencies within it to a degree that those processes become self-perpetuating without constant nurturing. Administrators do not have to worry about putting themselves out of business. Even in smoothly functioning systems, unusual circumstances arise constantly that require special attention.

It is particularly important that special care be exercised

when problems arise, as they often do, that consist in violations of the bonds of community. MacIntyre points out that
such problems must be resolved if the community is to survive
(p. 142). Administrators are supposed to act as watchdogs on
behalf of the community to guard against such violations, but
sometimes they themselves can be the cause of the problem.
MacIntyre portrays managers as malignant, as actively devising
means of coercing, ordering, and deluding others into following
directions. Another harmful approach sometimes seen in university administrators is utter disregard for effects of situations and
decisions on faculty members and other university personnel,
complete obliviousness even to the thought that perhaps the nature of effects should be of concern. Ralph Ellison observed
that direct insults can be more easily dealt with than being considered invisible. Administrators may adopt an attitude of obliviousness because they are by nature insensitive, because the
responsibilities of their jobs overwhelm them, or for other reasons. In any case, administrators who care nothing about the
persons who compose their university community can weaken
the bonds of community by making individuals feel that they
are nonentities.

In consultive decision making, sovereignty is a central
concept. Sovereignty of ideas can take precedence at times, as,
for example, when a groundswell of public opinion becomes apparent in favor of a particular solution to a problem. At other
times, sovereignty of the institutional hierarchy takes the lead.
This should be encouraged, for example, under circumstances
that threaten the traditional role of a particular unit. When the
hierarchy enters into conflict to a degree that is potentially destructive, then process takes precedence. The sovereignty of
process is recognized as driving decisions under such circumstances. But process can go wrong, too. It can include an improper selection of participants and be conducted according to
improper rules. Sometimes outcomes are impossible to implement or are antithetical to the goals of the institution or some
of its units. When that happens, an administrator must refuse to
be a party to the results, and since he bears legal authority for
the institution, his refusal to approve measures is generally

enough to block them. In such cases, processes are usually re-
formed and reinstituted, with charges to review committees
more carefully defined. An administrator, if all goes well, serves
in a ministerial role, but he must remain ready to take the initiative if necessary.

A process that is effective is effective because members of
the university community understand it, have access to it, accept it as legitimate, participate in it, and abide by its outcomes.
A governance nanny makes sure all these conditions are met.
Like it or not, a governance nanny also acts as a role model,
showing by example the respect that must be shown to process,
the hard work that must go into maintaining it, and the importance of abiding by its legitimate outcomes. Administrators are
responsible for shaping the culture of their universities to be in
congruence with tradition. This is not done by manipulating
people but by reminding them what sort of institution they are
a part of and by showing them by example how to play responsible roles.

The practice of administration involves sharing authority,
not abdicating it. MacIntyre points out (p. 88) that Machiavelli
believed that the influence of *Fortuna* in human events could
not be eliminated. Outcomes can rarely be predicted with certainty. Nevertheless, if reliable processes are in place, acceptable
outcomes can usually be achieved.

7

Dealing with Crises
Effectively

University administrators often say that, in their work, urgent problems routinely drive out important matters. At universities, crisis decision making is frequently concerned with matters that are merely urgent, rather than important. Issues that would have long-term impact on an institution, such as new programs or modification of policies on academic freedom or tenure, may be studied for years by various deliberative bodies. Although such issues are extremely important to an institution's mission and future, they should not be regarded as crises. Some crises occur over trifles; others occur over affairs beyond institutional control. Many are centered on concerns of individuals rather than on matters of principles or policies.

From time to time, crises occur that are both urgent and important. Budget reductions ordered by state legislatures may create such crises. Programs may be threatened, faculty members may be terminated, and graduate student support may be decimated by reductions in state subsidies. In some states, institutions have been merged by legislative edicts, resulting in incredible disturbances of programs and personnel. Less critical issues that may reach crisis proportions if mishandled include planned retrenchment of faculties due to declines in enrollment,

172

escalating costs of library books and periodicals, and shrinking federal student aid and research funds. Not only are these issues vitally important to the individuals who are affected by them, but many are beyond institutional control. Planning ahead with extensive consultation to agree on necessary changes in programs and policies and exploring alternative markets and funding sources that may help meet deficits are the best ways to avert developing crises regarding such issues.

Most crisis decision making must occur under one or more of the following conditions:

1. *Time constraints.* The time available for decision making and action is reduced during a crisis, sometimes so much that the idea of forgoing consultation is tempting. To do so is a mistake on several counts. Persons who are constitutionally empowered to be consulted, such as faculty senate leaders or trustees, will feel bypassed. Even worse, because they are not given an opportunity to become familiar with the facts of a case or with the deliberations that have led to a decision, they cannot be expected to support the final outcome. No matter how urgent a problem may appear to be, an effort should always be made to sound out opinion, rather than lose the sense of participation and authorization that consultation provides. Calling meetings of the board of trustees or the full faculty may be ill advised or impossible, but meetings of appropriate committees can usually be convened at short notice, or at least the leaders of interested constituencies can be contacted personally.

Time constraints are often created artificially. Special-interest groups may portray an issue as far more urgent than it really is in an effort to convince higher powers to turn their attention to it. A doomsday administrative style is also not uncommon. Administrators who wish to goad their staffs to action may predict disaster to be the result of continued procrastination. This approach is never effective for long and in fact may backfire, since "crying wolf" may convince the naive but amuses the experienced. Just as invoking time constraints may occasionally induce quicker settlement of issues, removing time constraints can be an effective means of deescalating a crisis to manageable status. Sometimes situations that appear irresolvable can be settled with surprising ease once all parties have agreed that the decisions over which they are at odds can be delayed until further deliberation has occurred. The very act of requiring appropriate consultation before decision making extends supposed deadlines and may deescalate a crisis to the status of a problem.

2. *Emotional component.* Crisis decision making often has a powerful emotional component that may be fueled by the demands of a situation and by the personalities and behavior of the actors involved in it. Pressure to do something as quickly as possible may be severe. Participants in a crisis may become emotionally charged because they believe moral or ideological principles are at stake. In fact, the most frequent causes of tension in crisis situations are faulty logic and irrelevant but annoying considerations interjected by participants—not abuse of principles.

Allowing administrative problems to be raised to the level of principle is usually a mistake. At most universities, principles relevant to the majority of problem situations have long since been established, and all that remains is to follow due process to implement the principles or provide new interpretations, when required. Each frustrated complainant wants to believe that his case is special, but administrators may have seen cases like it before. Explaining to complainants why it is in their best interests to follow existing rules or procedures and waiving certain requirements as circumstances warrant do much to alleviate frustration. Merely explaining rules and procedures, why they are necessary and appropriate, and what the effects on the institution and on complainants would be if they were not followed often calms complainants sufficiently to begin to deal rationally with their problems and to allow appropriate collegial procedures or established bureaucratic routines to be engaged. A majority of complainants do not understand university rules and regulations or how to register complaints or appeals. Much of their emotion may dissolve once they are told what routes lie open to them and how to proceed. Conversely, declaring a moratorium on change in policy can heighten the emotions associated with a situation by adding a sense of confrontation to the picture. Refusal to discuss policy may appear to constitute refusal to respond to demands and may be viewed as conservative posturing in favor of the status quo. How an administration expresses its position may be more important than what it says or does in response to problems.

In rare cases in which questions of principle arise, administrators should weigh competing alternatives and see that a combination of policy revision and remedial action is carried through, which, with luck, will provide long-term resolution not only of the problem at hand but of problems like it that may arise in the future. Changing policies may require deliberation and revision by a university's faculty senate, by its curriculum committee, or even by its board of trustees. Administrators should not take it on themselves to capitulate on fundamental policies or principles but should direct major issues that arise to appropriate deliberative bodies.

Some universities take the position that any administrative decision made under duress is void, thus limiting the arsenal of techniques that is available to protesters. This rule also limits the range of responses that administrators can make. Crisis management is an art, the exercise of which is occasionally impossible because circumstances are too extreme. More often, crisis management only appears impossible because the details of the situation are unfamiliar to the administrator who is assigned to handle it. Administrators may panic under pressure and may decide that they have no choice but to give in to complainants. A rule that review by higher authority is required to ratify concessions made under duress can offset this tendency.

Sometimes administrators respond to pressure by "flying to Bermuda"—that is, by choosing to ignore entirely a disturbing affair. Fellow administrators must be aware of this syndrome and be ready to help out if needed. A panicky president can cause more damage than a crisis itself.

3. *Public attention.* In crisis decision making, public attention may modify the issues at stake, the processes by which they are resolved, and the behavior of spokespersons for constituencies. Often, an issue that could be addressed in a routine fashion becomes a crisis because, for some reason, it is called to the attention of the public. Some crises are created by constitu-

encies to increase public awareness of key issues such as discrimination or academic freedom. Manipulating the media and acting out psychodramas behind the scenes to influence the behavior of influential figures in the administration and faculty are techniques commonly used to create crises.

Little change in institutional principles, policies, or processes usually results from such confrontational episodes. Sometimes an institution may be asked to grant an exception or a pardon or to declare a moratorium on action regarding a case that precipitated a crisis. Seasoned participants do not expect, however, that significant change will occur without extended deliberations. Because appropriate deliberative bodies must consider particular issues and recommend remedial actions, creators of crises may not be able to affect outcomes directly or in detail. But demonstrations, petitions, and letters of protest remind deliberative bodies to place issues on their agendas. Such actions also remind them that their deliberations will be watched and tested by an interested public.

4. *Extrauniversity component.* Crisis decision making often contains an element of political or philosophical competition among ideologies or value systems. In such cases, a confrontation may be a reflection of societal or international problems that may not be subject to resolution at the institutional level. This kind of confrontation requires special appreciation of the interests of the local groups that have joined in the protest to determine what actions might be undertaken to meet their needs. Obvious methods of dealing with problems are often overlooked both by administrators and by protesters. For example, frequently the best possible response to a complaint is to listen sympathetically to concerns and to discuss what, if anything, can be done to improve local conditions relating to the broader issues at stake. Once people realize that they are not helpless, that they are able to influence their world, they may be directed to more fruitful pursuits than complaining to university administrators. Groups can be told how to lobby legislators to change the laws of their state or nation or how to present issues to their faculty senates to bring about appropriate changes in campus policies.

Unfortunately, following good advice often does not have the intended effect; that is, desired changes may not result from the lobbying efforts that have been recommended. Even if advice given by administrators does not happen to work, attitudes of the complainants will be reshaped by the process of actively trying to bring about change instead of merely trying to bully others into doing it. At the very least, they will be forced to acknowledge that the administration is subject to the policies of the faculty senate, the board of trustees, and larger social units and is rarely free to make sweeping changes in policies or practices. Administrators are never viewed as compatriots by protesters. But administrators who are able to help complainants identify the root causes of their problems and how best to resolve them may come to be viewed as responsible facilitators.

Crisis and Conflict

Crisis and conflict may occur alone or simultaneously in a situation. A problem may arise that captures public attention, is emotion-laden, and demands immediate solution to avoid dire consequences, but neither its origin nor its solution may involve conflict. The problem may have been the product of a naturally occurring phenomenon such as demographic change in enrollment patterns, and everyone on campus may agree that only one particular means of dealing with the problem is appropriate. Alternatively, bitter conflict may fester within an organization for years without reaching a crisis point at which something must be done.

Gortner (1981, p. 135) defines conflict as "the struggle over resources or ideas, between two or more parties, caused by the perception on the part of the contending parties that both or all cannot have what they desire." Blake and Mouton (1969, pp. 65–68) list five means by which an individual may resolve a conflict that can no longer be ignored or suppressed: "(a) withdrawing from the situation, (b) smoothing over the issue, (c) forcing a 'win or lose' resolution, (d) compromising, or (e) employing a problem-solving attitude in seeking an 'integrative' solution."

In summarizing the positive and the negative effects that conflict may have, Gortner claims: "Within an organization, we are interested in the way that conflict affects productivity, stability, and adaptability. Whether the conflict has a positive or negative impact on the organization depends on the way that management handles the situation. If the conflict becomes personalized, if it causes people to neglect their normal tasks, or if it leads to proliferation of rules, regulations, and written communication, the conflict is deleterious to the organization. If, on the other hand, the manager is able to use skillfully the structures, roles, norms, and rules that exist within the organization to control conflict, the conflict will lead to healthy, meaningful, exploratory behavior that is a tonic for both the organization and the individuals involved" (pp. 162-163).

As Gortner points out, not all conflicts are negative events, although for many people the term carries a negative connotation. Certain problems within an organization may drag on for undisclosed reasons without being resolved. Dealing with them periodically just enough to sweep them back under the carpet becomes a familiar part of administrative routine. Problems may be endemic because a bureaucratic practice is faulty or because a policy is ill conceived. Other difficulties may occur because students' needs are undergoing change and their institution's faculties and programs have not evolved in pace with the demands being placed on them. To shake personnel out of their routines, to direct them to solving problems rather than to merely patching up the casualties that problems produce, may require conflict or even a crisis to overcome their inertia.

A crisis or a conflict may reveal a need for change in an institution's systems or processes or in its distribution of functions. A difficult tenure case may expose defects in the criteria being followed to award tenure, in the review process, or in the appeals system. Even if change comes too late to help in a current tenure case, the event may be used as a reason to direct to appropriate deliberative bodies the problem of correcting the defects in process. A crisis may also reveal a need for organizational change by making it clear that existing distribution of functions, authority, or personnel is not appropriate to meet the demands placed on them. Having ruled on a tenure case before its being appealed, for example, a vice-president for academic affairs may be compromised in handling the mechanics of the appeal. This technical function may better be assigned to a deputy or to university counsel, depending on the infrastructure of the institution and its past practices. Half a century ago, Mary Parker Follett (1940) perceived that we should put conflict to work for us instead of condemning it. The same may be said of crises.

Of course, persons who stand to lose a great deal understandably may have difficulty viewing a crisis or a conflict as anything but a potential disaster. The same event may be viewed by other persons as a grand opportunity for personal or professional gain or advancement. If a crisis involves a covert power struggle, one party may rejoice at the difficulties being encountered by a long-time opponent. Or a crisis may present an opportunity for an ambitious administrator to demonstrate his ability to invent creative solutions. Not only individuals but entire constituencies may benefit from crises. A crisis over a tenure-award process may help all untenured faculty members. A crisis over an innovative interdisciplinary curriculum, such as an urban studies program, may produce changes in the procedures governing interdepartmental cooperation to the benefit of all university programs—old, new, traditional, and interdisciplinary.

Unfortunately, changes that are stimulated by a crisis do not automatically result in more appropriate collocation of functions, authority, responsibilities, resources, and talent. Whereas a crisis or conflict may be an excellent stimulus for inducing change, it may also produce high stress that makes evaluating appropriate outcomes and mobilizing support for them unusually difficult. While a crisis or a conflict may open the way for changes that are desperately needed, the hard work required to define the exact changes that are necessary and subsequently to implement them may not be reduced one whit.

Conflict Model of Decision Making

All crisis managers should be aware of the points at which mistakes are likely to occur in decision-making processes and the means of avoiding those mistakes that may be called into play. The conflict model of decision making developed by Janis and Mann (1977, pp. 69-71) is helpful in identifying many potential difficulties. According to Janis and Mann, the model applies "only to decisions that have real consequences for the decision maker and thereby generate some discernible manifestations of psychological stress" (p. 69). The conflict referred to in the name of the model may be termed internal conflict, as opposed to external conflict that occurs between individuals or groups. Internal conflict results from being faced with a threatening situation and having to decide how best to respond to it.

The model portrays a decision maker under stress as asking himself a series of four questions:

1. *Are the risks serious if I do not change?* Janis and Mann postulate that a decision maker who is faced with an emergency will first seek information about the losses he is likely to suffer if he continues in his present course. As with each question in the series, if the answer is negative, the decision-making process is terminated, and the decision is enacted. If the answer is positive, the next question in the series is asked. In this case, if no serious risk occurs if the decision maker continues in his present course, then he enters a state of *unconflicted adherence* and goes on as before. If a serious risk is involved, he asks the next question:

2. *Are the risks serious if I do change?* In this step, information first is processed regarding serious risks that could result from a particular change in behavior. If no harm is perceived, that behavior is adopted, and the decision maker enters a state of *unconflicted change*. If harm is perceived, the decision maker asks the third question:

3. *Is it realistic to hope for a better solution?* The decision maker looks for signs that additional or unused resources may be available. If they are not available, the decision maker may avoid making a decision, or he may enact the decision of Step Two, in spite of the risks involved, and try to convince himself he did the right thing. Such a decision maker has entered a state of *defensive avoidance*. If additional or unused resources do seem to be available, the decision maker asks:

4. *Is there sufficient time to search and deliberate?* In

this case, if the answer is negative, the decision maker halts the search process and moves into a state of *hypervigilance,* which often leads to maladaptive reactions such as panic. If the answer is positive, the decision moves into a state of *vigilance,* which involves thorough search, appraisal, and contingency planning.

Even in the skeletal form in which the model is presented here, it is useful in pointing out some types of ineffectual behavior that a university administrator may display in a crisis. In general, too little stress is counterproductive because the person is not motivated to carry out a thorough search and evaluation process. Too much stress, however, can short-circuit the process by making the person "too upset to think straight." In the middle area of enough but not too much stress, a variety of problems can occur. Janis and Mann describe the types of mistakes that can be made at each of the four steps in their model in terms of criteria for high-quality decision making. For example, a decision maker in a state of defensive avoidance does not thoroughly canvass objectives or alternatives, does not evaluate consequences of current or alternative policies, does not search for new information or assimilate it without bias, does not reevaluate consequences, and does not plan for implementation and contingencies. That is, he meets none of the usual criteria of high-quality decision making. But a decision maker in a state of vigilance carries out all these procedures before making up his mind and acting.

Janis and Mann claim (p. 87) that when improper or incomplete information processing takes place in a state of defensive avoidance, the form of avoidance that is adopted depends on both personal and situational factors. Defensive avoidance may manifest itself in a decision maker's behavior as procrastination, as putting off making a decision in the usually vain hope that events will work out favorably of their own accord. Or a decision maker may defensively try to avoid making a decision by buck passing—by transferring the decision to someone else, either up or down the line of authority.

Bolstering is another type of defensive avoidance that may take many forms, some of which Janis and Mann discuss (pp. 86-87, 91-95, 125-129). A decision maker may exaggerate the favorable consequences and minimize the unfavorable consequences of his decision to reassure himself that he is doing the right thing. In the process of constructing rationalizations, he may process information incorrectly by paying no attention to threats, by neglecting to analyze ambiguous information, by simply forgetting unpleasant information, or by willfully misperceiving or misinterpreting information. A decision maker may also bolster his decision by denying that he has doubts or negative feelings about his decision. Sometimes he may do this in the face of considerable evidence that he is making a fool of himself. Or he may bolster his decision by telling himself that if his decision does lead to unfavorable consequences, they will happen so far in the future that he need not worry about them at present. Pretending that no one will know about his decision or understand his reasons for making it is another common means of bolstering.

Misjudging the importance of a situation is common among new administrators. A problem that may frighten them into a state of hypervigilance might strike seasoned administrators as routine. Other problems that do alarm experienced administrators may not even be noticed by newer colleagues. An administrator who is sufficiently experienced to recognize trouble when he sees it may make any number of errors in choosing among alternative solutions to a problem. He may commit himself wholeheartedly (unconflicted change) to an alternative course that may turn out to have utterly disastrous consequences. Or he may give responsibility for making a decision to an assistant or refer it to his boss. If he makes the decision himself, he may expend far more energy trying to prove that his choice was correct than he expended in the decision process itself. Or he may be so satisfied with the choice he has made that he does not bother to engage in contingency planning, in figuring out what he should do if his chosen course is ineffective or is blocked by unforeseen obstacles.

As has been mentioned earlier, consultation presupposes that group decision making has certain advantages over individual decision making. Groups are more efficient if a task can be divided. Members of cooperative groups correct one another's errors, stimulate creativity through competition, and provide emotional support to keep one another working toward completion of tasks. Broadening the base of decision making through consultation with representatives of constituencies also broadens satisfaction with decisions and aids implementation. These same advantages can occur in crisis decision making, although time constraints greatly reduce the extent of group deliberation and the breadth of constituencies that can be consulted. Even so, time saved in implementation may more than make up for time devoted to consultation. In universities, few crises occur that are so urgent that decision processes cannot be extended to allow at least minimal consultation.

During a crisis, involving interested parties and experts in decision making can produce more accurate evaluation of the risks of the situation and various alternative solutions, allow more complete searches for possible solutions, and lead to more precise definition of what constitutes a satisfactory outcome. Groups may excel at identifying means of implementing decisions and at contingency planning, as well. Moreover, group members can give one another emotional support that may be essential to enduring the stress of crises.

Groups can cause problems in crises, however, that can have severely negative effects on outcomes. A group collectively can become hypervigilant, panic under an overload of stress, fail to examine alternatives, or fail even to try to implement a solution. Fortunately, crises on university campuses do not often reach such extremes. Groups of administrators may, however, enter a pattern of defensive avoidance that Janis (1972) calls "groupthink." In groupthink, a group is not actually engaged in decision making, although its members believe they are. Instead, they are justifying a choice that was made before the beginning of the process, often by an authoritarian administrator. Janis and Mann describe the groupthink phenomenon as follows (1977, pp. 398-399):

> A set of antecedent conditions . . . give rise
> to the symptoms of groupthink, which in turn,

leads to defective policy-making procedures. . . .
These unfavorable [antecedent] conditions include
directive leadership, insulation of the group, and
lack of methodical procedures for search and appraisal. . . . When these conditions are present in a
cohesive group at a time when decisional stress is
high, the striving for concurrence fosters the pattern of defensive avoidance, with characteristic
lack of vigilance, unwarranted optimism, sloganis-
tic thinking, suppression of worrisome defects, and
reliance on shared rationalizations that bolster the
least objectionable alternative. The bolstered alternative is often the one urged by the leader. When
the other conditions that foster a collusive pattern
of defensive avoidance are also present, the leader's
initial bias in favor of the preferred alternative remains uncorrected even when his advisers have access to impressive evidence showing his preference
to be inferior to other feasible courses of action.

Janis and Mann list measures they believe can be taken to
prevent groupthink (pp. 399-400). Consultation may achieve
much the same purpose. The leader of a consultive process cannot expect to be directive—that is, to announce to the group
what he thinks should be done and expect the group to rubber-
stamp his opinion. No experienced consultive body would permit such behavior, which is antithetical to the *raison d'etre* of
the group. Furthermore, no consultive body is insulated. A consultive body consists of representatives of constituencies who
are expected to be constantly in touch with those they represent and with others in the university community. Finally, if the
group is ad hoc, the leader of a consultive process is expected to
set forth at the beginning of the process methical procedures
for search and appraisal. If the group is well established, it
should have its own rules.

Silence in a group may not imply agreement. Acceding to
the wishes of an aggressive leader can occur because everyone is
tired of fighting or is afraid. Possibly, group members may not
care what happens. Other problems that can occur in groups include unanimous locking into a position that is untenable and
leaves no room for compromise. When this occurs, it often hap-

pens because group members have decided to take a stand on an issue of some traditional importance, such as academic freedom or competitive admissions. A deadlocked group can intensify a crisis rather than deescalate it. Or a group may split asunder over competing principles, as, for example, when one faction consists of educational progressives and the other of educational traditionalists. When the deliberative process is deadlocked, no helpful outcome can be produced. In both cases, one or more expanded subcommittees may have to be appointed and each assigned to consider a different aspect of the problem. The dual goal at such a point must be to solve the task to which the consultive body is assigned while protecting the consultive process from being harmed permanently by the irresponsible behavior of the group.

Administrators of consultive processes nearly always are technically free to ignore the recommendations of consultive bodies, but generally in crisis situations they will not find it wise to do so if a sound consultive tradition has been built up within the institution. If such is the case, participants understand the process and how to fulfill their responsibility before being presented with the problem. They represent constituencies whose cooperation is necessary to implement the solution. Most important, they make it impossible for a macho administrator to sacrifice himself and his institution to the myth that decisiveness itself is a virtue. Decisions made in haste, without full knowledge of the circumstances or support of those affected, can be disastrous.

For their part, during crises administrators encourage deliberative bodies to follow proper procedures and to avoid wasting time with activities not related to task accomplishment. They feed deliberative bodies all information that is needed to function effectively. Administrators take necessary steps to prevent defensive avoidance reactions such as groupthink from appearing in the group, while the group, in turn, may correct any number of errors in decision-making processes that the administrator might make if on his own. Interplay between deliberative bodies and administrators can offset the weaknesses of each.

Maintaining Procedures and Process

The consultive process is sorely tried in crisis situations in which it must operate under severe time constraints and public scrutiny. Maintaining the integrity of the consultive process through crises is feasible if an institution has established a tradition of consultation and has organized consultive bodies with well-defined jurisdictions. During a crisis, instead of waiting for the next regularly scheduled meeting of a senate committee, a meeting may be called on a few hours' notice. An executive session that is closed to the media may be convened in an office without a formally structured agenda, instead of being held as an open meeting with an established agenda in the traditional meeting room. Much consultation may be done informally by telephone. In a crisis, rules may be suspended, issues may not be defined clearly, participants may be tense and distracted, and the range of parties who are contacted may be diminished, but even so, lines of communication can be maintained.

A tradition of consultation can speed response without neglecting usual processes by providing a climate of mutual trust and willingness to work together to reach solutions. On many campuses, only a small portion of the university community is even aware of the existence of various councils, committees, policies, and processes or understands how they operate. As consultation with such structures becomes a tradition, and consultive processes are reported again and again in campus newspapers, the university community learns to rely on consultation as a trustworthy problem-solving mechanism. People will use familiar mechanisms that they know are reliable instead of turning to other means which may be less effective and more disruptive and which may violate fundamental university traditions.

When a burning crisis is occurring, constituencies in the university community should be told that consultation with appropriate structures is underway and that progress reports will be issued at appropriate intervals. Making decisions that affect the university behind closed doors in complete secrecy without telling those who will be affected by a decision, generally, is poor practice. An administrative rule of thumb that nearly always holds true is that if a decision must be made in secret, it is probably not the right decision.

At the same time, especially on emotionally charged issues that may have politically significant consequences, all parties may prefer that exploratory discussions remain confidential, especially the initial positions taken by persons who are consulted. Personal trust must not be violated as representatives of constituencies weigh alternatives, argue all sides of issues, and move through the intellectual exercises that are necessary to reach appropriate outcomes. Shortening consultation to a day or two instead of the ordinary month or two often leads people to make ill-considered remarks or to draw conclusions prematurely without sound evidence. All parties should be protected until they have had a chance to gather full information on the matter at hand and ponder the situation sufficiently to feel prepared to be held accountable for their opinions. At such time, a public session may be announced on relatively short notice to address their concerns formally. "Sunshine" laws requiring all sessions to be public can be counterproductive in crises. Care must be taken to avoid compromising persons in crisis situations, because making enemies is of no help whatsoever in crisis management.

Regardless of the issue on which a crisis is focused, once media coverage becomes significant, numerous constituents will voice opinions. A subject that normally would not interest trustees, alumni, city council, state government, or social agencies can command attention in political domains far beyond the campus, once it becomes a feature story. The views of individuals involved, the political climate, the nearness of elections, and prevailing sympathetic or hostile public sentiment on an issue influence the reactions of constituencies. The liberal or conservative stances of the most influential parties to a crisis will also be a factor.

In most crises, external constituencies do not understand the issues at stake or the processes being used to deal with them. Frequently, this occurs because the media misunderstands or simply misreports the conflict. Persistent public relations efforts and distribution of accurate information will neutralize most external constituencies. It is not sufficient to label an affair none of their business and expect them to leave the university alone. If ignored, many constituencies have the political leverage to affect state allocations or the activities of regulatory agencies or to exert other influence that can affect university support.

An open administrative style that fosters trust and good will and suggests accessibility is also important in times of crisis. Lines of communication with leaders of various constituencies can become strong enough to resist the tendency of constituencies to assume defensive, closed stances toward an administration when under stress. Often, administrators with reputations for integrity are able to operate through communications channels that usually close during crises to neutralize protesting constituencies by trying to understand their demands and cope with them. The earlier action can be taken to resolve a crisis, the better. When resolution is delayed, representatives of constituencies and administrators become increasingly inclined to make intemperate statements and to engage in public posturing for the news media. Individuals and groups can then become trapped by their public utterances, since retaining their power bases may be difficult if they appear to vacillate or even show willingness to compromise after having committed themselves.

In crisis situations, time pressures can appear so great that the difference between success and failure in undertaking communications can sometimes be measured in hours. An administrator who has not established reliable communication channels cannot be effective in nipping problems in the bud. Of course, many administrators do not find much reward in taking preventive action. Usually few people are aware of developing crises or understand potential consequences of conflict. No one except those administrators directly involved may appreciate the quiet, herculean efforts often required to avoid escalation of disputes. Administrators like to see their pictures in the paper as much as the next person, and to be depicted as tough negotiators in tense confrontations is an image that pleases many of them and may help their careers. In an age in which so many equate notoriety with success, it is amazing that so many dedicated administrators continue to work quietly behind the scenes to try to solve problems before they reach the flash point.

Avoiding ad hoc procedures and structures is preferred, even in crises. If an ad hoc structure is required, both its establishment and its membership should be blessed by existing deliberative bodies. For example, an ad hoc committee may be appointed by the chairman of a faculty senate, or membership on such a committee may be approved by both administrators and protesters, and the chairman of the faculty senate may agree to chair the ad hoc group. This legitimizes the group's existence and operation.

Ad hoc processes may produce outcomes that cannot be sustained, because they may assign to administrators powers which they should not have or do not want or which belong rightfully to a senate tenure committee, a college curriculum committee, a board facilities committee, or some other group. In such a situation, no one will be satisfied with the outcomes of ad hoc processes, no matter what solution is adopted. Recriminations may be heard for years about decisions that were or were not made, compromised principles, or violated processes. More than likely, one or more parties to a dispute will demand that the decision be reviewed through conventional channels. Moreover, if consultation is bypassed when important issues surface, its effectiveness during less troubled times is diminished. Status may be earned and lost relatively easily in times of stress, not only by individuals but by processes and procedures.

If established processes are not followed, contractual rights to due process may be violated, and subsequently courts of law may find that damage was done by the ad hoc process that was adopted. In a democratic society, all parties representing both sides of an issue must understand the ground rules and processes that are in effect in working toward a settlement. Preexisting committee and council structures can be explained and adhered to more easily than can a new system invented on the spot, which is bound to be unsatisfactory to one or all parties to a dispute. In many cases, as when a tenure and review issue is at stake, procedures to be followed have been carefully spelled out in documents approved by a faculty senate, by a board of trustees, and, if appropriate, by a state system. Procedures so legitimized must be adhered to in crisis situations, although they may be accelerated somewhat and preparations may be foreshortened.

When established processes and fixed ground rules exist, dealing with a crisis does not require administrators actually to resolve the issues at stake. Instead, one of their primary responsibilities is to explain the processes and ground rules to all parties and to set dates on which various stages in the process will be initiated. Most parties to a dispute feel reassured if they are provided with written guidelines that spell out in detail well-established ground rules that were approved some time before by legitimizing authorities and have stood the tests of time and repeated usage. Ad hoc rules designed for a particular case may favor one party over another, whether or not they are tailored to do so.

To assume that complainants will gratefully and sedately adhere to established processes and practices can be a mistake. To assume that hidebound, traditional processes and practices do not need to be modified or should not be modified is another mistake. A complaining party may disdain accepted processes or justifiably demand changes in them. Responding takes time, whether it involves insisting that accepted processes be followed or negotiating particular changes. Complainants may have to be educated about the implications of the changes in policies they are advocating. Often they do not understand the effects on rights and privileges that could result from their efforts and may, in fact, be arguing for changes that could be detrimental to their status as a constituency or to the cause they espouse. Exhaustive philosophical debate, in which a faculty senate or other deliberative body may wish to play a role, may also be necessary. Added to this may be hours of argument that is pointless in itself but may be necessary to wear down complainants to a point at which they are satisfied to abide by legitimate, established procedures, to support feasible and appropriate changes, or to withdraw from the fray. All these matters add additional stress to the crisis situation.

Assuming that established processes are followed, numerous details regarding procedures remain to be defined and perhaps negotiated by administrators to speed resolution of a crisis. Who may appear as witnesses, how many advisers a complainant may have in a hearing room at any one time, how much time will be allowed for preparing and presenting positions and arguments, and many other procedural details can be negotiated. The premise that power to recommend outcomes, to approve decisions, and to hear appeals should not be dislocated from proper loci must be nonnegotiable, however. Issues that under normal circumstances fall under the jurisdiction of collegiate bodies or appeals panels remain there under crisis conditions. Administrators should not interfere with due process, but often they can expedite matters for deliberative bodies by providing counsel and secretarial assistance, information on relevant precedents and established procedures, and other support services.

Sometimes a deliberative body fails to behave responsibly under crisis conditions. This can place enormous pressure on an administrator. He may feel obliged to try to protect the consultive process by putting forth a ruling which is as congruent as possible with the faulty recommendation of the deliberative body and which, at the same time, is fair to all parties in the dispute, is acceptable to the board of trustees or other authorities that outrank him, does not set precedents that could have unfortunate consequences, and will not be rejected by the university community at large. A reputation for personal integrity is essential under such circumstances, especially if significant numbers of faculty members are avoiding a responsible role in governance. They may be inclined to believe that their representatives are behaving properly in spite of evidence to the contrary because they are not inclined to take responsibility to do anything about it.

An administrator may find it necessary under any number of circumstances to negotiate settlements. He may deny tenure to an individual but award to him a staff appointment outside the tenure stream or a cash settlement. He may decline to approve establishment of a degree program or center that a special-interest group is advocating but may agree instead to fund a noncredit or elective course or a research program. In all cases, negotiation and compromise should be regarded as standard elements in an administrator's arsenal of approaches to conflict resolution. To resort to such approaches does not give an administrator free rein to do whatever may be necessary to achieve the settlement he desires. The need for negotiation and compromise simply reflects limitations that human institutions and individuals share regarding their inability to change quickly or in practice always to live up to the standards they set for themselves or admire in principle.

Strauss (1978) has defined negotiation extremely broadly. He believes negotiations enter into the daily lives of individuals and into the operation of their institutions. He states that negotiation is "one of the possible means for 'getting things accomplished' ... for 'making things work' or making them 'continue to work' ... negotiation ... always implies some tension between parties, else they would not be negotiating" (p. 11). In crises, handling negotiations through consultation can produce acceptable results because consultation provides necessary checks and balances. Because an administrator negotiating a settlement is responsible for solving the problem at hand without creating further problems, the solution he devises must not be disruptive. It must be the result of consultation with grievants to find out what will suit them, it must be the result of consultation with affected parties to find out whether they approve of proposed changes, and it must be the result of consultation with various administrators to check on whether solutions fit the missions of the institution, are affordable, and do not produce disturbances of structure or function that could give rise to major complaints.

Strategic and Tactical Considerations

Dressel (1981, pp. 177–181) has made some cogent observations about crisis management. One difficulty encountered in crisis management is understanding the true nature of a crisis, a task that may require hardheaded honesty. As an example, Dressel mentions crises that have occurred at various state-supported institutions because (so the institutions have claimed) their state governments have tried to intervene to improper extents in their affairs. Dressel suggests that often the true cause of this kind of crisis is irresponsible behavior by universities, not by states. A second challenge to administrators is to be able to anticipate crises. Dressel says, "Few administrators who have been at an institution over a period of time with no serious problems can adjust to a crisis situation. Unwilling to recognize the development in its earlier stages, they also are incapable of dealing with it when it bursts into full bloom. Thus it is commonplace for new administrators to be brought in to manage crises" (p. 179).

A third problem Dressel identifies that is encountered in dealing with crises is identifying the most significant matters on which to concentrate one's energy. These elements must be central to resolution of the problem, and they must be of such a nature that something can be done about them. Dressel cautions that solutions to these central issues cannot be merely expedient. They must serve the long-term goals of the institution. Communication is the final difficulty in crisis management that Dressel discusses. He states, "When confidence and security are disturbed and mutual trust has disappeared, the restoration of completely open, forthright, and honest communication is likely to be the most crucial issue. Indeed, most crisis situations in colleges and universities result, in some part, from failure in some aspect of communication. Information has been ignored, misinterpreted, or held back from those who might have acted upon it" (p. 181).

Matters of a strategic nature also enter into management of crises. To cope with a crisis, administrators must be able to define their own objectives clearly, as well as the objectives of all parties to the dispute. Objectives are never simple. Personal goals of members of the negotiating team may be contradictory. For example, the overriding interest of a conflict manager may be simply to end the conflict. He may become too overwhelmed by stress to work toward concrete, positive goals that serve the best interests of his institution. He may be willing to agree to nearly any settlement that does not damage the public image of his university or its representatives. Another administrator on the negotiating team may have quite different goals. He may be concerned above all with preserving administrative prerogatives, with avoiding displacement of hierarchal authority, and with barring capitulation as a means of crisis resolution. Yet another administrator may be concerned primarily with long-term institutional goals and in order to maintain the values and purposes of his university may be willing to sacrifice significant short-term gains.

Institutional concerns may seem of negligible importance to an administrator on the negotiating team who is interested in trying to change society's values. Outcomes may be more important than processes to such a person, and local skirmishes are of less interest than producing changes in the broader community to which they are related. Social change may seem irrelevant, however, to a colleague who joined the negotiating team for self-serving purposes—to consolidate a leadership role and gain personal power. He may have little in common with a colleague who has joined the team because his personal values or principles seem to be at stake in the dispute, and who has only minor interest in the particular case that happens to be involved or in personal gain. Defining the goals of just the administrative negotiating team, not to mention the goals of other parties to a dispute, can be a complicated matter.

A clear understanding of institutional needs and objectives is also essential. Often, particular outcomes that may occur must be a secondary concern. For example, whether a particular person is awarded tenure or a particular program is approved is usually of less importance to an institution than whether due process is followed in reaching the decision or whether constituencies will regard the process as fair and will abide by the outcome. An institution always wants to avoid damage to its reputation. If possible, it tries to placate external constituencies, particularly those that can affect its financial condition. It avoids outcomes that involve burdensome costs or other liabilities.

Art is involved in achieving an optimal balance of conflicting goals in resolution of a crisis. Factors that must be borne in mind include university traditions, institutional long-term and short-term welfare, the well-being of individuals and programs involved, the potential for change in policy that exists, legal and financial considerations, and the eccentricities of particular cases. Participants may reverse stereotypical attitudes, as when a faculty behaves contrary to the norm and recommends immediate termination of a troublesome colleague, or a university counsel argues that the faculty member must be kept in university employ for some time to come because the terms of his employment constitute a binding contract. Media treatment of an issue may cost an institution much credibility in the eyes of the public, even though due process is followed, a fair settlement is reached, and all parties are satisfied. Sometimes threats to university goals cannot be identified in time to take protective action.

Ethically and professionally, to compromise due process, intentionally damage individuals, or neglect to guard basic university traditions is always reprehensible, although to do so to get sympathetic press coverage or to placate aggressive attorneys may be tempting. Usually, attorneys can be distracted from using approaches that challenge institutional processes and traditions on promotion and tenure or other such matters by directing their attention to checking all the details involved in implementation of outcomes. Print media can also be dealt with through sensitive public relations and intelligently handled contacts with editors. If they are not more ambitious than professional, reporters try to report the truth, but it can be a grave mistake to assume that reporters, just because they are employed as such, are expert in understanding the pertinent facts of a case and expressing them in print.

Managing television coverage is another matter. Once television reporters have identified an apparent weakness in institutional or personal conduct, nothing but waiting until the story becomes old news can stop them from exploiting the situation. A simple but effective means of exerting some control over television reports is to select articulate spokesmen for the university to make themselves available for thirty-second "talking head" news spots. No matter what question reporters ask one of these spokesmen, he repeats the university's position, rephrasing it often to avoid behaving like an automaton. Thus, no matter which segment of the interview is included in a report, views of the institution are likely to be expressed. This approach does not control the quality of reports, statements by opponents, or commentaries, but it increases the likelihood that both sides of an issue will be reported. The assumption, especially in a crisis, is always that the university is probably at fault. A television reporter who is paid to reveal wrongdoing is not pleased to be presented with facts to the contrary or with information proving that although a mistake was made, steps have been taken to rectify it.

Spokesmen for a university who appear on public relations or local talk shows are not able to rely on the "repeat announcement" approach just described, which is useful only in situations in which most of the tape that is shot ends up on the cutting-room floor. Administrators who appear on television shows where they must engage in extended conversations with interviewers, critics of their institution, or persons who have brought charges against it should not be evasive or untruthful. Nor should they behave as the researchers and teachers they were trained to be, for whom professional behavior involves analyzing all sides of issues while maintaining a detached attitude. Administrators are paid to defend positions taken by their universities, not to dissect them publicly in a detached fashion. Television reporters and audiences, by and large, do not understand professorial behavior and may interpret detached analysis as an admission of guilt.

To manage a conflict effectively requires coping with the needs and interests of all parties, including the complainant, the appeals panel, and parties who are being consulted on the case. This last group may include the faculty of a department of which the complainant is a member or faculty members from departments throughout the institution who are opposed to proposed policy or program changes. It may also include deans, the vice-president for academic affairs, financial and legal officers, the president, or members of the board of trustees, to name the most obvious.

Throughout a conflict, morale of the faculty and student body must be considered. A case that is mishandled, especially if it involves civil rights, sports, or other subjects that command widespread public attention, can color the attitudes of affected constituents toward their institution for years to come. None of these considerations should be allowed to interfere with the proper deliberative body taking jurisdiction or with due process being followed through established procedures. But the need to balance diverse interests influences the sequence of consultation that is appropriate, routing of the news and information releases that keep all parties abreast of latest developments, public and private statements made about the issue at hand by various parties, the care with which records are kept for possible subsequent court review, and other considerations.

For most crises, understanding the immediate effects of the solution that is applied is less important than understanding the long-term implications of the solution and the means by which it was selected. Capitulating to a special-interest group or making an exception for a complainant may seem to be an easy way out of a bothersome problem, but such action may set a precedent or compromise a principle and have severe repercussions later on. For example, the consequence of granting tenure to someone to whom the departmental review process recommended denying tenure could be that, in the future, no other department in a school would bother going to the trouble of rejecting difficult tenure cases. Or if a decision is reached not to terminate a program that a consultive body has recommended be dismantled because it no longer serves a useful purpose, that consultive body may not be inclined thereafter to recommend retrenchment actions.

Constituents pay surprisingly close attention to the resolution of cases, particularly in crisis settings. Actions that are taken influence expectations in future problem situations. When existing policy supports a certain kind of behavior, but actual behavior is quite different, actual behavior may send a more powerful message. If a central administration displays a lack of decisiveness or courage following receipt of recommendations from a deliberative body, that deliberative body subsequently should not be expected to be decisive or courageous. An atmosphere must be generated in a crisis, just as in any other decision-making situation, that will encourage appropriate behavior thereafter when similar situations occur.

The impact of crises on survivors must also be considered. A decision to grant tenure to a faculty member in a department that does not want him may create a climate in which scholarly productivity and collegial relations may be damaged for a decade. A controversial figure might be tenured in another department or be told to report to a dean rather than be left in a department following a divisive crisis with its members. To avoid poisonous recriminations or the disruption of work for a protracted period that may result, settling a suit out of court may be wiser than pursuing a winning case. To set up consultive mechanisms, encourage their operation, and then bypass their recommendations may have more negative effects than not engaging in consultation would have had. The reputations of all who took part will be damaged, and their interest in further responsibility will be greatly reduced.

A tactical question that must be considered in any crisis involves the particular arrangements that would facilitate the work of the consultive council or review body. Convening a body at its usual time and place and with an agenda of ordinary form may create a business-as-usual atmosphere that supports thoughtful deliberation. If size or location of the meeting room that is usually used or the timing of the meeting is not conducive to proper consideration of issues at hand, then changes may be appropriate. Meetings with community groups may be more productive if held in the evening, in a large room, with microphones and crowd control provided. Even when no threat of violent protest exists, rooms may be inappropriate that have only one exit, lack telephones, a communications system, or restrooms, are too small, or can be reached by only one elevator. A hearing panel may require appropriate tables for lawyers and a recording secretary. It may deliberate at an isolated location with controlled access at a time that is not widely publicized. Just as in negotiations in various kinds of conflict situations, the setting, timing, and conveniences provided to various parties all have consequences that should be anticipated.

By definition, a crisis that involves vicious disagreement challenges a democratic administrative style based on the assumption that people can reach compromise with each other. Limits exist, of course, to what can be accomplished through any decision-making style, process, or outcome. Sometimes goals of warring parties are so antithetical that any compromise, no matter how fair, will be unsatisfactory to both sides. Everyone involved in such a situation must be aware of this fact and be prepared to bear the consequences. The consultive process is not intended to make all parties happy or merely to placate them but to reach wise decisions that have, under the circumstances, the best possible long-term consequences for the institution. Such decisions are often unpopular. Sometimes they consist in those alternatives that are disliked the least by all parties.

Ironically, administrators may find it necessary to lecture a consultive body on the need for rational, unprejudiced decision making and then, as soon as a decision has been made, begin immediately to bolster the choice—that is, to praise its positive aspects and to denigrate its negative aspects. This behavior is both inconsistent and necessary. The decision may be the best possible choice under the circumstances, and yet implementing it may be so difficult and chances of its succeeding may seem so slim that blind optimism is required for success. In any case, consultation to determine a solution should never be viewed as the final step or end point in management of a crisis. It may be, in fact, the first step of a process that may lead, on the one hand, to implementation of a solution or, on the other hand, to confrontations in broader forums such as the courts, the city streets, or the political arena.

When review panels must be formed, members of the panels and the decision makers who will receive their recommendations should be involved in deliberations on the processes and mechanisms of review to be followed. They must be insulated from communications, evidence, and public statements that might compromise their appearance of neutrality or prejudice their judgment. Other line officers, staff, legal counsel, and officials of the faculty senate play key roles in the communication networks that facilitate review processes. The state of heightened emotion that parties to crises often experience is fertile ground for the growth of suspicion and paranoia concerning the next moves of opponents. It also may seem to justify attempting to manipulate the situation, or particular actors in it, to selfish ends, because everyone else may appear to be trying to do the same thing. This atmosphere requires that the review committee and all line officers scrupulously avoid even the appearance of conflict of interest or prejudice.

Leaders of an institution are responsible in a crisis setting for ensuring that consultation goes forward evenhandedly, with no partiality shown to any constituency involved. If the consultive process is disrupted, compromised, or used to exert leverage in key decisions, immediate and forceful intervention may be required. If troublemakers can be identified early in the process, steps often can be taken to neutralize the tactics they seem most likely to use, and the process may be protected. Alliances that have formed to exert pressure improperly may have to be reminded of their conflicting interests. Telephoning key political or community leaders, newspaper editors, and owners of television stations may be necessary to deescalate a crisis by reducing manipulation of events by media. Reporters may be barred from a hearing room to reduce posturing by witnesses.

Crowd control may be required as well, for similar reasons. This may be accomplished by limiting spectators at a hearing to those who take the trouble to obtain tickets in advance or simply by forbidding spectators altogether. If public access is required, placing loudspeakers or closed-circuit television screens in a series of smaller rooms to which spectators are admitted may be preferable to holding the hearing in a single room large enough to admit all who wish to attend. This not only eases the general problem of crowd control, it prevents crowds from interfering with deliberations. Whatever actions are taken, they must have the dual effect of protecting deliberative processes while not themselves offering unfair advantage to one of the parties involved in consultation.

Throughout settlement of a crisis or resolution of a conflict, administrators must prepare to deal with every likely outcome in a fashion that meets their responsibility to their institution. If any chance exists that an appeal of a decision may be taken to court, university counsel must be asked to observe cru-

cial parts of the proceedings or at least check all records and preparations. Proper records must also be built to defend the institution, its officers, and its board of trustees in case they are
named as defendants. University counsel must be sure that all
parties understand their rights, should that appear necessary.

Some constituencies have a right to know more than others about particular matters. Under certain conditions, an administrator is behaving irresponsibly if he releases information
about individuals, programs, or pending decisions. In a tenure or
dismissal case, the complainant has the news advantage because,
as plaintiff or appellant, he can say nearly anything he wants to
say. The university can speak only with regard to the process
that will be followed and to the rights to appeal that exist. Not
until all proceedings have run their course, the hearing board
has made a recommendation, and authorized administrators and
the board of trustees have acted—and perhaps not even then—
can spokesmen for an institution comment on a case. To behave
otherwise compromises deliberative processes and may do permanent damage to persons connected with the problems involved.

Postcrisis Inventory

After a crisis has passed, a post mortem should be undertaken to determine whether the situation was handled intelligently. Changes in policy or processes may be required to prevent future crises of the same kind. Examination of the policies
and processes of crisis management is also important. Identifying the points at which no one was sure what to do next, as distinct from the points at which waiting and doing nothing was
the proper action, is crucial. Processes should be defined to the
point that general directions can be given that cover as many
contingencies as possible. The behavior of personnel who handled the crisis, particularly their styles and strategies for coping,
must be reviewed in terms of the effects they may have had on
the outcome. Analyzing the effectiveness of existing practices,
policies, and programs and the responsibilities and behavior under pressure of various officers and office staff is the best way
to prepare for the next crisis.

Administrative style varies enormously, as does the capacity of an administration to divide responsibility and work as a team. If administrators determine that, in the crisis just past, management was decentralized improperly so that uncoordinated and counterproductive behavior occurred, correction is possible. Some members of the administrative team can be replaced, and the duties of others can be changed or defined more clearly. One staff officer may be assigned the duty of becoming the nerve center through which communications among all constituencies must flow. Appellants and petitioners discuss with this person concerns about processes and policies. Contacts with leaders of each constituency are also carried forward through this person. Needless to say, the person chosen to act as nerve center must understand decision-making and consultive processes. He must be respected by the deliberative body, the university administration, and various constituencies, must have a reputation for fairness, must be unaffected personally or professionally by whatever outcome occurs, and must not be involved in any way in its implementation. University counsel is sometimes appointed to this coordinating role, but in most cases an academic officer is more useful because he understands better the implications of the issues at stake.

Not only coordination of processes but the processes themselves should be examined in a post mortem. Were certain steps in the process counterproductive or unclear? Were there mechanical problems that interfered with deliberations? Crises vary greatly, but guidelines can be prepared to deal with certain types of problems. One important goal of a post mortem is to improve policies so that, without compromising principles, frequency of problems decreases. If this is not possible, the existence of guidelines provides a certain comfort to those who must deal with the problems that develop.

A post mortem should identify any damage that may have been done to collegial relations in a department or in a faculty senate or to the relationships among external constituencies and the university. If personal animosities are the only aftermath, time may be all that is required to dissolve them. Discussions of the crisis and its aftermath may be required, however, by parties such as the council of deans or the faculty

senate to allow members to ventilate pent-up opinions and emotions, to make suggestions for changes in policies and procedures, to understand one another's positions, and to overcome
any misunderstandings, clashes of temper, or ego damage that
occurred during the crisis. After some crises, relationships are
permanently breached between persons who disagreed on appropriateness of outcomes or on means of obtaining them. Re-
organizations, reassignments, or changes in duties may ease
these tensions. Taking people home to dinner and listening
sympathetically to their descriptions and explanations of the
tensions, insults, achievements, and failures that were part of
the crisis may help them put it behind them and get on with
business.

Someone who has had no stake in the outcome of a dispute, who is too busy to worry about other people's problems,
who does not identify with his institution, or who takes fair
play, due process, and democratic governance for granted may
not be able to understand fully the personal wounds and satis-
factions that may result from being involved in a major campus
upheaval. The ivory tower contains some of the sharpest minds
in the world, whose acuity of perception and analytic skills have
been finely honed. When they squabble among themselves,
heavy-caliber intellectual weaponry and professional reputations
may be called into play. Wounds to ego may be deep and may
affect professional performance for some time to come. Bringing such a battle to a close while not allowing it to harm the
institution that has been serving as the battlefield can be rewarding.

Crisis managers frequently burn out, become convinced
that no one will ever be satisfied no matter what settlement is
reached, and decide in despair to give up the role. Deans may
age, become resentful, and allow their values to become less in-
stitutionally oriented. Faculty members may become less naive
and simplistic regarding their opinions and values after seeing
those principles put into practice. An entire institution may be
sufficiently unsettled to rethink its goals, redefine its priorities,
and change its programs. Or a crisis or a confrontation may
change nothing. It may leave all parties all the more convinced of

the correctness of their positions and of the rank stupidity or duplicity of the opposition. These attitudes must be moderated if peace is to be more than short-term. Forums may be held to continue discussions of underlying issues, or programs may be started to meet the needs of special-interest groups. Crises do not begin when harsh words start to fly, and they do not end when the last newspaper stories have been filed.

The consultive process must be centrally involved in effecting necessary changes during the aftermath of a crisis. Through action by the faculty senate and other deliberative bodies, policies are modified and new interpretations and models emerge. The aftermath of a crisis can be an excellent time to ask deliberative bodies to consider how various mediation techniques must be used to deal with future crises, whether appointing an ombudsman as a full-time mediator to avert crises might not be worthwhile, whether rules governing arbitration should be codified, whether community relations officers should be appointed and how their duties should be defined, and other matters. Issues such as these cannot be dealt with while a crisis is occurring, and no one wants to bother with them after a crisis has been forgotten. Consultation plays a significant role in addressing particular crises, but it plays a far more significant role when it can be used to develop means of avoiding recurrence of problems or resolving them with minimal trauma to all parties.

In crises as in normal times, there are two major reasons for engaging in consultation. First, the university community is eternally concerned not merely with what is done in response to problems but with the processes by which solutions are chosen. A correct solution arrived at by improper processes is likely to be rejected flatly, whereas an imperfect solution arrived at by proper processes may not be condemned. Second, because consultation can be a difficult mode of decision making, some feel that the reason that best justifies engaging in it is a conviction that people have a basic right to take part in making decisions that affect their personal and professional lives and that this right should not be given over to campus authoritarians even during crises.

8

Strengths of Participatory Management: Overcoming Potential Drawbacks

≈✓≈✓≈✓≈✓≈✓≈✓≈✓≈✓≈✓≈✓≈✓≈✓≈

Yukl (1981, p. 208) echoes Strauss (1978) when he states, "Participatory management . . . is consistent with American ideals of equality, democracy, and individual dignity." Yukl lists (pp. 208-209) additional factors to explain why participatory management can improve motivation, performance, and satisfaction of subordinates:

1. Under participatory management, subordinates understand and accept decisions better. When subordinates are anxious about the implications of decisions, participation gives them opportunities for catharsis and chances to protect their interests (Coch and French, 1948; Maier, 1963; Strauss, 1963).
2. Participation leads to greater identification with decisions and to greater commitment to implement them (Anthony, 1978; Coch and French, 1948; Strauss, 1963).
3. Participation increases understanding by subordinates of both objectives of decisions and plans to achieve them. Implementation of decisions and modification of plans when necessary are easier as a result (Bass, 1970).

205

4. Task motivation is increased by participation because through participation subordinates understand that effort will be rewarded and that lack of effort will lead to negative outcomes (Mitchell, 1973).

5. Participation is consistent with the needs of mature subordinates for autonomy, achievement, self-identity, and psychological growth. Because autocratic leadership does not meet these needs, it tends to cause frustration, resentment, and apathy (Argyris, 1964, 1973; McGregor, 1960).

6. When group decisions are the result of legitimate decision making processes, the group applies social pressure to dissenters to accept, or at least comply with, the decisions (Likert, 1961; Strauss, 1978).

7. When groups cooperate in solving common problems, mutual understanding, team identity, and coordination are strengthened (Anthony, 1978).

8. When subordinates and their managers have different objectives, consultation and joint decision making provide opportunities for resolving conflicts and increasing acceptance by subordinates of decisions (Anthony, 1978; Strauss, 1978).

9. Because participation utilizes expertise and analytical skills of subordinates as well as leaders, it can result in better decisions (Anthony, 1978; Maier, 1963; Vroom and Yetton, 1973).

Although Yukl calls this list of potential benefits of participatory management "impressive," he notes (pp. 209-210) that other writers (Anthony, 1978; Locke and Schweiger, 1979; Lowin, 1968; Strauss, 1963, 1978) have pointed out certain potential disadvantages and limitations of participation:

1. Participatory procedures take much more time than autocratic procedures. Therefore, participation results in wasted time and is not useful in emergencies.

2. Because participation raises subordinates' expectations about influencing decisions, subordinates may assume a right to participate in making wider ranges of decisions than leaders wish to allow.

3. Participatory leaders may be viewed by subordinates as weak leaders lacking in expertise, initiative, and self-confidence.
4. Extreme forms of participation such as rule by committee may result in decisions of lower quality if subordinates lack expertise, are apathetic, or have goals or values incompatible with those of their leaders.
5. Because group decision making diffuses responsibility, reward for achievement and blame for failure are difficult to assign. As a result, groups may choose risky alternatives that may have unfortunate consequences for their organizations (Clark, 1971; Vinokur, 1971).
6. Participatory decision procedures are difficult to lead effectively, and if led by leaders who lack required skills, they may result in decisions that are worse than if the leaders had made autocratic decisions.

Overcoming Potential Drawbacks
of Consultive Leadership

Yukl's point about the time requirements of participatory decision making bears further discussion because slowness of the process can be a major problem with consultation. Whereas individuals may make decisions on certain topics after brief deliberation, the same decisions with the same outcomes attained through consultation may consume hours of deliberation before closure is reached. Consultive processes are extremely time-consuming, not only in terms of actual hours used but also in terms of duration. A single administrator may be able to approve a policy in a day, but consultation may require a series of meetings spread out over months. Everyone involved is affected to some extent, but administrators bear the brunt of the problem. To compensate, sophisticated staffing is needed. Capable deputies must be available either to oversee consultive processes or to handle other matters while senior administrators are engaged in consultation. Even so, demands of time for consultation may limit the number of assignments that senior administrators can accept.

When use of the consultive process is widespread, numbers of administrators need not be increased, but those in place must make very wise use of their time, giving priority to issues of lasting significance. Constituencies may assign senior spokespersons to issues so that the burden of shepherding draft policies through committees does not always fall on the administrator who is coordinating the total process. Penalties associated with widespread consultation can also be controlled by appointing to committee chairs energetic and capable persons who can be counted on to prepare minutes, to see that written position papers are drafted and circulated, to negotiate compromises, and to make advances between formal meetings of consultive bodies. Not every senior administrator need be invited to participate in all deliberations or to attend every consultive session.

The point should be noted, moreoover, that extra time spent in consultation need not be regarded as "wasted," as Yukl characterizes it. By legitimizing policies and by widening bases of support or compliance, consultation can have a net effect of speeding implementation of goals. In some cases, in fact, decisions made unilaterally by authoritarian leaders may stand little chance of ever being implemented. In other cases, when consultation is not undertaken, implementation can be stalled for some time because the persons responsible do not understand how to implement the decision or because they lack motivation. Dissatisfaction, low involvement, and inefficiency can cripple implementation. Blake, Mouton, and Williams argue that the extra time spent on consultation can be well worth it. They claim that most crises can be avoided or their impact reduced through consultation (1981, p. 299). Miles echoes this claim by stating that "crises should arise less often and consensus should be more quickly reached when they do arise" (1974, p. 264).

Miles adds two additional points regarding the positive effects of the time spent in consultation. First, participation induces workers to become goal-oriented and to exercise self-direction and self-control. Managers need not spend time exercising control over such workers. Miles states: "The manager increases his total control over the accomplishment of departmental objectives by encouraging self-control on the part of his subordinates. . . . When subordinates are concerned with accomplishing goals and exercising self-direction and self-control, their combined efforts will far outweigh the results of the exercise of any amount of control by the manager" (p. 262). Second, Miles makes a point about information flow that is related to the issue of time requirements for consultation. Consultation requires improved information flow to everybody throughout an organization. This is expensive and takes time. "However," Miles claims, "information collected and *used* at lower levels may be less costly than information collected for use at upper levels that is subsequently ignored or missed" (p. 264). At any level of an organization, improved information flow through consultation can improve understanding and motivation, which can affect creativity and productivity.

Difficulty may be encountered in performing experiments comparing the efficiencies of authoritarian decision making and consultation. Time spent in decision making as such during a consultive process may be hard to isolate from time spent in such matters as extended information gathering, gaining understanding of the implications of alternative decisions, working through details of compromises reached by mutual accommodation, allaying anxiety about effects of proposed changes and providing opportunities for catharsis for representatives of affected constituencies, developing commitment to the decision that results from group processes, protecting the self-interest of each member of the deliberative body as well as the interests of the constituency each represents, and understanding the plan to be used to implement the decision reached and the difficulties that may be encountered. Many authoritarian administrators do not consider it necessary to engage in all these steps when making decisions.

In comparing efficiencies of authoritarian and consultive decision making, it also should be noted that persons who engage in consultation routinely become increasingly skilled and efficient at negotiation. Administrators are usually better negotiators, not only because they have opportunities to become more experienced, but probably because they become administrators in the first place because they possessed some talent of that sort. Similarly, constituencies tend to pick spokespersons who are articulate and persuasive to begin with and who become even more facile with experience. Administrators or leaders of constituencies who are charismatic and aggressive can influence outcomes significantly.

Likewise, experienced deliberative bodies require far less time to reach mutually satisfactory conclusions than do groups inexperienced in consultation. When establishing consultive processes and creating new advisory bodies, administrators may have to spend more time educating participants than in any other element of the process. Even civilized, sensitive, rational people may have difficulty learning to behave in deliberative bodies in ways that help to solve existing problems instead of using them as springboards to create new ones. Time spent in educating consultive bodies can significantly reduce the time spent in fruitless disagreement and posturing.

Responsibilities of a member of a participatory decision-making group include (1) focusing discussion on the problem at hand, which means not using the group setting either as a forum for discussing extraneous issues or for building a personal power base, serving ego needs, or dealing with other matters of individual concern, (2) behaving in a civil fashion, realizing that the *raison d'etre* of the group is reasoned discourse, not making *ad hominem* attacks or committing other fallacies merely to assert oneself, (3) remembering that the rights of individuals and constituencies end where the rights of other individuals and constituencies begin, (4) remembering that few issues that arise on university campuses are matters of life and death and that even in true crises cool heads have an advantage in effective problem solving, (5) spending sufficient time doing homework to understand the causes and implications of the problem at hand, (6) protecting the integrity of the consultive process by agreeing to serve on deliberative groups when needed, by examining all sides of every issue as impartially as possible, by not abusing the patience of others, by trying to reach decisions that serve the best interests of the university as a whole, over and above the needs of particular constituencies involved, and by helping to execute decisions reached through mutual accommodation, and (7) accepting the advisory role of deliberative bodies and the limits of power vested in them while appreciating their role in the broader governance system. Fortunately, once people understand what is expected of them, group efficiency improves markedly. Members begin coming to meetings bringing analyses of problems, supportive data, and proposals for creative solutions. Most people enjoy being influential and working together toward common goals. Consultation can provide positive feedback to participants that encourages them to make processes optimally effective.

To remain effective, even experienced consultive groups need sound leadership. As Yukl points out in his list of potential drawbacks of participatory management, deliberative bodies, sometimes with the best of intentions, may extend their range of decisions beyond the scope their charters allow and may have to be reminded of their proper role. Leaders also may be required to encourage the maintenance of traditional trustee and administrative jurisdictions as well as faculty jurisdiction—whether in the department, school, or faculty senate—to increase the probability that each faculty member and unit discharges its professional responsibilities satisfactorily; that academic freedom is maintained; that the common burden of instruction is shared equitably; that professional standards are satisfied, including accreditation requirements; and that property and contractual rights of faculty members are guarded.

As groups become experienced, leadership skill becomes less crucial in achieving maximum benefit from consultation, assuming that group members continue to fulfill their responsibilities. Also, experienced groups rarely make the mistake of perceiving consultive leaders as weak merely because they consult. On the contrary, they learn from experience to appreciate the courage and strength that are required to undertake consultation routinely. In short, the disadvantages to participation that Yukl lists do not outweigh the advantages; certainly they are not enough to prompt one to turn to authoritarianism as a more effective approach.

During consultation, leaders have little difficulty accurately assigning praise or blame for outcomes, since the traditional hierarchy is not disrupted by displacement of foci of authority and responsibility. In any case, as was noted in Chapter One, in consultation achieving satisfactory outcomes is considered more important than assigning praise or blame for them.

A number of other potential disadvantages of consultation exist in addition to those Yukl included. For example, as discussed in Chapter Five, quantity and quality of faculty input can pose a serious challenge to consultive processes. Most faculty members will participate in governance processes if approached directly, but relatively few take the initiative in becoming involved. Personalities of those who choose or are persuaded to participate greatly influence outcomes of consultive processes. Undue weight may be given to the opinions of an articulate or charismatic leader who may not be well informed or understand the implications of alternatives. Selection of spokespersons for constituencies is critical, since capacity to influence outcomes may be a function of the personal style of representatives more than the legitimacy of their views or the relative importance of the constituencies they represent. An important characteristic to be sought in spokespersons is a conviction that a solution to the problem at stake not only should be but can be reached. Further, spokespersons must be willing and able to represent views of constituencies accurately. Otherwise, legitimacy of processes, outcomes, or both may be subject to challenge.

Spokespersons should communicate regularly with their constituencies, not only to remain in touch with their opinions, but to involve them in the consultive process so that the likelihood that they will support its outcomes is increased. If a spokesperson does not reflect the views of his constituency, other parties to a deliberation may wish to broaden the points of access or representation before proceeding further or even seek a replacement if the constituency becomes alarmed by its representative's behavior. Administrators should consult with spokespersons and other ranking members of constituencies to determine which of the possible outcomes stand a chance of approval. No purpose is served by wasting the time and energy of the group in exploring alternatives that will not be accepted when others will serve as well. If others will not serve as well, then groups might devote themselves to producing acceptable compromises.

Serious problems can occur during consultation if not all constituencies are represented or if some constituencies are represented out of proportion to their interests. Exclusion from consultation of persons or groups with final authority on issues can also lead to difficulties. For example, trustees concerned with students' writing proficiency can create a campus crisis by deciding to reinstitute an English-composition requirement for entering freshmen in contradiction to a curriculum voted into effect by faculty members. Although boards of trustees may be empowered to approve such matters, faculties are empowered by tradition and usually by their senate or collegiate bylaws to decide them. An equally touchy problem arises when, by nature of the composition of a deliberative council, undue weight is given to the opinion of a constituency that is relatively unaffected by a proposed policy. An example of this situation would occur if student members of university councils were permitted to vote on faculty appeals policies. Problems of representation are dealt with by leaders of consultive processes either directly through appointments procedures or through educating constituencies about the impact that particular decision alternatives will have on their interests.

Engaging in consultation is difficult, if not impossible, if one's direct superior or the president or vice-president for academic affairs of an institution is authoritarian. An authoritarian administrator cannot allow others to be involved in his decision making, for he regards it as an erosion of his status. Stimulating change in the behavior of any superior is difficult, but authoritarians are particularly set in their ways. Gortner (1981, p. 256) states, "Perhaps the reason many managers use negative control systems is that the change of incentive or management requires that the manager's style and philosophy must change. This type of change is a difficult one for many managers to make, because they consider the recognition of a need for change as an admission of guilt, weakness, or failure, and they find it easier to make others change than to change their own behavior."

The major problem with trying to conduct consultive

processes within one's area, on the one hand, and to be responsive to an autocrat, on the other, is, of course, that an autocrat feels no obligation to respond to or even acknowledge recommendations forwarded to him from consultive groups. This renders consultation fruitless. Some authoritarian presidents will permit consultation to occur within particular units if it is confined to issues that they have stated should be dealt with by the governance structure of those units. But extremely authoritarian leaders interfere at will in the business of units, giving orders without bothering to find out what has already been decided by unit leaders or to determine the opinions of various members of the unit on the issues involved. Faculty members will not waste their time offering advice if it is consistently ignored. If a superior demands that his personal interests rather than the needs of the institution be kept at the forefront of all decisions, if he refuses to listen to advice or concerns of others, if he refuses to approve outcomes that he did not conceive of personally, or if, in destructive displays of arrogance, he approves decisions of consultive bodies only to withdraw support and dismantle outcomes after the decisions have been implemented, a culture in which consultation can flourish cannot develop within a university community. Anyone committed to engaging in consultation should make it a point during job interviews to discover the governance style of all administrators with whom he would have to work, particularly his immediate superior, the vice-president for academic affairs, and/or the president. His own consultive working style should also be discussed, and superiors should be queried about the weight they are willing to give to the results of properly conducted deliberations of consultive bodies.

Unfortunately for administrators who are not particularly skilled in leading consultive processes, deliberative bodies have a potential for generating heat as well as light. If not properly managed, the consultive process may raise this potential to the flash point. A policy that an unwary administrator views as innocuous may seem threatening to a constituency for innumerable reasons. Once an alarm has been sounded, it can grow exponentially in volume as each side hears the views and arguments of the other. A leader's ability to call attention to all sides of an issue must be coupled with an ability to put each viewpoint in perspective *vis-à-vis* the needs of competing groups and draw all parties together toward compromise. Calling a meeting just to allow complaints to be aired may do more harm than good if no progress is made, because a concentrated dose of criticism can make a situation seem worse than it is. Meetings also raise expectations, and raised expectations that are not met even by token improvement lead to bitterness. When resources are especially tight, for example, mere expressions of interest can rekindle enough hope to persuade some faculty members to hold fast to their projects until better days arrive. Nearly everyone responds positively to sincere expressions of interest in his work. If better days do not arrive and an administrator was foolish enough to ask for advice without stating clearly that he was not promising anything specific for the future, hope may have reached such a pitch that not rewarding it would be cruel. This might give an administrator a reputation for being deceitful and callous that could stay with him for a long time.

Ill-conceived or poorly drafted policy changes are likely to be revealed as such by consultation. To avoid such problems, administrators are wise to do extensive homework before engaging in consultive processes. They should try to identify all likely sources of opposition and make ready not only to rebut objections, perhaps even before they are raised, but also to offer positive support of key components of their positions, some of which may be accepted even if other components are received with disfavor. Sometimes consultation touches off deep emotional reactions in participants. Grudges can be harbored silently even by advocates of consultation who have voted in favor of particular issues. Individuals and groups may not feel a measure meets their needs adequately. There are times, and such occasions are not infrequent, when all participants agree that a compromise that has been reached is inadequate. In such cases, participants may start again, or a new group may be formed to make a fresh effort. A leader should remind an unsuccessful group that without their analysis of the problem and efforts to reach mutual accommodation, potential for success of future groups is diminished.

Another potential disadvantage of consultation is that

alert constituencies may identify proposed changes in policies or programs as vehicles for accomplishing tangential goals or objectives that serve their selfish interests or broaden their power bases. They may launch into rhetoric or heated debates not because they care about the issues at stake but because they wish to strengthen opposition to related changes that will affect them negatively. They may foster support for their own interests by pretending to support the interests of others. As a result, proposed changes of little interest to the academic community at large can become foci for full-scale brouhahas.

Consultive processes are also vulnerable to manipulation by chairmen of deliberative bodies. The role of committee chairman can easily be transformed during the course of deliberations from merely a convening role into a position of control. Construction of agendas, preparation of minutes and records, distribution of position papers, management of speakers, time limits and sequences of presentations, and control of other procedural matters can influence outcomes greatly. For this reason, chairmen must be chosen with care, primarily on the basis of their willingness and ability to serve the committee rather than manipulate it. As Dalton has observed, "Anyone who deals with others in a responsible position is in danger of becoming manipulative. His only effective means of dealing with this danger is an intelligent awareness of his own actions and motives and an openness in his dealings with others. . . . We are all in the business of influencing others. It is not our understanding or consciousness which presents the real moral issues, but our motives and methods. These can be better scrutinized when made explicit" (1974, p. 425).

All parties to the consultive process must constantly remain aware of its vulnerability to abuse. Manipulative administrators know that in an institution accustomed to consultation, an action is easily legitimized by labeling it a product of consultive processes while paying little heed either to established procedures or to the spirit of accepted practice. By such means, unprincipled administrators are able to foist on an institution policies of their own design. These policies may be ill conceived and self-serving, or they may be judgments worthy of Solomon, but their intrinsic value or lack thereof may be less important than the abuse of the consultive process that has taken place.

The leader of a consultive process should not use the process to increase his personal influence and security within the institutional hierarchy. He should not relate to deliberative bodies in ways that imply personal authority over them. He should avoid acts that render their deliberations void, such as appointing to a deliberative body only persons whose advice he knows he will like or persons whom he can control by telling them behind the scenes what outcomes he expects the committee to endorse. He should avoid acts such as refusing to provide funding for solutions forwarded by a deliberative body that would be effective but are not quite what he had intended. He should not use a two-faced approach, telling the sponsors of a measure that he supports it, then speaking against it later when it is reviewed by a faculty senate or board of trustees. He should avoid *ad hominem* attacks under all circumstances. An authoritarian administrator may rejoice when a deliberative body does not function effectively, makes errors in judgment, or cannot reach consensus, because an ineffective deliberative body is less likely to interfere with his decisions on current matters. A consultive administrator is satisfied when the consultive process is functioning smoothly and outcomes are acceptable.

Games played in ivory towers are not unlike games played by political parties, corporations, bureaucracies, or unions. Unfortunately, on any large campus, power brokers abound who are always on the lookout for issues and controversies that can be manipulated to add funds, personnel, authority, or influence to the fiefdoms they have built for themselves. The consultive process can be used by such people to excellent advantage in fighting personal vendettas or building power bases. Abuse of power is indigenous to all human activities, including deliberative processes. It may arise not only in consultation but in all alternatives. No form of governance, including the consultive process, can substitute for responsible, civil, moral behavior.

Constant use of the consultive process is necessary to protect and preserve the process itself. Constituents must be reassured that the administration of their institution supports and believes in consultation and can be trusted not to resort unexpectedly to authoritarian action. Frequent use of the process is also needed to build constituents' confidence that the consultive process can be relied on to resolve favorably situations in which their interests are at stake. Groups that lack confidence in consultation will seek to legitimize and institutionalize strategies that they believe will protect their interests better. Common strategies include mobilization of interest groups from outside the university, approval of stifling constitutional constraints, routine disruption of meetings of governing bodies, and initiation of an unending process of forming and reforming coalitions to maintain balance of power.

Even in an institution where consultation is solidly established and is viewed by a majority of constituencies as legitimate and more effective than the alternatives, it must be used without exception in deciding major policy and program issues. Otherwise, confidence quickly diminishes and alternative means of protecting group interests immediately appear. Outrage at the failure of administrators to consult the faculty senate or other governing body when drafting changes in a tenure code or a faculty appeals system, for example, can be enough to turn into union supporters some faculty members who previously were opposed to adversarial approaches.

Strengths of Consultive Leadership

A fundamental goal of the consultive process is to develop wise policy and effective programs by improving the quality of the decisions that produce them. Through increased communication among personnel at every level of every division of an institution, a broader range of more accurate information can be obtained about problems that exist and solutions that will be effective. Needs of constituencies can be identified, and expertise of persons responsible for implementing decisions can be made available. Even experienced university administrators can gain more balanced and accurate perspectives of problems by consulting persons who work daily in the areas in which the problems are occurring. In any institution, persons can be identified who will improve decisions by bringing different analytic perspectives to bear on issues. In some cases, consultation may occur only in the initial stages of policy development during which the problem to be addressed is defined. Even so, improvement can result. Often, changes needed in policies or programs cannot be fully understood until all elements of the underlying issues have been explored. Consultation also furthers understanding of immediate and long-term implications of various alternative solutions to problems. This, in turn, increases the likelihood that sound strategies will be selected to resolve them. Generally, decisions reached by consultation are feasible in terms of costs and are not rejected by higher authorities as ineffective.

Consultation involves opening decision-making processes to concerned constituencies holding diverse points of view in the hope that reasoned discourse and patient, far-ranging discussion may lead to consensus on issues or to better mutual understanding of the needs, goals, and interests of each group involved. By giving each constituency an opportunity to learn about the values and priorities of its competitors, the consultive process performs a function that transcends particular issues. That is, participants become capable of identifying common ground and reconciling differences when other issues must be addressed and other councils are convened.

Consultation assumes that although the interests of constituencies in a particular issue vary and their stakes in the outcome differ, neither the issue nor the outcome is unique. Matters brought to consultive councils have been examined at the same or at other institutions at some time or other. Frequently, a consultive council will be asked to reexamine an issue that has been brought before it in the past. The consultive process typically includes review of experiences of other faculties or institutions, including collation of data concerning costs of alternative solutions, pertinent laws or rules, and successful and unsuccessful policies or practices that have been developed elsewhere. Some assistance in data collection or literature searches is often requested by consultive bodies. When all participants share understanding of pertinent facts, laws, data, and experience of other institutions, deliberative processes proceed more quickly and the quality of exchanges improves substantially. These effects are due in part to having built a common vocabulary and assumptions concerning the problem. It is frustrating to be on the brink of agreement, only to discover that all along various parties have assumed vastly different definitions of terms or interpretations of statements in policy drafts. It is even more disturbing to have differences surface after the policy has been made official and widely publicized.

At the same time, calculated and deliberate ambiguity of key statements in policy drafts can frequently benefit all parties, if a skilled negotiator is in charge and if all parties acquiesce to such an approach. Evolution of such policy drafts must be watched carefully, however. The importance of changes in emphasis of draft statements or planning documents as consultation progresses may not always be evident to inexperienced observers. Consultation may result in new policy statements being buried in the text of an original draft that treat wholly unrelated topics or even reverse the original intent of the draft. Careful review of all drafts is necessary to ensure that qualifying clauses or limitations have not effectively blocked attainment of original goals. Examination of deletions from drafts and of the reasons given for eliminating the sections is sometimes more instructive than examination of the statement that survived negotiations. For example, parties with polar positions may concur that a particular element should be changed, but for totally different reasons. Examination of these reasons may yield significant insight into fundamental differences between the parties that must be dealt with if consensus is ever to be reached.

Often, to settle an emotion-laden issue, substance may be decided in favor of one party to a dispute, while rhetoric is given to the opponent. Many judges and labor negotiators regard this mode of settlement as standard practice. Small-group processes often include psychodrama and posturing deserving of Academy Awards. Not only is such behavior to be expected, it may be necessary to gain support from other constituencies. Allowing parties to ventilate and to express their viewpoints may be necessary to achieve resolution. Some people must get moral or philosophical issues off their chests before they are able to appreciate other points of view or become pragmatic in negotiations. If all parties to consultation understood that emotional gyrations are common, the hyperbole and exaggeration that occur would not easily distract participants from their tasks.

Policy or program changes typically induce anxiety, which sometimes takes the form of anger. In extreme cases, political action groups form to protest changes. The consultive process has the great advantage of providing opportunities for discussion of changes and giving affected persons time to adjust their thinking. Both measures tend to reduce irrationality and emotional reaction. The chances that a decision will be effective are sometimes enhanced if time is allowed to elapse between announcement of the decision and its implementation. During this period, administrators are wise to lie low while constituencies examine the proposed policy. Most policies appear less threatening as they become more familiar. Negative emotional responses can also be reduced by discussion as each side listens to evidence and arguments that are put forth in support of opposing views. A policy or program change that initially strikes a constituency as counterproductive or nonsensical may seem quite reasonable and acceptable if during a process of consultation the full story is told of why the change is appropriate and needed.

A further advantage of consultive processes lies in the opportunities they offer to meet the needs of minorities. Although federal funds have been withdrawn from many programs developed in the 1960s and 1970s to benefit minorities, much can continue to be done at universities to further the cause of equal rights at modest cost. Females and representatives of minority groups should be involved in informal decision-making processes of all kinds throughout the institution. Until significant numbers of females and members of minority groups are appointed to influential positions and become spokespersons for offices or for constituencies that are not sexually or racially defined, they will continue to be left out of many important decisions. Care must also be taken to place women and blacks or other minority persons on councils and task forces at all levels, regardless of the issues being considered. The best way for individuals to gain the experience they need to assume leadership roles is to work in such groups. To stimulate permanent change, leaders must be trained who understand the processes by which institutional affairs are ordinarily conducted and how to resolve issues within such systems.

Being involved in consultive processes can also have positive effects on other constituents in the university community. Including bureaucrats in consultive processes is essential, for example, because often they are important actors in implementation of decisions. If they are included in decision-making groups charged with developing policies, they will understand better what is required of them to implement policies in the spirit in which they are developed. Bureaucrats need not always be made voting members of groups in which tradition dictates that another constituency holds authority, but they should be included so that they have a chance to learn the nuances of why decisions are made as they are. The operation of virtually every university committee or other decision-making structure could be improved by including on it appropriate bureaucrats.

Too often bureaucrats are subtly encouraged to believe that in order to get their work done, their offices must maintain combative stances against offices of other bureaucrats and against administrators, faculty members, and students. The problem occurs not only because many bureaucrats may be more concerned with protecting their office routines than with serving consumers but because many persons at universities behave impatiently and rudely when forced to deal with red tape. If bureaucrats can be shown how their work can be made easier by improved communications with feeder offices and with user constituencies, they may be quick to make appropriate changes.

By the act of participating in consultation, constituencies declare themselves willing to come to terms with their opponents. Partisans may view willingness to consult as caving in on issues from the beginning, contrary to the best interests of the constituency. Therefore, a constituency sometimes feels obliged to undertake aggressive posturing for the benefit of the campus or local news media before declaring itself willing to "concede" to engage in consultation. But unlike adversarial collective bargaining, consultation does not lend itself to denouncing representatives of opposing groups or to rejecting feasible alternatives merely because opponents support them. The rational behavior expected on university campuses, combined with the apathy toward governance that is common there, tends to make agreements that are reached by representatives of constituencies on policy, plans, or programs as binding as if they had been voted on by entire memberships.

A further benefit of established consultive processes is that their mechanisms and routines serve a function of control. Many disruptions occur in universities because problem-solving mechanisms do not exist across areas and units. As new kinds of problems arise that affect different mixes of constituencies, major disruptions can be avoided if faculty and staff are accustomed to engaging in consultation to solve problems and are motivated to do so by past successes. Existence of well-established consultive networks improves control by increasing the likelihood that relevant information exchange will occur and that consultation will automatically be used to elicit cooperation to resolve problems as they arise. Such institutionalized behavior makes it less likely that complainants will turn to less rational or more aggressive forms of negotiation until appropriate channels of expressing interest, of lodging appeals, or of seeking redress have been exhausted. For consultation to be effective, however, personnel must want to solve their problems. If too many prefer only to complain, as is often the case, no governance mechanism can function. Civilized governance falters when individuals cease to be responsible and exercise self-control.

Controversy often puts intense demands on the consultive process, but the consultive process is an effective response to controversy. Pressure created by a rebellious constituency can be offset by opening communication channels to competitors. Although opening communications to all and sundry involves an implicit risk that all and sundry may decide to enter the fray, this does not occur, as a rule, because most constituencies do not care to become involved. When it does occur, competitors tend to attack each other instead of the policy or administrator that instigated the disagreement. This is all well and good in that administrators and proposed policies may emerge unscathed. But after a major confrontation, no constituency may be willing to support any policy, regardless of its worth, until some time has passed and tempers have cooled. Well-mannered, logical, goal-directed controversy is essential to development of sound policy. Unrestrained conflict not only can destroy specific proposals, it can make cooperation in developing more appropriate policies impossible.

Sometimes administrators must organize meetings of unsympathetic constituencies to give them a chance to air their concerns and to become acquainted with the needs and interests of the institution. Occasionally, when positions of rival parties will not be changed by anything else that can be done, a public relations effort must be undertaken to try to reduce hostility and to allow parties to understand better the needs of their adversaries. The consultive process has an educational effect and, once begun, can lead to establishment of policy that reassures each party about the intentions of its rivals without lessening its own authority or independence. Such a product is not likely to be forthcoming in the absence of consultation. Conflict mediation should not be undertaken without careful consideration of the impact of the process. It may have no effect whatever on settling conflicts between single-issue special-interest groups that have little interest in resolving their differences.

Rational behavior, like honesty, is necessary for sound participatory governance. As every administrator has learned, however, objections raised by constituencies are not always rational. Ignoring irrational behavior is an easy but ineffective way to deal with it. Uninformed persons in influential positions in a university, on its board of trustees, or on the staff of its campus or community newspaper may take invalid charges seriously when issued by dissenting employees. Usually, education of both participants and observers about issues and implications of alternative solutions occurs as part of consultive processes, so that everyone concerned becomes capable of distinguishing valid from invalid charges, and escalation of emotions can be forestalled or redirected.

Use of the consultive process promotes consensus. This is an important asset, since general support for change in policies or programs allows implementation to occur in a positive environment that limits interference and resistance. Individuals and groups are more likely to obey a new rule or actively help to implement a new program if they know that their advice helped shape the rule or program and that it has been endorsed by all constituencies affected. Consultation not only legitimizes decisions and facilitates implementation of them, it reveals the range of opinion that exists regarding goals and outcomes that are expected to result from new rules for programs. Widely divergent attitudes tend to converge during the consultive process, and suspicion and resistance tend to be reduced. Reservations harbored by constituents who persistently refuse to support a policy or program change can be identified and understood. New rounds of consultation may then be initiated, or an alternative approach may be followed to cope with these objections.

In striving for consensus, consultation has advantages over systems that depend on majority rule. Techniques such as circulation of position papers, questionnaires and surveys, and personal interviews are used extensively during consultation to survey opinion on issues. As a side effect, these measures inform the university community about the issues. In addition, Nichols's comments on the tradition of majority vote are interesting:

No organization in America makes more use of committees than the college or university. However more often than not those committees resolve their disputes by majority.

Decision by majority vote is the pattern in faculty organizations. . . . Academics typically vote almost as readily as they eat, sleep, and go to work.

Participatory management is more than votes. A majority vote can leave a dissatisfied and angry minority. Group agreement is a higher goal and is central to the Japanese quality-circle ideal. The methods for reaching consensus differ from the politics of producing majorities. A genuinely participatory procedure seeks an outcome in which everybody is a winner because each has had a voice in the decision.

A cacophony of competitive factions is common in higher education. Voting tends, by its very nature, to focus on academic interest groups rather than to produce an environment in which people's best ideas are heard and valued. That is a world away from the Japanese spirit of cooperation. If you can't get enough votes to win, it is just possible that you won't really have to listen to what the other person has to say.

Participatory management focuses on groups rather than individuals. It is cooperative rather than adversarial. It prizes teamwork more than competition. Many businesses have discovered that, like an athletic team, they need unity within to whip the competition without. So does higher education [1982, p. 72].

One of the most important advantages of consultive processes is their power to build a sense of community on a university campus. Devotion to common goals, pooling of abilities, knowledge, and resources, mutual accommodation and cooperation, and commitment to outcomes of group deliberations all are elements of consultive processes that can reduce campus tensions and provide all constituencies with the complex support systems they require to function effectively.

In addition to its other positive qualities, consultation also is an effective means of legitimizing an administrative action or policy before implementation or submission to an authorizing board. Whether or not widespread support for the move is generated, at least destructive confrontation can be avoided. Many constituents will comply with a policy that they do not favor if their opinions have been heard and considered. Furthermore, an authorizing board may endorse an administrative initiative that it does not understand and has not had time to investigate if it knows that proper authorities and affected parties have been involved in developing the proposed action. If a board can be assured that all possible alternatives have been thoroughly explored, its endorsement can often be obtained even if consensus was not reached by all parties consulted. An administrator can avoid being strongly criticized for unpopular actions if many groups have participated through consultive processes in making the decisions. Groups that have been enlisted as supporters of an unpopular decree not only deflect barbs but lose their ability to serve as foci around which opposition may be mobilized. A lone administrator may be relatively easy to attack, but by demonstrating the support of leaders of diverse constituencies who have played a role in drafting a policy, he can reassure potential opponents and diminish his suitability as a target. By spreading responsibility and diverting criticism, he also can implement some unpopular but necessary actions that otherwise would meet with implacable opposition.

Campus life is possessed of great inertia, however. Even when appropriate authorities endorse a policy campus life may continue entirely unchanged after revisions supposedly have gone into effect, because significant numbers of persons simply decide not to acquiesce to the changes or heed them. Of course, a new tenure code approved by trustees is unlikely to be ignored, but a fully approved new degree program, curriculum, service agency, research center, administrative structure, or bureaucratic routine can be ignored and often is treated by constituencies as if it had never come into existence. The loose regulatory environment of campuses allows scholars to withdraw into themselves and to continue their teaching, research, and study routines without perceptible effect one way or the other on their working conditions or careers. Sometimes resistance to change can be dealt with by allowing implementation of policy to occur in stages, with relatively loose enforcement at the beginning of the process. Enforcement then progresses through a series of approximations and is phased in with grandfather clauses until the policy is entirely in effect. Although half measures can be worse than none, allowing outcomes to evolve through successive stages may be the only viable approach to implementation. Sudden, rigid enforcement of a radically new policy can mobilize so much opposition that it may have to be withdrawn.

A last important benefit of consultation that should be

mentioned is its usefulness in providing candid feedback on the progress that units are currently making. Through the channels of communication with administrators, or governing boards that they provide, constituencies can report successes or problems they are encountering in achieving established goals. Maintaining open communication channels can convince constituencies that the administration values the advice and comments it receives from them and can reduce anxiety about proposed changes. At the same time, it can strengthen the public image of leaders of various constituencies by giving them opportunities to bring forth evidence of their leadership, to show that they really are in charge and deserve to be. Governance bodies, too, can be strengthened by being consulted. Suppose, for example, that an administration refers a proposed policy draft on periodic evaluation of quality to a faculty senate, not only to secure advice or to legitimize the proposed policy, but to indicate that the administration values the senate's advice. This imputes power to the senate, which, in turn, increases its standing in the eyes of the faculty. A strong, highly regarded, active faculty senate can gain influence over an administration that faculty members rightfully should have.

Closing Comments

Because universities are steeped in the tradition of collegial governance in academic affairs, they are a particularly fertile medium for establishing and nurturing consultation as a parallel tradition. Consultive or participatory decision making may fail, as any form of democratic governance may fail, owing to lack of interest by faculty members. It may also fail if authoritarian senior administrators refuse to support it. On campuses where faculty members and leaders alike are willing to fulfill their responsibilities to their institutions while guarding their professional welfare in the process, consultation can result in wise and effective policies and practices. It requires that certain factors in the university culture be emphasized: awareness by all members of their interdependence, willingness to work together, commitment to institutional goals, and mutual trust.

These qualities do not exist only in the imaginations of utopian dreamers, but are possessed by many administrators and faculty members.

Authoritarian leaders who are inclined to issue orders without seeking opinions from experts or from those who will be affected by their decisions usually do not elicit the best efforts subordinates are capable of producing. When large numbers of employees become less productive, their institutions suffer. Authoritarian leaders can have an even more damaging effect on their institutions, however. The modern world is exceedingly complex, and many administrators, authoritarian and participatory, are not equal to the challenges associated with effective decision making. This is neither shameful nor surprising. Too many competing goals and values must be reconciled, and too many complex agendas of diverse constituencies must be met. Decision making rarely can be a simple process of determining a solution to a problem and requiring subordinates to enact it. Affected constituencies must accept a solution as legitimate, experts and persons responsible for implementing a decision must be convinced that it actually can solve the problem at hand, and appropriate role differentiation and balance among power centers must be maintained across campus. Unilateral decision making by authoritarian administrators who refuse to consult can result in unwise choices based on incorrect or inadequate information, or poor understanding of the needs, values, and goals of constituencies. If subordinates, affected constituencies, and other campus power centers do not adopt an authoritarian's dream, it will fail to be implemented. An authoritarian approach is particularly inappropriate during periods of redefinition of mission, plans, and priorities, when difficult decisions on resource allocations are required.

Rule by committee is no better, however. Administrators may preside over their institutions by playing titular roles legitimized by governance structures and by endorsing decisions that apparently are the result of consensus by members of those structures. In some cases, governance structures are charged with responsibility for a broad range of decision making, a state of affairs that administrators may interpret as restricting their role as leader and casting them instead in an implementing role *vis-à-vis* the structures. For such administrators, governance structures are refuges; their existence is used as an excuse not to lead. Rule by committee tends to result in decisions that involve minimal change and do not threaten the interests of the constituencies represented by members of the committee. Such decisions may not address satisfactorily the problems they were intended to resolve. Difficult decisions that could affect interests perceived as vital by one or more constituencies represented on the committee may be tabled, referred to subcommittees for further study, or sent on to other committees.

By contrast, leadership is an integral component of any consultive process. Consultation functions best under the guidance of a proactive leader who is willing to express his dreams, define missions, encourage representatives of constituencies and experts on problems at hand to take part in deliberations, articulate difficulties that may be encountered in reaching consensus on and implementing solutions, prepare agendas for action, and assist in implementation. A skilled leader of consultive processes does not pretend to know all the answers or perceive optimal goals or solutions in detail. He predefines outcomes only to the extent of articulating the general direction of the investigations that will be undertaken and the principles that will be followed. He talks extensively with leaders of key constituencies, asks advice of heads of governance bodies, seeks counsel of those bodies, and respects their jurisdictions.

Although he does not give orders to leaders and governance bodies, he also does not abdicate his responsibility to make difficult choices when others refuse to be involved; nor will he accept decisions forwarded to him for his approval that are ineffective. He respects effective processes of shared decision making that have become traditional in his institution and avoids actions that might weaken them. His purpose is to assist and guide representatives of constituencies and fellow administrators in arriving at effective decisions that most are willing to help implement. He provides leaders of constituencies and governance bodies with opportunities, information, and premises and perspectives necessary for them to execute their responsibilities properly. Sometimes they do not do so, and on such occasions he must have the fortitude and persistence to begin again, to extend consultation to broader audiences under refined guidelines. Above all, a leader of consultive processes tries to make the processes successful. He proposes, initiates, actively participates, and does anything necessary to help the processes move forward. With each success, consultation becomes better established and more effective. A sense of shared effort and accomplishment builds trust and mutual respect among leaders and subordinates, constituencies and governing bodies, administrators and faculty members.

Persons who are expert at guiding consultive processes serve both as leaders and as administrators. Their goal is to orchestrate processes that result in outcomes that are wiser than simply the sum of the wisdom of the participants. Leading consultive processes requires energy, patience, integrity, and an ability to listen. Some individuals are able to train themselves to acquire the traits needed to become leaders of consultive processes. Certainly search committees, administrators, and boards of trustees can learn to place more emphasis on finding candidates for senior administrative posts who possess, in addition to traditional scholarly credentials, the traits, skills, and experience required to help diverse interest groups work together successfully.

The criticism most often leveled at consultive leadership is that it is extremely time-consuming. Yet authoritarian administrators are not evaluated on this criterion as often as they should be. If objective postmortems were undertaken to determine actual accomplishments of authoritarian administrators, no doubt they would turn up many instances of orders being issued, followed by long periods of months or even years during which repeated efforts are made to force implementation of the directives, only to have them rejected in the end by boards and councils, or die more quiet deaths owing to widespread lack of interest. Would engaging in consultation from the beginning have taken any longer or consumed more time of administrators and their staffs? Well-conceived and well-established consultive processes can routinely allow excellent outcomes to emerge that are widely supported and successfully implemented. That, after all, is the final test of excellence of leadership and administration.

References

Adler, D. A. *Governance and Collective Bargaining in Four-Year Institutions, 1970-1977.* Academic Collective Bargaining Information Service Monograph No. 3, 1977.

American Association for Higher Education. *Faculty Participation in Academic Governance.* Washington, D.C.: National Education Association, 1967.

American Association of University Professors, American Council on Education, and Association of Governing Boards of Universities and Colleges. "Statement on Government of Colleges and Universities." *AAUP Bulletin,* 1966, *52*(4), 375-379. Also in *AAUP Policy Documents and Reports.* Washington, D.C.: American Association of University Professors, 1977.

American Association of University Professors. "Student Participation in College and University Government." *AAUP Bulletin,* 1970, *56*(1), 33-35. Also in *AAUP Policy Documents and Reports.* Washington, D.C.: American Association of University Professors, 1977.

Anthony, W. P. *Participative Management.* Reading, Mass.: Addison-Wesley, 1978.

Argyris, C. *Integrating the Individual and the Organization.* New York: Wiley, 1964.

Argyris, C. *Management and Organizational Development.* New York: McGraw-Hill, 1971.

Argyris, C. "Personality and Organization Theory Revisited." *Administrative Science Quarterly,* 1973, *18,* 141-167.

Argyris, C., and Schön, D. A. *Theory in Practice: Increasing Professional Effectiveness.* San Francisco: Jossey-Bass, 1974.

Bachman, J. G., Smith, C. G., and Slesinger, J. A. "Control, Performance, and Satisfaction: An Analysis of Structural and Individual Effects." *Journal of Personality and Social Psychology,* 1966, *4,* 127-136.

Baldridge, J. V., and others. *Policy Making and Effective Leadership: A National Study of Academic Management.* San Francisco: Jossey-Bass, 1978.

Bales, R. F., and Strodtbeck, F. L. "Phases in Group Problem Solving." *Journal of Abnormal Social Psychology,* 1951, *46,* 485-495.

Bass, B. M. "When Planning for Others." *Journal of Applied Behavioral Science,* 1970, *6,* 151-171.

Bennis, W. G. *Organizational Development: Its Nature, Origins, and Prospects.* Reading, Mass.: Addison-Wesley, 1969.

Bennis, W. G. *The Unconscious Conspiracy.* New York: AMACOM, 1976.

Blake, R. R., and Mouton, J. S. *The Managerial Grid.* Houston: Gulf, 1964.

Blake, R. R., and Mouton, J. S. *Building a Dynamic Corporation Through Grid Organization Development.* Reading, Mass.: Addison-Wesley, 1969.

Blake, R. R., Mouton, J. S., and Williams, M. S. *The Academic Administrator Grid: A Guide to Developing Effective Management Teams.* San Francisco: Jossey-Bass, 1981.

Bowers, D. G., and Seashore, S. E. "Predicting Organizational Effectiveness with a Four-Factor Theory of Leadership." *Administrative Science Quarterly,* 1966, *11,* 238-263.

Carnegie Commission on Higher Education. *A Digest of Reports of the Carnegie Commission on Higher Education.* New York: McGraw-Hill, 1974.

Carnegie Foundation for the Advancement of Teaching. *The Control of the Campus: A Report on Governance of Higher Education.* Lawrenceville, N.J.: Princeton University Press, 1982.

Clark, B. R. "Faculty Authority." *AAUP Bulletin,* 1961, *47*(4), 293-302.

Clark, R. D. "Group Induced Shift Toward Risk." *Psychological Bulletin,* 1971, *76,* 251-270.

Cleveland, H. "The Decision Makers." *Center Magazine,* September/October 1973, pp. 9-18. Based on H. Cleveland, *The Future Executive.* New York: Harper & Row, 1972.

Cleveland, H. "The Macrotransition in American Life." *AAHE Bulletin,* 1982, *34*(9), 11-13.

Coch, L., and French, J. R. P., Jr. "Overcoming Resistance to Change." *Human Relations,* 1948, *1,* 512-532.

Cohen, M. D., and March, J. G. *Leadership and Ambiguity: The American College President.* New York: McGraw-Hill, 1974.

Corson, J. J. *Governance of Colleges and Universities.* New York: McGraw-Hill, 1960.

Dalton, G. W. "Influence and Organizational Change." In D. A. Kolb, I. M. Rubin, and J. M. McIntyre (Eds.), *Organizational Psychology: A Book of Readings.* Englewood Cliffs, N.J.: Prentice-Hall, 1974.

Dressel, P. L. *Administrative Leadership: Effective and Responsive Decision Making in Higher Education.* San Francisco: Jossey-Bass, 1981.

Drucker, P. F. *Management: Tasks, Responsibilities, Practices.* New York: Harper & Row, 1974.

Duberman, M. "An Experiment in Education." *Daedalus,* 1968, *97*(1), 318-341.

Dunnette, M. D. *Handbook of Organizational Psychology.* Chicago: Rand McNally, 1976.

Ellison, R. *The Invisible Man.* New York: Random House, 1952.

Etzioni, A. *Modern Organizations.* Englewood Cliffs, N.J.: Prentice-Hall, 1964.

Fiedler, F. E. "A Contingency Model of Leadership Effectiveness." In L. Berkowitz (Ed.), *Advances in Experimental Social Psychology.* Vol. 1. New York: Academic Press, 1964.

Fiedler, F. E. *A Theory of Leadership Effectiveness*. New York: McGraw-Hill, 1967.

Follett, M. P. *Dynamic Administration: The Collected Papers of Mary Parker Follett*. (H. C. Metcalf and L. Urwick, Eds.) New York: Harper, 1940.

Georgopoulos, B. S., Mahoney, G. M., and Jones, N. W., Jr. "A Pathological Approach to Productivity." *Journal of Applied Psychology*, 1957, *41*, 345-353.

Glenny, L. A. *State Budgeting for Higher Education: Interagency Conflict and Consensus*. Berkeley: Center for Research and Development in Higher Education, University of California, 1976.

Glenny, L. A., and others. *Coordinating Higher Education for the '70s*. Berkeley: Center for Research and Development in Higher Education, University of California, 1971.

Gortner, H. F. *Administration in the Public Sector*. New York: Wiley, 1981.

Halpin, A. W., and Winer, B. J. *The Leadership Behavior of the Airplane Commander*. Columbus: Ohio State University Research Foundation, 1952.

Hare, A. P. *Handbook of Small Group Research*. New York: Free Press, 1976.

Hersey, P., and Blanchard, K. H. *Management of Organizational Behavior*. Englewood Cliffs, N.J.: Prentice-Hall, 1977.

Hickman, C. A. "Faculty Participation in Academic Governance." *Proceedings*, 2nd Minnesota Intercollegiate Faculty Conference, March 1968. Quoted in Mason, H. L., *College and University Governance: Handbook of Principles and Practice*. New Orleans: Tulane University, 1972.

Hollender, E. P. "Leadership and Social Exchange Processes." In K. Gergen, M. S. Greenberg, and R. H. Willis (Eds.), *Social Exchange: Advances in Theory and Research*. New York: Winston-Wiley, 1979.

House, R. J. "A Path Goal Theory of Leader Effectiveness." *Administrative Science Quarterly*, 1971, *16*, 321-339.

House, R. J., and Dessler, G. "The Path Goal Theory of Leadership: Some Post Hoc and A Priori Tests." In J. Hunt and L. Larson (Eds.), *Contingency Approaches to Leadership*. Carbondale: Southern Illinois University Press, 1974.

House, R. J., and Mitchell, T. R. "Path-Goal Theory of Leadership." *Contemporary Business,* Fall 1974, pp. 81–98.

Jacobs, T. O. *Leadership and Exchange in Formal Organizations.* Alexandria, Va.: Human Resources Research Organization, 1970.

Janis, I. L. *Victims of Groupthink.* Boston: Houghton Mifflin, 1972.

Janis, I. L., and Mann, L. *Decision Making: A Psychological Analysis of Conflict, Choice and Commitment.* New York: Free Press, 1977.

Jencks, C., and Riesman, D. *The Academic Revolution.* New York: Doubleday, 1968.

Katz, R. L. "Skills of an Effective Administrator." *Harvard Business Review,* January–February 1955, pp. 33–42.

Kemerer, F. R., and Baldridge, J. V. *Unions on Campus: A National Study of the Consequences of Faculty Bargaining.* San Francisco: Jossey-Bass, 1975.

Kipling, R. *Just So Stories.* New York: Doubleday, 1902.

Koestler, A. *Janus.* New York: Random House, 1978.

Lazarsfeld, P. A., and Thielens, W., Jr. *The Academic Mind.* New York: Free Press, 1958.

Lewin, K., and Lippitt, R. "An Experimental Approach to the Study of Autocracy and Democracy: A Preliminary Note." *Sociometry,* 1938, *1,* 292–300.

Likert, R. *New Patterns of Management.* New York: McGraw-Hill, 1961.

Likert, R. *The Human Organization: Its Management and Value.* New York: McGraw-Hill, 1967.

Locke, E. A., and Schweiger, D. M. "Participation in Decision Making: One More Look." *Research in Organizational Behavior,* 1979, *1,* 265–339.

Lowin, A. "Participative Decision-Making: A Model, Literature Critique, and Prescriptions for Research." *Organizational Behavior and Human Performance,* 1968, *3,* 68–106.

McCarthy, J., and Ladimer, I. *Resolving Faculty Disputes.* New York: American Arbitration Association, 1981.

McClelland, D. *Power: The Inner Experience.* New York: Irvington, 1975.

McClelland, D., and Burnham, D. H. "Power is the Great Motivator." *Harvard Business Review,* March–April 1976, pp. 100–110.

McConnell, T. R. "Faculty Government." In H. L. Hodgkinson and L. R. Meeth (Eds.), *Power and Authority: Transformation of Campus Governance.* San Francisco: Jossey-Bass, 1971.

MacCrimmon, K. R., and Taylor, R. N. "Decision Making and Problem Solving." In M. D. Dunnette (Ed.), *Handbook of Organizational Psychology.* Chicago: Rand McNally, 1976.

McGregor, D. *The Human Side of Enterprise.* New York: McGraw-Hill, 1960.

McGregor, D. "Theory Y: The Integration of Individual and Organizational Goals." In R. A. Sutermeister, *People and Productivity.* New York: McGraw-Hill, 1969.

MacIntyre, A. *After Virtue.* Notre Dame, Ind.: University of Notre Dame Press, 1981. (Copyright University of Notre Dame Press and Duckworth & Co. Ltd., London.)

Maier, N. R. F. *Problem Solving Discussions and Conferences: Leadership Methods and Skills.* New York: McGraw-Hill, 1963.

Mann, F. C. "Toward an Understanding of the Leadership Role in Formal Organization." In R. Dubin and others (Eds.), *Leadership and Productivity.* San Francisco: Chandler, 1965.

Mayhew, L. B. *Legacy of the Seventies: Experiment, Economy, Equality, and Expediency in American Higher Education.* San Francisco: Jossey-Bass, 1977.

Miles, R. E. "Human Relations or Human Resources?" In D. A. Kolb, I. M. Rubin, and J. M. McIntyre (Eds.), *Organizational Psychology: A Book of Readings.* Englewood Cliffs, N.J.: Prentice-Hall, 1974.

Millett, J. D. *The Academic Community.* New York: McGraw-Hill, 1962.

Millett, J. D. *New Structures of Campus Power: Success and Failures of Emerging Forms of Institutional Governance.* San Francisco: Jossey-Bass, 1978.

Miner, J. B. *Studies in Management Education.* Atlanta, Ga.: Organizational Measurement Systems Press, 1965.

Miner, J. B. "Twenty Years of Research on Role Motivation

Theory of Managerial Effectiveness." *Personnel Psychology,* 1978, *31,* 739-760.

Mintzberg, H. *The Nature of Managerial Work.* New York: Harper & Row, 1973.

Mitchell, T. R. "Motivation and Participation: An Integration." *Academy of Management Journal,* 1973, *16,* 660-679.

Mortimer, K. P., and McConnell, T. R. *Sharing Authority Effectively: Participation, Interaction, and Discretion.* San Francisco: Jossey-Bass, 1978.

Nichols, D. A. "Can 'Theory Z' Be Applied to Academic Management?" *The Chronicle of Higher Education,* September 1, 1982, p. 72. (Reprinted with permission. Copyright 1982 by The Chronicle of Higher Education, Inc.)

Ouchi, W. G. *Theory Z.* Reading, Mass.: Addison-Wesley, 1981.

Pfiffner, J., and Sherwood, F. *Administrative Organization.* Englewood Cliffs, N.J.: Prentice-Hall, 1960. Also in R. T. Golembiewski, and others (Eds.), *Public Administration.* Chicago: Rand McNally, 1976, pp. 471-481.

Porter, L. W., and Roberts, K. H. "Communication in Organizations." In M. D. Dunnette (Ed.), *Handbook of Organizational Psychology.* Chicago: Rand McNally, 1976.

Powers, D. R. "Reducing the Pain of Retrenchment." *Educational Record,* 1982, *63*(3), 8-12.

Schein, E. *Process Consultation: Its Role in Management Development.* Reading, Mass.: Addison-Wesley, 1969.

Schenkel, W. "Who Has Been in Power?" In H. L. Hodgkinson and L. R. Meeth (Eds.), *Power and Authority: Transformation of Campus Governance.* San Francisco: Jossey-Bass, 1971.

Selznick, P. *Leadership in Administration: A Sociological Interpretation.* New York: Harper & Row, 1957.

Smith, C. G., and Tannenbaum, A. S. "Organizational Control Structure: A Comparative Analysis." *Human Relations,* 1963, *16,* 299-316.

"State Laws, Ruling in Yeshiva Case Blamed for Slowing the Pace of Faculty Unionization." *Chronicle of Higher Education,* May 5, 1982, p. 6.

Stogdill, R. M. "Personal Factors Associated with Leadership: A

Survey of the Literature." *Journal of Psychology,* 1948, *25,* 35–71.

Stogdill, R. M. *Handbook of Leadership: A Survey of Theory and Research.* New York: Free Press, 1974.

Strauss, A. *Negotiations: Varieties, Contexts, Processes, and Social Order.* San Francisco: Jossey-Bass, 1978.

Strauss, G. "Some Notes on Power Equalization." In H. J. Leavitt (Ed.), *The Social Science of Organizations: Four Perspectives.* Englewood Cliffs, N.J.: Prentice-Hall, 1963.

Strauss, G. "Managerial Practices." In J. R. Hackman and J. L. Suttle (Eds.), *Improving Life at Work.* Santa Monica, Calif.: Goodyear, 1977.

Townsend, R. *Up the Organization.* New York: Knopf, 1970.

University of Maryland. *The Post–Land Grant University: The University of Maryland Report.* (M. Moos, Director.) Delphi: University of Maryland System, 1981.

University of Pittsburgh. *Guidelines on Academic Integrity and Statement on Faculty Responsibilities.* In-house publication, University of Pittsburgh, 1974.

University of Pittsburgh. *University Policies Relating to Reorganization or Termination of Academic Programs.* In-house publication, University of Pittsburgh, 1979.

Van Gieson, N., and Zirkel, P. A. "Fiscal Exigency." *Educational Record,* October 1981, pp. 75–77.

Vinokur, A. "Review and Theoretical Analysis of the Effects of Group Processes upon Individual and Group Decisions Involving Risk." *Psychological Bulletin,* 1971, *76,* 231–250.

Vroom, V. H. *Work and Motivation.* New York: Wiley, 1964.

Vroom, V. H., and Mann, F. "Leader Authoritarianism and Employee Attitudes." *Personal Psychology,* 1960, *13,* 125–129.

Vroom, V. H., and Yetton, P. W. *Leadership and Decision Making.* University of Pittsburgh Press, 1973.

Walker, D. E. *The Effective Administrator: A Practical Approach to Problem Solving, Decision Making, and Campus Leadership.* San Francisco: Jossey-Bass, 1979.

Yukl, G. A. *Leadership in Organizations.* Englewood Cliffs, N.J.: Prentice-Hall, 1981.

Yukl, G. A., and Nemeroff, W. "Identification and Measurement of Specific Categories of Leadership Behavior: A Progress Report." In J. G. Hunt and L. L. Larson (Eds.), *Crosscurrents in Leadership*. Carbondale: South Illinois University Press, 1979.

Index

243

www.ingramcontent.com/pod-product-compliance
Lightning Source LLC
Chambersburg PA
CBHW031243090426
42742CB00007B/299